The Britannica Guide to

Electricity **and**

Magnetism

PHYSICS EXPLAINED

The Britannica Guide to
Electricity and
Magnetism

EDITED BY ERIK GREGERSEN, ASSOCIATE EDITOR,
SCIENCE AND TECHNOLOGY

Britannica®
Educational Publishing

IN ASSOCIATION WITH

ROSEN
EDUCATIONAL SERVICES

Published in 2011 by Britannica Educational Publishing
(a trademark of Encyclopædia Britannica, Inc.)
in association with Rosen Educational Services, LLC
29 East 21st Street, New York, NY 10010.

Distributed exclusively by Rosen Educational Services.
For a listing of additional Britannica Educational Publishing titles, call toll free (800) 237-9932.

First Edition

Britannica Educational Publishing
Michael I. Levy: Executive Editor
J.E. Luebering: Senior Manager
Marilyn L. Barton: Senior Coordinator, Production Control
Steven Bosco: Director, Editorial Technologies
Lisa S. Braucher: Senior Producer and Data Editor
Yvette Charboneau: Senior Copy Editor
Kathy Nakamura: Manager, Media Acquisition
Erik Gregersen: Associate Editor, Science and Technology

Rosen Educational Services
Jeanne Nagle: Senior Editor
Nelson Sá: Art Director
Cindy Reiman: Photography Manager
Nicole Russo: Designer
Matthew Cauli: Cover Design
Introduction by Erik Gregersen

Library of Congress Cataloging-in-Publication Data

The Britannica guide to electricity and magnetism / edited by Erik Gregersen.—1st ed.
   p. cm.—(Physics explained)
"In association with Britannica Educational Publishing, Rosen Educational Services."
Includes bibliographical references and index.
ISBN 978-1-61530-305-2 (lib. bdg.)
1. Electricity—Popular works. 2. Magnetism—Popular works. I. Gregersen, Erik. II. Title:
Guide to electricity and magnetism. III. Title: Electricity and magnetism.
QC527.B83 2011
537—dc22

                                                                            2010017168

Manufactured in the United States of America

Cover, p. iii © www.istockphoto.com/Daniel Brunner

On page x: X-rays are but one useful application of electromagnetic radiation, which occurs
when electric and magnetic fields travel together through space, independent of matter.
Hemera Technologies/AbleStock.com/Thinkstock

Pages xviii, 1, 29, 89, 122, 174, 215, 248, 263, 265, 267 Wood/CMSP/Collection Mix: Subjects/
Getty Images

Contents

Introduction   x

**Chapter 1: An Introduction to
Electricity and Magnetism**   1
  Historical Background   2
  Early Observations and Applications   3
  Emergence of the Modern Sciences of
  Electricity and Magnetism   4
    Pioneering Efforts   5
    Invention of the Leyden Jar   6
    Formulation of the Quantitative Laws
    of Electrostatics and Magnetostatics   8
  Foundations of Electrochemistry and
  Electrodynamics   10
    Experimental and Theoretical Studies
    of Electromagnetic Phenomena   13
    Discovery of the Electron and Its
    Ramifications   20
    Special Theory of Relativity   22
  Development of Electromagnetic
  Technology   24

Chapter 2: Electricity   **29**
  Electrostatics   29
    Electric Charge   30
    Static Electricity   31
    Capacitance   47
    *Dielectric Constants of Some Materials
    (At Room Temperature)*   53
  Direct Electric Current   55
    *Electric Resistivities (At Room
    Temperature)*   60
    Conductors, Insulators, and
    Semiconductors   60

39

46

47

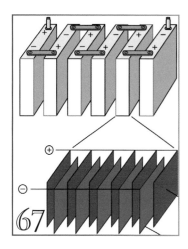

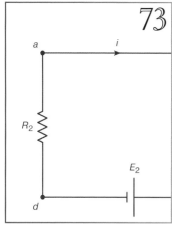

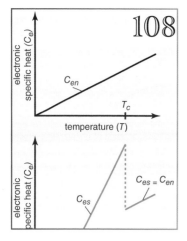

Electromotive Force	64
Direct-Current Circuits	68
Resistors in Series and Parallel	70
Kirchhoff's Laws of Electric Circuits	72
Alternating Electric Currents	74
Transient Response	75
Alternating-Current Circuits	76
Reactance	83
Electrical Units	85
Ampere	85
Coulomb	85
Electron Volt	86
Faraday	86
Henry	86
Ohm	87
Siemens	87
Volt	88
Watt	88
Weber	88

Chapter 3: Electric Properties of Matter 89

Piezoelectricity	89
Electro-Optic Phenomena	92
Thermoelectricity	93
Thermionic Emission	95
Secondary Electron Emission	96
Photoelectric Conductivity	97
Electroluminescence	98
Bioelectric Effects	100
Pyroelectricity	102
Superconductivity	103
Discovery	103
Thermal Properties of Superconductors	105
Magnetic and Electromagnetic Properties of Superconductors	111

Higher-Temperature
Superconductivity 117

Chapter 4: Magnetism **122**

Fundamentals 122
Typical Magnetic Fields 126
Magnetic Field of Steady Currents 126
Magnetic Forces 131
Lorentz Force 132
Repulsion or Attraction Between
Two Magnetic Dipoles 136
Magnetization Effects in Matter 140
Magnetohydrodynamics 145
Magnetic Properties of Matter 146
Induced and Permanent Atomic
Magnetic Dipoles 149
Diamagnetism 151
Paramagnetism 153
Ferromagnetism 154
Curie Temperatures for Some
Ferromagnetic Substances 157
Antiferromagnetism 160
Néel Temperature of
Antiferromagnetic Substances 161
Ferrimagnetism 161
Magnets 162
Magnetization Process 163
Powder Magnets 168
High Anisotropy and Alnico
Alloys 169
Rare-Earth 169
Barium Ferrites 170
Permeable Materials 170
Magnetic Units 172
Gauss 172
Oersted 173
Tesla 173

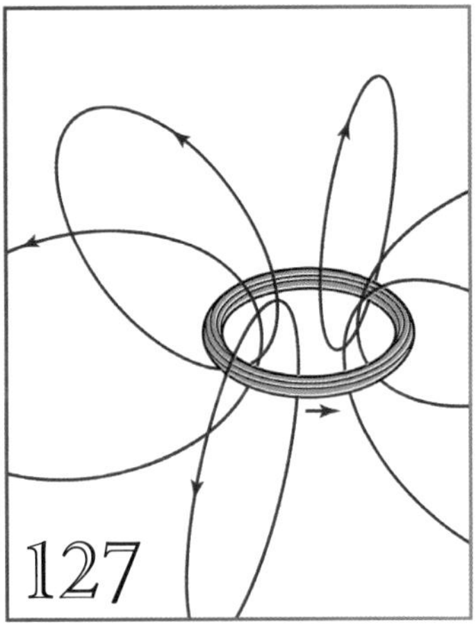

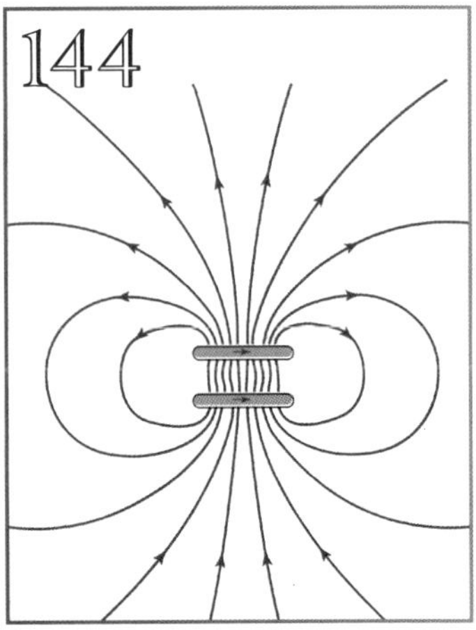

127

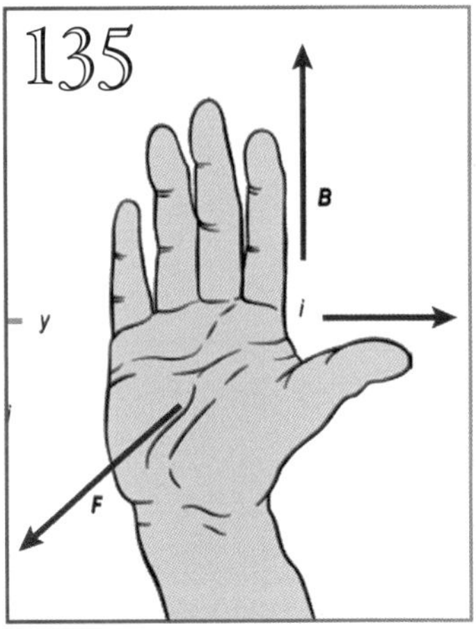

135

144

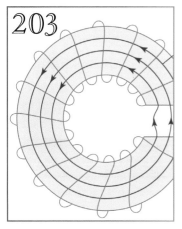

Chapter 5: The Fundamentals of Electromagnetism   **174**

    Coulomb's Law   176

    Principle of Charge Conservation   178

    Electric Fields and Forces   179

    Magnetic Fields and Forces   185

    Interaction of a Magnetic Field with a Charge   187

    Effects of Varying Magnetic Fields   190

        Faraday's Law of Induction   191

        Self-Inductance and Mutual Inductance   194

    Effects of Varying Electric Fields   197

    Electromagnets   202

        Solenoids   205

        Relays   207

        Design of Large Electromagnets   209

        Principal Applications   210

    Conclusion   213

Chapter 6: Biographies   **215**

    André-Marie Ampère   215

    François Arago   219

    Jean-Baptiste Biot   221

    Charles-Augustin de Coulomb   222

    Michael Faraday   223

    Luigi Galvani   227

    William Gilbert   231

    Joseph Henry   232

    Fleeming Jenkin   233

    Gustav Robert Kirchhoff   234

    James Clerk Maxwell   235

    Louis-Eugène-Félix Néel   239

    Georg Simon Ohm   240

    Hans Christian Ørsted   241

Jean-Charles-Athanase Peltier   242
Peter Peregrinus of Maricourt   242
John Henry Poynting   243
William Sturgeon   244
Alessandro Volta   245
Wilhelm Eduard Weber   246
Sir Charles Wheatstone   246

Appendix: Other Concepts   **248**
Ammeter   248
Barkhausen Effect   249
Displacement Current   249
Electric Displacement   250
Electron Optics   252
Ferrite   252
Ferroelectricity   254
Galvanometer   255
Gauss's Law   255
Gunn Effect   256
Magnetic Mirror   257
Magnetic Monopole   257
Magnetic Pole   258
Magnon   259
Pinch Effect   260
Polaron   260
Seebeck Effect   261
Skin Effect   261
Space Charge   261
Thomson Effect   262

Glossary   263
Bibliography   265
Index   267

242

247

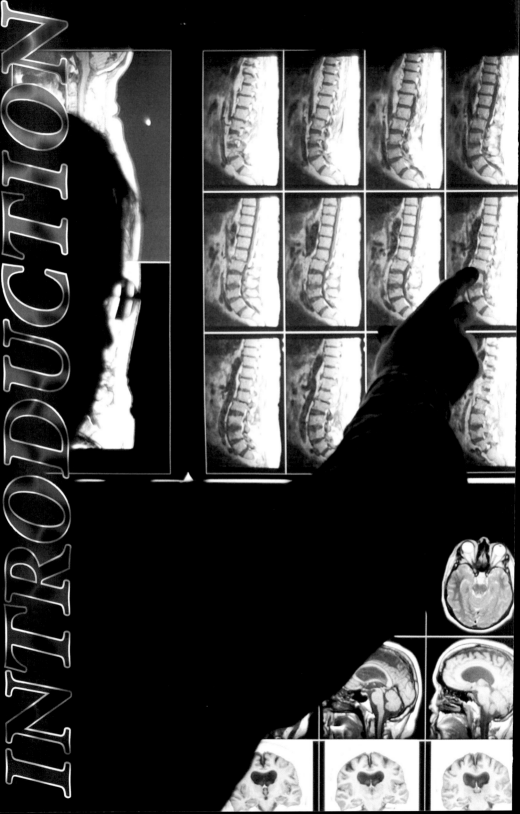

INTRODUCTION

W hen they think of electricity, most people probably think of many of the appliances and electronic equipment in their homes, ranging from light bulbs to refrigerators to computers. They also may think of the outlets, fuse boxes, and wires that deliver the electricity, or even the static that builds up on clothes that just come out of the dryer. Perhaps they think of something more grandiose, like a bolt of lightning tearing across a stormy sky.

What animates these appliances, flows through the wires, sticks the clothes together, and lights up the sky has its root in a basic property of matter called electric charge. Electricity and magnetism are actually two faces of electric charge. Electricity is sparks and shocks; magnetism seems something else entirely. The simple bar magnet works only on certain metals. On larger scales there is the attraction of the compass to the north pole of Earth's magnetic field.

This book examines electricity and magnetism, two physical phenomena that underlie much of the technology that makes the modern world work. The biographies of leading figures in electromagnetic science also are discussed in detail.

For all their differences, both these phenomena have one thing in common: moving electric charges. Charge is fundamental. Matter is either charged or uncharged. This property of charge also comes in a bit called an elementary charge, or -1 e. This property is quantized. That is, charge is almost always observed in integer multiples of e; for example, -4 e or -5 e is possible, but -4.5 e, -4.6 e, or any amount of charge between -4 and -5 are not. (There is an exception in the quarks, the subatomic particles that make up the proton and the neutron. Quarks have charge of 2/3 or -1/3 e. However, free quarks are never observed outside of particle accelerators and so do not affect this book's discussion of electricity.)

The study and the use of electricity involves the observation and manipulation of these charges. The carrier of the charge, -1 e, is the electron. The electron is one of the lightest subatomic particles and one of the key components of atoms, along with neutrons and protons.

Like masses, charges have a force between them that is an inverse square law. The force decreases as the distance is squared; if two charges are moved twice as far apart as they were previously, the force between them is one-quarter of what it was before. In the case of masses, the force is that of gravity. For charges, the force is called the Coulomb force. Objects can have either positive or negative charge. This means that unlike gravity, the charge can be either attractive or repulsive. A positive charge attracts a negative charge, and vice versa. A positive charge repels a positive charge, and a negative charge repels a negative charge. If it was possible for negative mass to exist, gravity would act like the Coulomb force and the universe would be very different.

The modern study of electricity began with the English doctor William Gilbert, who was physician to Queen Elizabeth I and King James I. In 1600, Gilbert coined the word "electricity" for the attraction that brought together two objects that had been charged by being rubbed together. He attributed this electricity to a fluid, which, because of his medical training, he called a "humour," after the fluids that were thought to influence personality. This may seem like a long way away from subatomic particles with fundamental irreducible properties. However, the basics of Gilbert's description contained the seed for the further study and explanation of electricity.

Once charges had been discovered, the next logical step was to somehow store them. This was done in 1745 when the Dutch mathematician Pieter van Musschenbroek invented the Leyden jar. This device was a glass jar containing water stopped up by a cork with a wire going through it. The jar was charged by connecting devices that generated static electricity to the wire. If the wire was touched, the jar discharged and gave the person touching the wire an electric shock. As was the case with many an 18th-century electrical apparatus, this was used to perform scientific tricks that were sometimes edifying and but sometimes ridiculous, such as being made into the shape of a cane and being placed into a rack to shock the unwary. As historian Jessica Riskin put it, "The Leyden jar ultimately became the whoopie cushion of the 1740s." Despite its ribald origins, the Leyden jar was the ancestor of the capacitor, a device usually consisting of two parallel plates that is used in many pieces of electrical equipment to store charge.

The other obvious thing to do with charge was to move it from one place to another, to make it flow. Such a flow is called a current. The current in most homes is known as alternating current, or AC, in which current flows in a periodic pattern of 60 cycles or Hertz per second. AC succeeded direct current (DC) in the late 19th century. The change to the more efficient AC from DC was one of the greatest technological feuds in American history, with the Wizard of Menlo Park, Thomas Alva Edison, on the side of direct current, and the eccentric inventor, Nikola Tesla on the side of alternating current. Both Edison and Tesla resorted to lurid demonstrations to bolster their case. Tesla lit lamps with alternating current that flowed through his body. One demonstration of Edison's showed the dangers of AC when he electrocuted an elephant in 1904, an event that was filmed for posterity.

Once charge can be stored and can flow, one can harness it for human needs. There are various ways this can be accomplished. Light comes from electricity. In old-fashioned filament bulbs, the resistance of the filament material to the flow of electricity heats the wire, causing it to emit light. In compact fluorescent bulbs, the interior, which contains argon and mercury vapor, is ionized and emits ultraviolet radiation, which is absorbed and reradiated by phosphors on the inside of the tube. Electrical energy can also be converted into mechanical energy to move an object. For example, in the home, an electric motor can be used to spin the blades of a blender. This requires electromagnetism.

The concept of magnetism was understood long before William Gilbert conducted his first experiments with electricity. "One feels the stone's own power," said the Roman poet Lucretius about the magnet. Hundreds of years before the Renaissance, before modern science, a 13th-century Frenchman, Peter Peregrinus of Maricourt, mapped a magnetic field. The magnet was spherical, and its field had two poles. By this time, the compass had come into use in navigation, and it was William Gilbert himself who realized the movement of the compass, its attraction to the North, meant that Earth was a giant magnet. Just as Peregrinus's small magnet had north and south poles, Earth's polar regions also had magnetic poles.

Unlike electricity, there is no "magnetic charge," no elementary particle that in itself carries some quantity of magnetism. Scientists have tried very hard to find such particles, called monopoles, without success. There are merely the north and south poles.

In the humble bar magnet, the moving charges are those of the electrons orbiting around the nuclei of the atoms in the material. These atoms have what is called a dipole moment, which is the product of the current of the moving electrons and the area of their orbits. These dipole moments give rise to the magnetic field. In the case of Earth, the mechanism is complicated (the "magnetic field" is produced by many different currents) but is mainly due to fluid iron moving because of the convection caused by temperature differences between colder and hotter areas in Earth's core. This movement creates an electric current and thus a magnetic field.

The connection between magnetism and electricity surprised 19th-century scientists. The discovery happened with one of those happy accidents that occur so often in science. While setting up some electrical equipment for a lecture in April 1820, the Danish physicist Hans Christian Oersted discovered that when a current passed through a wire, a nearby compass needle moved. English physicist Michael Faraday took the next logical step and produced an electric current by changing a magnetic field. The discovery of this type of charge, called induction, led to the first electromagnetic generators. These generators originally were used to spark the powerful light of arc lamps and subsequently the gentler radiance of incandescent lamps.

Since magnetic fields could cause currents and currents could cause magnetic fields, it was only a matter of time before they could be mathematically described in a single theory. In 1864 the Scottish physicist James Clerk Maxwell did just that using four simple equations. To state them in simple English, rather than in the more abstruse terms of vector calculus that they are usually stated in, they are: 1) the electric field diverges outward from electric charges, 2) there are no magnetic monopoles, 3) an electric field arises from a changing magnetic field, and 4) a magnetic field arises from a changing electric field. Not only did these equations explain how the compass needle moved in Oersted's demonstration, they also gave a speed for how fast this effect traveled. That speed was 300,000 kilometres per second—the speed of light, which had been known since the 17th century. Light was an electromagnetic wave.

Although it may seem as if electricity and magnetism should march toward their unification in electromagnetism, there are many interesting byways that make this happen, such as superconductivity. The same resistance of an incandescent lamp's filament to the flow of electric current operates in every wire and electrical device, causing some loss of efficiency. A material in which the resistance is zero is called superconducting. Many materials can be superconductors, but they usually have to be very cold, at temperatures close to absolute zero. Scientists have embarked on the quest for a material that would be superconducting at room temperature, but they have not gotten there yet.

Some of the leading personalities in the history of electromagnetic science were not single-minded savants but figures who ranged over the whole of what was then physical science. For example, Coulomb studied the strength of materials and frictional forces. In fact, he used the same apparatus, a torsion balance, for many of his experiments. Maxwell, the great unifier of electricity and magnetism, made great advances in the study of thermodynamics. He also demonstrated a process of colour photography.

The study of electricity and magnetism is but one part of the broad field of physics, but it contains much of what makes science rich and interesting. From the simple sparks and magnets have emerged one of the key forces of the universe.

CHAPTER 1
AN INTRODUCTION TO ELECTRICITY AND MAGNETISM

Electricity and magnetism are two aspects of electro-magnetism, the science of charge and of the forces and fields associated with charge. Electricity and magnetism were long thought to be separate forces. It was not until the 19th century that they were finally treated as interrelated phenomena. In 1905 Albert Einstein's special theory of relativity established beyond a doubt that both are aspects of one common phenomenon. At a practical level, however, electric and magnetic forces behave quite differently and are described by different equations. Electric forces are produced by electric charges either at rest or in motion. Magnetic forces, on the other hand, are produced only by moving charges and act solely on charges in motion.

Electric phenomena occur even in neutral matter because the forces act on the individual charged constituents. The electric force, in particular, is responsible for most of the physical and chemical properties of atoms and molecules. It is enormously strong compared with gravity. For example, the absence of only one electron out of every billion molecules in two 70-kg (154-pound) persons standing two metres (two yards) apart would repel them with a 30,000-ton force. On a more familiar scale, electric phenomena are responsible for the lightning and thunder accompanying certain storms.

Electric and magnetic forces can be detected in regions called electric and magnetic fields. These fields are fundamental in nature and can exist in space far from the charge or current that generated them.

HISTORICAL BACKGROUND

Electric and magnetic forces have been known since antiquity, but they were regarded as separate phenomena for centuries. Magnetism was studied experimentally at least as early as the 13th century; the properties of the magnetic compass undoubtedly aroused interest in the phenomenon. Systematic investigations of electricity were delayed until the invention of practical devices for producing electric charge and currents. As soon as inexpensive, easy-to-use sources of electricity became available, scientists produced a wealth of experimental data and theoretical insights. As technology advanced, they studied, in turn, magnetism and electrostatics, electric currents and conduction, electrochemistry, magnetic and electric induction, the interrelationship between electricity and magnetism, and finally the fundamental nature of electric charge.

Remarkably, electric fields can produce magnetic fields and vice versa, independent of any external charge. Maxwell's equations still provide a complete and elegant description of electromagnetism down to, but not including, the subatomic scale. The interpretation of his work, however, was broadened in the 20th century. Einstein's special relativity theory merged electric and magnetic fields into one common field and limited the velocity of all matter to the velocity of electromagnetic radiation. During the late 1960s, physicists discovered that other forces in nature have fields with a mathematical structure similar to that of the electromagnetic field. These other forces are the nuclear force, responsible for the energy released in nuclear fusion, and the weak force, observed in the radioactive decay of unstable atomic nuclei. In particular, the weak and electromagnetic forces have been combined into a common force called the electroweak force. The goal of many physicists to unite all of the fundamental forces, including gravity, into one grand unified theory has not been attained to date.

EARLY OBSERVATIONS AND APPLICATIONS

The ancient Greeks knew about the attractive force of both magnetite and rubbed amber. Magnetite, a magnetic oxide of iron mentioned in Greek texts as early as 800 BCE, was mined in the province of Magnesia in Thessaly. Thales of Miletus, who lived nearby, may have been the first Greek to study magnetic forces. He apparently knew that magnetite attracts iron and that rubbing amber (a fossil tree resin that the Greeks called *ēlektron*) would make it attract such lightweight objects as feathers. According to Lucretius, the Roman author of the philosophical poem *De rerum natura* ("On the Nature of Things") in the 1st century BCE, the term magnet was derived from the province of Magnesia. Pliny the Elder, however, attributes it to the supposed discoverer of the mineral, the shepherd Magnes, "the nails of whose shoes and the tip of whose staff stuck fast in a magnetic field while he pastured his flocks."

The oldest practical application of magnetism was the magnetic compass, but its origin remains unknown. Some historians believe it was used in China as far back as the 26th century BCE; others contend that it was invented by the Italians or Arabs and introduced to the Chinese during the 13th century CE. The earliest extant European reference is by Alexander Neckam (1157–1217) of England.

The first experiments with magnetism are attributed to Peter Peregrinus of Maricourt, a French crusader and engineer. In his oft-cited *Epistola de magnete* (1269; "Letter on the Magnet"), Peregrinus describes having placed a thin iron rectangle on different parts of a spherically shaped piece of magnetite (or lodestone) and marked the lines along which it set itself. The lines formed a set of meridians of longitude passing through two points at opposite ends of the stone, in much the same way as the lines of longitude on Earth's surface intersect at the North and South poles. By analogy, Peregrinus called the points the poles of the magnet. He further noted that when a magnet is cut into pieces each piece still has two poles. He also observed that unlike poles attract each other and that a strong magnet can reverse the polarity of a weaker one.

EMERGENCE OF THE MODERN SCIENCES OF ELECTRICITY AND MAGNETISM

The founder of the modern sciences of electricity and magnetism was William Gilbert, physician to both Elizabeth I and James I of England. Gilbert spent 17 years experimenting with magnetism and, to a lesser extent, electricity. He assembled the results of his experiments and all of the available knowledge on magnetism in the treatise *De Magnete, Magneticisque Corporibus, et de Magno Magnete Tellure* ("On the Magnet, Magnetic Bodies, and the Great Magnet of the Earth"), published in 1600. As suggested by the title, Gilbert described Earth as a huge magnet. He introduced the term "electric" for the force between two objects charged by friction and showed that frictional electricity occurs in many common materials. He also noted one of the primary distinctions between magnetism and electricity: The force between magnetic objects tends to align the objects relative to each other and is affected only slightly by most intervening objects, while the force between electrified objects is primarily a force of attraction or repulsion between the objects and is grossly affected by intervening matter. Gilbert attributed the electrification of a body by friction to the removal of a fluid, or "humour," which then left an "effluvium," or atmosphere, around the body. The language is quaint, but, if the "humour" is renamed "charge" and the "effluvium" renamed "electric field," Gilbert's notions closely approach modern ideas.

PIONEERING EFFORTS

During the 17th and early 18th centuries, as better sources of charge were developed, the study of electric effects became increasingly popular. The first machine to generate an electric spark was built in 1663 by Otto von Guericke, a German physicist and engineer. Guericke's electric generator consisted of a sulfur globe mounted on an iron shaft. The globe could be turned with one hand and rubbed with the other. Electrified by friction, the sphere alternately attracted and repulsed light objects from the floor.

Stephen Gray, a British chemist, is credited with discovering that electricity can flow (1729). He found that corks stuck in the ends of glass tubes become electrified when the tubes are rubbed. He also transmitted electricity approximately 150 metres through a hemp thread supported by silk cords and, in another demonstration, sent electricity even farther through metal wire. Gray concluded that electricity flowed everywhere.

From the mid-18th through the early 19th centuries, scientists believed that electricity was composed of fluid. In 1733 Charles François de Cisternay DuFay, a French chemist, announced that electricity consisted of two fluids: "vitreous" (from the Latin for "glass"), or positive, electricity; and "resinous," or negative, electricity. When DuFay electrified a glass rod, it attracted nearby bits of cork. Yet, if the rod touched the pieces of cork, the cork fragments were repelled and also repelled one another. DuFay accounted for this phenomenon by explaining that, in general, matter was neutral because it contained equal quantities of both fluids. If, however, friction separated the fluids in a substance and left it imbalanced, the substance would attract or repel other matter.

INVENTION OF THE LEYDEN JAR

In 1745 a cheap and convenient source of electric sparks was invented accidentally by Pieter van Musschenbroek, a physicist and mathematician in Leiden, Neth. Later called the Leyden jar, it was the first device that could store large amounts of electric charge. (Ewald Georg von Kleist, a German cleric, independently developed the idea for such a device in 1745 but did not investigate it as thoroughly as did Musschenbroek.)

The Leyden jar devised by the latter consisted of a glass vial that was partially filled with water and contained a thick conducting wire capable of storing a substantial amount of charge. One end of this wire protruded through the cork that sealed the opening of the vial. The Leyden jar was charged by bringing this exposed end of the conducting wire into contact with a friction device that generated static electricity. When the contact was broken, a charge could be demonstrated by touching the wire with the hand and receiving a shock. (The Leyden jar is of importance as a prototype of capacitors, which are widely used in radios, television sets, and other electrical and electronic equipment.)

Within a year after the appearance of Musschenbroek's device, William Watson, an English physician and scientist, constructed a more sophisticated version of the Leyden jar; he coated the inside and outside of the container with metal foil to improve its capacity to store charge. Watson transmitted an electric spark from his device through a wire strung across the River Thames at Westminster Bridge in 1747.

The Leyden jar revolutionized the study of electrostatics. Soon "electricians" were earning their living all over Europe demonstrating electricity with Leyden jars. Typically, they killed birds and animals with electric shock or sent charges through wires over rivers and lakes. In 1746 the abbé Jean-Antoine Nollet, a physicist who popularized science in France, discharged a Leyden jar in front of King Louis XV by sending current through a chain of 180 Royal Guards. In another demonstration, Nollet used wire made of iron to connect a row of Carthusian monks more than a kilometre long; when a Leyden jar was discharged, the white-robed monks reportedly leapt simultaneously into the air.

In the United States, Benjamin Franklin sold his printing house, newspaper, and almanac to spend his time conducting electricity experiments. In 1752 Franklin proved that lightning was an example of electric conduction by flying a silk kite during a thunderstorm. He collected electric charge from a cloud by means of wet twine attached to a key and thence to a Leyden jar. He then used the accumulated charge from the lightning to perform electric experiments.

Franklin enunciated the law now known as the conservation of charge (the net sum of the charges within an isolated region is always constant). Like Watson, he disagreed with DuFay's two-fluid theory. Franklin argued that electricity consisted of two states of one fluid, which is present in everything. A substance containing an unusually large amount of the fluid would be "plus," or positively charged. Matter with less than a normal amount of fluid would be "minus," or negatively charged. Franklin's one-fluid theory, which dominated the study of electricity for 100 years, is essentially correct because most currents are the result of moving electrons. At the same time, however, fundamental particles have both negative and positive charges and, in this sense, DuFay's two-fluid picture is correct.

Joseph Priestley, an English physicist, summarized all available data on electricity in his book *History and Present State of Electricity* (1767). He repeated one of Franklin's experiments, in which the latter had dropped small corks into a highly electrified metal container and found that they were neither attracted nor repelled. The lack of any charge on the inside of the container caused Priestley to recall Newton's law that there is no gravitational force on the inside of a hollow sphere. From this, Priestley inferred that the law of force between electric charges must be the same as the law for gravitational force—i.e., that the force between masses diminishes with the inverse square of the distance between the masses. Although they were expressed in qualitative and descriptive terms, Priestley's laws are still valid today. Their mathematics was clarified and developed extensively between 1767 and the mid-19th century as electricity and magnetism became precise, quantitative sciences.

Formulation of the Quantitative Laws of Electrostatics and Magnetostatics

Charles-Augustin de Coulomb established electricity as a mathematical science during the latter half of the 18th century. He transformed Priestley's descriptive observations into the basic quantitative laws of electrostatics and magnetostatics. He also developed the mathematical theory of electric force and invented the torsion balance that was to be used in electricity experiments for the next

100 years. Coulomb used the balance to measure the force between magnetic poles and between electric charges at varying distances. In 1785 he announced his quantitative proof that electric and magnetic forces vary, like gravitation, inversely as the square of the distance. Thus, according to Coulomb's law, if the distance between two charged masses is doubled, the electric force between them is reduced to a fourth. (The English physicist Henry Cavendish, as well as John Robison of Scotland, had made quantitative determinations of this principle before Coulomb, but they had not published their work.)

The mathematicians Siméon-Denis Poisson of France and Carl Friedrich Gauss of Germany extended Coulomb's work during the 18th and early 19th centuries. Poisson's equation (published in 1813) and the law of charge conservation contain in two lines virtually all the laws of electrostatics. The theory of magnetostatics, which is the study of steady-state magnetic fields, also was developed from Coulomb's law. Magnetostatics uses the concept of a magnetic potential analogous to the electric potential (i.e., magnetic poles are postulated with properties analogous to electric charges).

Michael Faraday built upon Priestley's work and conducted an experiment that verified quite accurately the inverse square law. Faraday's experiment involving the use of a metal ice pail and a gold-leaf electroscope was the first precise quantitative experiment on electric charge. In Faraday's time, the gold-leaf electroscope was used to indicate the electric state of a body. This type of apparatus consists of two thin leaves of gold hanging from an insulated metal rod that is mounted inside a metal box. When the rod is charged, the leaves repel each other and the deflection indicates the size of the charge. Faraday began his experiment by charging a metal ball suspended on an insulating silk thread. He then connected the gold-leaf electroscope to a metal ice pail resting on an insulating block and lowered the charged ball into the pail. The electroscope reading increased as the ball was lowered into the pail and reached a steady value once the ball was within the pail. When the ball was withdrawn without touching the pail, the electroscope reading fell to zero. Yet, when the ball touched the bottom of the pail, the reading remained at its steady value. On removal, the ball was found to be completely discharged. Faraday concluded that the electric charge produced on the outside of the pail, when the ball was inside but not in contact with it, was exactly equal to the initial charge on the ball.

He then inserted into the pail other objects, such as a set of concentric pails separated from one another with various insulating materials like sulfur. In each case, the electroscope reading was the same once the ball was completely within the pail. From this, Faraday concluded that the total charge of the system was an invariable quantity equal to the initial charge of the ball. The present-day belief that conservation is a fundamental property of charge rests not only on the experiments of Franklin and Faraday but also on its complete agreement with all observations in electric engineering, quantum electrodynamics, and experimental electricity. With Faraday's work, the theory of electrostatics was complete.

FOUNDATIONS OF ELECTROCHEMISTRY AND ELECTRODYNAMICS

The invention of the battery in 1800 made possible for the first time major advances in the theories of electric current and electrochemistry. Both science and technology developed rapidly as a direct result, leading some to call the 19th century the age of electricity.

The development of the battery was the accidental result of biological experiments conducted by Luigi
Galvani. Galvani, a professor of anatomy at the Bologna
Academy of Science, was interested in electricity in fish
and other animals. One day he noticed that electric
sparks from an electrostatic machine caused muscular
contractions in a dissected frog that lay nearby. At first,
Galvani assumed that the phenomenon was the result of
atmospheric electricity because similar effects could be
observed during lightning storms. Later, he discovered
that whenever a piece of metal connected the muscle
and nerve of the frog, the muscle contracted. Although
Galvani realized that some metals appeared to be more
effective than others in producing this effect, he concluded incorrectly that the metal was transporting a fluid,
which he identified with animal electricity, from the nerve
to the muscle. Galvani's observations, published in 1791,
aroused considerable controversy and speculation.

Alessandro Volta, a physicist at the nearby University
of Pavia, had been studying how electricity stimulates the
senses of touch, taste, and sight. When Volta put a metal
coin on top of his tongue and another coin of a different
metal under his tongue and connected their surfaces with
a wire, the coins tasted salty. Like Galvani, Volta assumed
that he was working with animal electricity until 1796
when he discovered that he could also produce a current
when he substituted a piece of cardboard soaked in brine
for his tongue. Volta correctly conjectured that the effect
was caused by the contact between metal and a moist
body. Around 1800 he constructed what is now known
as a voltaic pile consisting of layers of silver, moist cardboard, and zinc, repeated in that order, beginning and
ending with a different metal. When he joined the silver
and the zinc with a wire, electricity flowed continuously
through the wire. Volta confirmed that the effects of his

pile were equivalent in every way to those of static electricity. Within 20 years, galvanism, as electricity produced by a chemical reaction was then called, became unequivocally linked to static electricity. More important, Volta's invention provided the first source of continuous electric current. This rudimentary form of battery produced a smaller voltage than the Leyden jar, but it was easier to use because it could supply a steady current and did not have to be recharged.

The controversy between Galvani, who mistakenly thought that electricity originated in the animal's nerve, and Volta, who realized that it came from the metal, divided scientists into two camps. Galvani was supported by Alexander von Humboldt in Germany, while Volta was backed by Coulomb and other French physicists.

Within six weeks of Volta's report, two English scientists, William Nicholson and Anthony Carlisle, used a chemical battery to discover electrolysis (the process in which an electric current produces a chemical reaction) and initiate the science of electrochemistry. In their experiment the two employed a voltaic pile to liberate hydrogen and oxygen from water. They attached each end of the pile to brass wires and placed the opposite ends of the wires into salt water. The salt made the water a conductor. Hydrogen gas accumulated at the end of one wire; the end of the other wire was oxidized. Nicholson and Carlisle discovered that the amount of hydrogen and oxygen set free by the current was proportional to the amount of current used. By 1809 the English chemist Humphry Davy had used a stronger battery to free for the first time several very active metals—sodium, potassium, calcium, strontium, barium, and magnesium—from their liquid compounds. Faraday, who was Davy's assistant at the time, studied electrolysis quantitatively and showed that the amount of energy needed to separate a gram of a substance from its compound is closely related to the atomic weight of the substance. Electrolysis became a method of measuring electric current; and the quantity of charge that releases a gram atomic weight of a simple element is now called a faraday in his honour.

Once scientists were able to produce currents with a battery, they could study the flow of electricity quantitatively. Because of the battery, the German physicist Georg Simon Ohm was able experimentally in 1827 to quantify precisely a problem that Cavendish could only investigate qualitatively some 50 years earlier—namely, the ability of a material to conduct electricity. The result of this work—Ohm's law—explains how the resistance to the flow of charge depends on the type of conductor and on its length and diameter. According to Ohm's formulation, the current flow through a conductor is directly proportional to the potential difference, or voltage, and inversely proportional to the resistance—that is, $i = V/R$. Thus, doubling the length of an electric wire doubles its resistance, while doubling the cross-sectional area of the wire reduces the resistance by a half. Ohm's law is probably the most widely used equation in electric design.

EXPERIMENTAL AND THEORETICAL STUDIES OF ELECTROMAGNETIC PHENOMENA

One of the great turning points in the development of the physical sciences was Hans Christian Ørsted's announcement in 1820 that electric currents produce magnetic effects. (Ørsted made his discovery while lecturing to a class of physics students. He placed by chance a wire carrying current near a compass needle and was surprised to see the needle swing at right angles to the wire.) Ørsted's fortuitous discovery proved that electricity and magnetism are linked. His finding, together with Faraday's subsequent discovery that a changing magnetic field produces an electric current in a nearby circuit, formed the basis of both James Clerk Maxwell's unified theory of electromagnetism and most of modern electrotechnology.

Once Ørsted's experiment had revealed that electric currents have magnetic effects, scientists realized that there must be magnetic forces between the currents. They began studying the forces immediately. A French physicist, François Arago, observed in 1820 that an electric current will orient unmagnetized iron filings in a circle around the wire. That same year, another French physicist, André-Marie Ampère, developed Ørsted's observations in quantitative terms. Ampère showed that two parallel wires carrying electric currents attract and repel each other like magnets. If the currents flow in the same direction, the wires attract each other; if they flow in opposite directions, the wires repel each other. From this experiment, Ampère was able to express the right-hand rule for the direction of the force on a current in a magnetic field. He also established experimentally and quantitatively the laws of magnetic force between electric currents. He suggested that internal electric currents are responsible for permanent magnets and for highly magnetizable materials like iron. With Arago, he demonstrated that steel needles become more strongly magnetic inside a coil carrying an electric current. Experiments on small coils showed that, at large distances, the forces between two such coils are similar to those between two small bar magnets and, moreover, that one coil can be replaced by a bar magnet of suitable size without changing the forces. The magnetic moment of this equivalent magnet was determined by the dimensions of the coil, its number of turns, and the current flowing around it.

William Sturgeon of England and Joseph Henry of the United States used Ørsted's discovery to develop electromagnets during the 1820s. Sturgeon wrapped 18 turns of bare copper wire around a U-shaped iron bar. When he turned on the current, the bar became an electromagnet capable of lifting 20 times its weight. When the current was turned off, the bar was no longer magnetized. Henry repeated Sturgeon's work in 1829, using insulated wire to prevent short-circuiting. Using hundreds of turns, Henry created an electromagnet that could lift more than one ton of iron.

Ørsted's experiment showing that electricity could produce magnetic effects raised the opposite question as well: Could magnetism induce an electric current in another circuit? The French physicist Augustin-Jean Fresnel argued that since a steel bar inside a metallic helix can be magnetized by passing a current through the helix, the bar magnet in turn should create a current in an enveloping helix. In the following decade many ingenious experiments were devised, but the expectation that a steady current would be induced in a coil near the magnet resulted in experimenters either accidentally missing or not appreciating any transient electric effects caused by the magnet.

Faraday's Discovery of Electric Induction

Faraday, the greatest experimentalist in electricity and magnetism of the 19th century and one of the greatest experimental physicists of all time, worked on and off for 10 years trying to prove that a magnet could induce electricity. In 1831 he finally succeeded by using two coils of wire wound around opposite sides of a ring of soft iron.

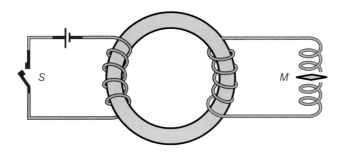

Faraday's magnetic induction experiment. When the switch S is closed in the primary circuit, a momentary current flows in the secondary circuit, giving a transient deflection of the compass needle M. Copyright Encyclopædia Britannica; rendering for this edition by Rosen Educational Services

The first coil was attached to a battery. When a current passed through the coil, the iron ring became magnetized. A wire from the second coil was extended to a compass needle a metre away, far enough so that it was not affected directly by any current in the first circuit. When the first circuit was turned on, Faraday observed a momentary deflection of the compass needle and its immediate return to its original position. When the primary current was switched off, a similar deflection of the compass needle occurred but in the opposite direction.

Building on this observation in other experiments, Faraday showed that changes in the magnetic field around the first coil are responsible for inducing the current in the second coil. He also demonstrated that an electric current can be induced by moving a magnet, by turning an electromagnet on and off, and even by moving an electric wire in Earth's magnetic field. Within a few months, Faraday built the first, albeit primitive, electric generator.

Joseph Henry had discovered electric induction quite independently in 1830, but his results were not published until after he had received news of Faraday's 1831 work, nor did he develop the discovery as fully as Faraday. In his paper of July 1832, Henry reported and correctly interpreted self-induction. He had produced large electric arcs from a long helical conductor when it was disconnected from a battery. When he had opened the circuit, the rapid decrease in the current had caused a large voltage between the battery terminal and the wire. As the wire lead was pulled away from the battery, the current continued to flow for a short time in the form of a bright arc between the battery terminal and the wire.

Faraday's thinking was permeated by the concept of electric and magnetic lines of force. He visualized that magnets, electric charges, and electric currents produce lines of force. When he placed a thin card covered with iron filings on a magnet, he could see the filings form chains from one end of the magnet to the other. He believed that these lines showed the directions of the forces and that electric current would have the same lines of force. The tension they build explains the attraction and repulsion of magnets and electric charges. Faraday had visualized magnetic curves as early as 1831 while working on his induction experiments; he wrote in his notes, "By magnetic curves I mean lines of magnetic forces which would be depicted by iron filings." Faraday opposed the prevailing idea that induction occurred "at a distance"; instead, he held that induction occurs along curved lines of force because of the action of contiguous particles. Later, he explained that electricity and magnetism are transmitted through a medium that is the site of electric or magnetic "fields," which make all substances magnetic to some extent.

Faraday was not the only researcher laying the groundwork for a synthesis between electricity, magnetism, and other areas of physics. On the continent of Europe, primarily in Germany, scientists were making mathematical connections between electricity, magnetism, and optics. The work of the physicists Franz Ernst Neumann, Wilhelm Eduard Weber, and H.F.E. Lenz belongs to this period. At the same time, Helmholtz and the English physicists William Thomson (later Lord Kelvin) and James Prescott Joule were clarifying the relationship between electricity and other forms of energy. Joule investigated the quantitative relationship between electric currents and heat during the 1840s and formulated the theory of the heating effects that accompany the flow of electricity in conductors. Helmholtz, Thomson, Henry, Gustav Kirchhoff, and Sir George Gabriel Stokes also extended the theory of the conduction and propagation of electric effects in conductors. In 1856 Weber and his German colleague, Rudolf Kohlrausch, determined the ratio of electric and magnetic units and found that it has the same dimensions as light and that it is almost exactly equal to its velocity. In 1857 Kirchhoff used this finding to demonstrate that electric disturbances propagate on a highly conductive wire with the speed of light.

MAXWELL'S UNIFIED THEORY OF ELECTROMAGNETISM

The final steps in synthesizing electricity and magnetism into one coherent theory were made by Maxwell. He was deeply influenced by Faraday's work, having begun his study of the phenomena by translating Faraday's experimental findings into mathematics. (Faraday was self-taught and had never mastered mathematics.) In 1856 Maxwell developed the theory that the energy of the electromagnetic field is in the space around the conductors as well as in the conductors themselves. By 1864 he had formulated his own electromagnetic theory of light, predicting that both light and radio waves are electric and magnetic phenomena. While Faraday had discovered that changes in magnetic fields produce electric fields, Maxwell added the converse: Changes in electric fields produce magnetic fields even in the absence of electric currents. Maxwell predicted that electromagnetic disturbances traveling through empty space have electric and magnetic fields at right angles to each other and that both fields are perpendicular to the direction of the wave. He concluded that the waves move at a uniform speed equal to the speed of light and that light is one form of electromagnetic wave. Their elegance notwithstanding, Maxwell's radical ideas were accepted by few outside England until 1886, when the German physicist Heinrich Hertz verified the existence of electromagnetic waves traveling at the speed of light; the waves he discovered are known now as radio waves.

Maxwell's four field equations represent the pinnacle of classical electromagnetic theory. The statements of these four equations are, respectively: (1) electric field diverges from electric charge, an expression of the Coulomb force, (2) there are no isolated magnetic poles, but the Coulomb force acts between the poles of a magnet, (3) electric fields are produced by changing magnetic fields, an expression of Faraday's law of induction, and (4) circulating magnetic fields are produced by changing electric fields and by electric currents, Maxwell's extension of Ampère's law to include the interaction of changing fields. The most compact way of writing these equations in the metre–kilogram–second (mks) system is in terms of the vector operators div (divergence) and curl. In these expressions the Greek letter rho, ρ, is charge density, J is current density, E is the electric field, and B is the magnetic field; here, D and H are field quantities that are proportional to E and B, respectively. The four Maxwell equations, corresponding to the four statements above, are: (1) div $D = \rho$, (2) div $B = 0$, (3) curl $E = -dB/dt$, and (4) curl $H = dD/dt + J$.

Subsequent developments in the theory have been concerned either with the relationship between electromagnetism and the atomic structure of matter or with the practical and theoretical consequences of Maxwell's equations. His formulation has withstood the revolutions of relativity and quantum mechanics. His equations are appropriate for distances as small as 10^{-10} centimetres—100 times smaller than the size of an atom. The fusion of electromagnetic theory and quantum theory, known as quantum electrodynamics, is required only for smaller distances.

While the mainstream of theoretical activity concerning electric and magnetic phenomena during the 19th century was devoted to showing how they are interrelated, some scientists made use of them to discover new properties of materials and heat. Weber developed Ampère's suggestion that there are internal circulating currents of molecular size in metals. He explained how a substance loses its magnetic properties when the molecular magnets point in random directions. Under the action of an external force, they may turn to point in the direction of the force; when all point in this direction, the maximum possible degree of magnetization is reached, a phenomenon known as magnetic saturation. In 1895 Pierre Curie of France discovered that a ferromagnetic substance has a specific temperature above which it ceases to be magnetic. Finally, superconductivity was discovered in 1900 by the German physicist Heike Kammerlingh-Onnes. In superconductivity electric conductors lose all resistance at very low temperatures.

DISCOVERY OF THE ELECTRON AND ITS RAMIFICATIONS

Although little of major importance was added to electromagnetic theory in the 19th century after Maxwell, the discovery of the electron in 1898 opened up an entirely new area of study: the nature of electric charge and of matter itself. The discovery of the electron grew out of studies of electric currents in vacuum tubes. Heinrich Geissler, a glassblower who assisted the German physicist Julius Plücker, improved the vacuum tube in 1854. Four years later, Plücker sealed two electrodes inside the tube, evacuated the air, and forced electric currents between the electrodes; he attributed the green glow that appeared on the wall of the tube to rays emanating from the cathode. From then until the end of the century, the properties of cathode-ray discharges were studied intensively. The work of the English physicist Sir William Crookes in 1879 indicated that the luminescence was a property of the electric current itself. Crookes concluded that the rays were composed of electrified charged particles. In 1898 another English physicist, Sir J.J. Thomson, identified a cathode ray as a stream of negatively charged particles, each having a mass $\frac{1}{1,836}$ smaller than that of a hydrogen ion. Thomson's discovery established the particulate nature of charge; his particles were later dubbed electrons.

Following the discovery of the electron, electromagnetic theory became an integral part of the theories of the atomic, subatomic, and subnuclear structure of matter. This shift in focus occurred as the result of an impasse between electromagnetic theory and statistical mechanics over attempts to understand radiation from hot bodies. Thermal radiation had been investigated in Germany by the physicist Wilhelm Wien between 1890 and 1900. Wien had virtually exhausted the resources of thermodynamics in dealing with this problem. Two British scientists, Lord Rayleigh (John William Strutt) and Sir James Hopwood Jeans, had by 1900 applied the newly developed science of statistical mechanics to the same problem. They obtained results that, though in agreement with Wien's thermo-dynamic conclusions (as distinct from his speculative extensions of thermodynamics), only partially agreed with experimental observations. The German physicist Max Planck attempted to combine the statistical approach with a thermodynamic approach. By concentrating on the necessity of fitting together the experimental data, he was led to the formulation of an empirical law that satisfied Wien's thermodynamic criteria and accommodated the experimental data. When Planck interpreted this law in terms of Rayleigh's statistical concepts, he concluded that radiation of frequency v exists only in quanta of energy. Planck's result, including the introduction of the new universal constant h in 1900, marked the foundation of quantum mechanics and initiated a profound change in physical theory.

By 1900 it was apparent that Thomson's electrons were a universal constituent of matter and, thus, that matter is essentially electric in nature. As a result, in the early years of the 20th century, many physicists attempted to construct theories of the electromagnetic properties of metals, insulators, and magnetic materials in terms of electrons. In 1909 the Dutch physicist Hendrik Antoon Lorentz succeeded in doing so in *The Theory of Electrons and Its Applications to the Phenomena of Light and Radiant Heat*; his work has since been modified by quantum theory.

SPECIAL THEORY OF RELATIVITY

The other major conceptual advance in electromagnetic theory was the special theory of relativity. In Maxwell's time, a mechanistic view of the universe held sway. Sound was interpreted as an undulatory motion of the air, while light and other electromagnetic waves were regarded as undulatory motions of an intangible medium called ether. The question arose as to whether the velocity of light measured by an observer moving relative to ether would be affected by his motion. Albert Abraham Michelson and Edward W. Morley of the United States had demonstrated in 1887 that light in a vacuum on Earth travels at a constant speed which is independent of the direction of the light relative to the direction of Earth's motion through the ether. Lorentz and Henri Poincaré, a French physicist, showed between 1900 and 1904 that the conclusions of Michelson and Morley were consistent with Maxwell's equations. On this basis, Lorentz and Poincaré developed a theory of relativity in which the absolute motion of a body relative to a hypothetical ether is no longer significant. Poincaré named the theory the principle of relativity in a lecture at the St. Louis Exposition in September 1904.

Planck gave the first formulation of relativistic dynamics two years later. The most general formulation of the special theory of relativity, however, was put forth by Einstein in 1905, and the theory of relativity is usually associated with his name. Einstein postulated that the speed of light is a constant, independent of the motion of the source of the light, and showed how the Newtonian laws of mechanics would have to be modified. While Maxwell had synthesized electricity and magnetism into one theory, he had regarded them as essentially two interdependent phenomena; Einstein showed that they are two aspects of the same phenomenon.

Maxwell's equations, the special theory of relativity, the discovery of the electronic structure of matter, and the formulation of quantum mechanics all occurred before 1930. The quantum electrodynamics theory, developed between 1945 and 1955, subsequently resolved some minute discrepancies in the calculations of certain atomic properties. For example, the accuracy with which it is now possible to calculate one of the numbers describing the magnetic moment of the electron is comparable to measuring the distance between New York City and Los Angeles to within the thickness of a human hair. As a result, quantum electrodynamics is the most complete and precise theory of any physical phenomenon. The remarkable correspondence between theory and observation makes it unique among human endeavours.

DEVELOPMENT OF ELECTROMAGNETIC TECHNOLOGY

Electromagnetic technology began with Faraday's discovery of induction in 1831. His demonstration that a changing magnetic field induces an electric current in a nearby circuit showed that mechanical energy can be converted to electric energy. It provided the foundation for electric power generation, leading directly to the invention of the dynamo and the electric motor. Faraday's finding also proved crucial for lighting and heating systems.

The early electric industry was dominated by the problem of generating electricity on a large scale. Within a year of Faraday's discovery, a small hand-turned generator in which a magnet revolved around coils was demonstrated in Paris. In 1833 there appeared an English model that featured the modern arrangement of rotating the coils in the field of a fixed magnet. By 1850 generators were manufactured commercially in several countries. Permanent magnets were used to produce the magnetic field in generators until the principle of the self-excited generator was discovered in 1866. (A self-excited generator has stronger magnetic fields because it uses electromagnets powered by the generator itself.) In 1870 Zénobe

Théophile Gramme, a Belgian manufacturer, built the first practical generator capable of producing a continuous current. It was soon found that the magnetic field is more effective if the coil windings are embedded in slots in the rotating iron armature. The slotted armature, still in use today, was invented in 1880 by the Swedish engineer Jonas Wenström. Faraday's 1831 discovery of the principle of the AC transformer was not put to practical use until the late 1880s when the heated debate over the merits of direct-current and alternating-current systems for power transmission was settled in favour of the latter.

At first, the only serious consideration for electric power was arc lighting, in which a brilliant light is emitted by an electric spark between two electrodes. The arc lamp was too powerful for domestic use, however, and so it was limited to large installations like lighthouses, train stations, and department stores. Commercial development of an incandescent filament lamp, first invented in the 1840s, was delayed until a filament could be made that would heat to incandescence without melting and until a satisfactory vacuum tube could be built. The mercury pump, invented in 1865, provided an adequate vacuum, and a satisfactory carbon filament was developed independently by the English physicist Sir Joseph Wilson Swan and the American inventor Thomas A. Edison during the late 1870s. By 1880 both had applied for patents for their incandescent lamps, and the ensuing litigation between the two men was resolved by the formation of a joint company in 1883. Thanks to the incandescent lamp, electric lighting became an accepted part of urban life by 1900. Since then, the tungsten filament lamp, introduced during the early 1900s, has become the principal form of electric lamp, though more efficient fluorescent gas discharge lamps have found widespread use as well.

Electricity took on a new importance with the development of the electric motor. This machine, which converts electric energy to mechanical energy, has become an integral component of a wide assortment of devices ranging from kitchen appliances and office equipment to industrial robots and rapid-transit vehicles. Although the principle of the electric motor was devised by Faraday in 1821, no commercially significant unit was produced until 1873. In fact, the first important AC motor, built by the Serbian-American inventor Nikola Tesla, was not demonstrated in the United States until 1888. Tesla began producing his motors in association with the Westinghouse Electric Company a few years after DC motors had been installed in trains in Germany and Ireland. By the end of the 19th century, the electric motor had taken a recognizably modern form. Subsequent improvements have rarely involved radically new ideas. However, the introduction of better designs and new bearing, armature, magnetic, and contact materials has resulted in the manufacture of smaller, cheaper, and more efficient and reliable motors.

The modern communications industry is among the most spectacular products of electricity. Telegraph systems using wires and simple electrochemical or electromechanical receivers proliferated in western Europe and the United States during the 1840s. An operable cable was installed under the English Channel in 1865, and a pair of transatlantic cables were successfully laid a year later. By 1872 almost all of the major cities of the world were linked by telegraph.

Alexander Graham Bell patented the first practical telephone in the United States in 1876, and the first public telephone services were operating within a few years. In 1895 the British physicist Sir Ernest Rutherford advanced Hertz's scientific investigations of radio waves and transmitted radio signals for more than one kilometre. Guglielmo Marconi, an Italian physicist and inventor, established wireless communications across the Atlantic employing radio waves of approximately 300- to 3,000-metre wavelength in 1901. Broadcast radio transmissions were established during the 1920s.

Telephone transmissions by radio waves, the electric recording and reproduction of sound, and television were made possible by the development of the triode tube. This three-electrode tube, invented by the American engineer Lee De Forest, permitted for the first time the amplification of electric signals. Known as the Audion, this device played a pivotal role in the early development of the electronics industry.

The first telephone transmission via radio signals was made from Arlington, Va., to the Eiffel Tower in Paris in 1915; a commercial radio telephone service between New York City and London was begun in 1927. Besides such efforts, most of the major developmental work of this period was tied to the radio and phonograph entertainment industries and the sound film industry. Rapid progress was made toward transmitting moving pictures, especially in Great Britain. Just before World War II, the British Broadcasting Corporation inaugurated the first public television service. Today, many regions of the electromagnetic spectrum are used for communications, including microwaves in the frequency range of approximately 7×10^9 hertz for satellite communication links and infrared light at a frequency of about 3×10^{14} hertz for optical fibre communications systems.

Until 1939 the electronics industry was almost exclusively concerned with communications and broadcast entertainment. Scientists and engineers in Britain, Germany, France, and the United States did initiate research on radar systems capable of aircraft detection and antiaircraft fire-control during the 1930s, however, and this marked the beginning of a new direction for electronics. During World War II and after, the electronics industry made strides paralleled only by those of the chemical industry. Television became commonplace, and a broad array of new devices and systems, most notably the electronic digital computer, emerged.

The electronic revolution of the last half of the 20th century has been made possible in large part by the invention of the transistor (1947) and such subsequent developments as the integrated circuit. This miniaturization and integration of circuit elements has led to a remarkable diminution in the size and cost of electronic equipment and an equally impressive increase in its reliability.

CHAPTER 2
ELECTRICITY

The phenomenon associated with stationary or moving electric charges is called electricity. Electric charge is a fundamental property of matter and is borne by elementary particles. In electricity the particle involved is the electron, which carries a charge designated, by convention, as negative. Thus, the various manifestations of electricity are the result of the accumulation or motion of numbers of electrons.

ELECTROSTATICS

Electrostatics is the study of electromagnetic phenomena that occur when there are no moving charges—i.e., after a static equilibrium has been established. Charges reach their equilibrium positions rapidly because the electric force is extremely strong. The mathematical methods of electrostatics make it possible to calculate the distributions of the electric field and of the electric potential from a known configuration of charges, conductors, and insulators. Conversely, given a set of conductors with known potentials, it is possible to calculate electric fields in regions between the conductors and to determine the charge distribution on the surface of the conductors. The electric energy of a set of charges at rest can be viewed from the standpoint of the work required to assemble the charges; alternatively, the energy also can be considered to reside in the electric field produced by this assembly of charges. Finally, energy can be stored in a capacitor. The energy required to charge such a device is stored in it as electrostatic energy of the electric field.

29

ELECTRIC CHARGE

Electric charge is a basic property of matter carried by some elementary particles. Electric charge, which can be positive or negative, occurs in discrete natural units and is neither created nor destroyed.

Electric charges are of two general types, positive and negative. Two objects that have an excess of one type of charge exert a force of repulsion on each other when relatively close together. Two objects that have excess opposite charges, one positively charged and the other negatively charged, attract each other when relatively near.

Many fundamental, or subatomic, particles of matter have the property of electric charge. For example, electrons have negative charge and protons have positive charge, but neutrons have zero charge. The negative charge of each electron is found by experiment to have the same magnitude, which is also equal to that of the positive charge of each proton. Charge thus exists in natural units equal to the charge of an electron or a proton, a fundamental physical constant.

A direct and convincing measurement of an electron's charge, as a natural unit of electric charge, was first made (1909) in the Millikan oil-drop experiment. Atoms of matter are electrically neutral because their nuclei contain the same number of protons as there are electrons surrounding the nuclei. Electric current and charged objects involve the separation of some of the negative charge of neutral atoms. Current in metal wires consists of a drift of electrons of which one or two from each atom are more loosely bound than the rest. Some of the atoms in the surface layer of a glass rod positively charged by rubbing it with a silk cloth have lost electrons, leaving a net positive charge because of the unneutralized protons of their nuclei. A negatively charged object has an excess of electrons on its surface.

Electric charge is conserved. In any isolated system, in any chemical or nuclear reaction, the net electric charge is constant. The algebraic sum of the fundamental charges remains the same.

The unit of electric charge in the metre–kilogram–second and SI systems is the coulomb, equivalent to the net amount of electric charge that flows through a cross section of a conductor in an electric circuit during each second when the current has a value of one ampere. One coulomb consists of 6.24×10^{18} natural units of electric charge, such as individual electrons or protons. One electron itself has a negative charge of $1.602176487 \times 10^{-19}$ coulomb. In the centimetre–gram–second system there are two units of electric charge: the electrostatic unit of charge, esu, or statcoulomb; and the electromagnetic unit of charge, emu, or abcoulomb. One coulomb of electric charge equals about 3,000,000,000 esu, or one-tenth emu.

An electrochemical unit of charge, the faraday, is useful in describing electrolysis reactions, such as in metallic electroplating. One faraday equals 9.64853399×10^{4} coulombs, the charge of a mole of electrons (that is, an Avogadro's number, $6.02214179 \times 10^{23}$, of electrons).

STATIC ELECTRICITY

This is a familiar electric phenomenon in which friction transfers charged particles from one body to another. If two objects are rubbed together, especially if the objects are insulators and the surrounding air is dry, the objects acquire equal and opposite charges and an attractive force develops between them. The object that loses electrons becomes positively charged, and the other becomes negatively charged. The force is simply the attraction between charges of opposite sign. The properties of this force are incorporated in the mathematical relationship known as

Coulomb's law. The electric force on a charge Q_1 under these conditions, due to a charge Q_2 at a distance r, is given by Coulomb's law,

$$F = k \frac{Q_1 Q_2}{r^2} \hat{r}. \tag{1}$$

The bold characters in the equation indicate the vector nature of the force, and the unit vector $\hat{r}$ is a vector that has a size of one and that points from charge Q_2 to charge Q_1. The proportionality constant k equals $10^{-7} c^2$, where c is the speed of light in a vacuum; k has the numerical value of 8.99×10^9 newtons-square metre per coulomb squared (Nm^2/C^2). A numerical example will help to illustrate the force on Q_1 due to Q_2. Both Q_1 and Q_2 are chosen arbitrarily to be positive charges, each with a magnitude of 10^{-6} coulomb. The charge Q_1 is located at coordinates x, y, z with values of 0.03, 0, 0, respectively, while Q_2 has

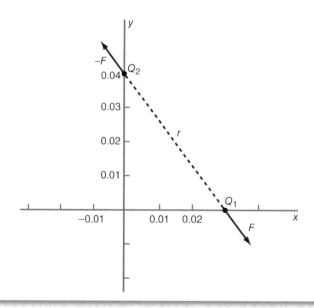

Electric force between two charges. Courtesy of the Department of Physics and Astronomy, Michigan State University; rendering for this edition by Rosen Educational Services

coordinates 0, 0.04, 0. All coordinates are given in metres. Thus, the distance between Q_1 and Q_2 is 0.05 metre.

The magnitude of the force F on charge Q_1 as calculated using equation (1) is 3.6 newtons. The force on Q_2 due to Q_1 is $-F$, which also has a magnitude of 3.6 newtons; its direction, however, is opposite to that of F. The force F can be expressed in terms of its components along the x and y axes, since the force vector lies in the xy plane. This is done with elementary trigonometry. Thus,

$$F = 2.16\hat{x} - 2.88\hat{y} \qquad (2)$$

in newtons. Coulomb's law describes mathematically the properties of the electric force between charges at rest. If the charges have opposite signs, the force would be attractive; the attraction would be indicated in equation (1) by the negative coefficient of the unit vector $\hat{r}$. Thus, the electric force on Q_1 would have a direction opposite to the unit vector $\hat{r}$ and would point from Q_1 to Q_2. In Cartesian coordinates, this would result in a change of

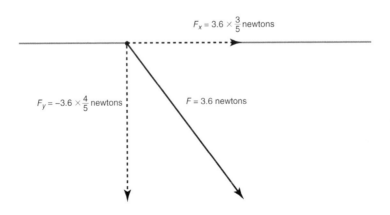

The x *and* y *components of the force* F. Courtesy of the Department of Physics and Astronomy, Michigan State University; rendering for this edition by Rosen Educational Services

the signs of both the x and y components of the force in equation (2).

How can this electric force on Q_1 be understood? Fundamentally, the force is due to the presence of an electric field at the position of Q_1. The field is caused by the second charge Q_2 and has a magnitude proportional to the size of Q_2. In interacting with this field, the first charge some distance away is either attracted to or repelled from the second charge, depending on the sign of the first charge.

CALCULATING THE VALUE OF AN ELECTRIC FIELD

In the example, the charge Q_1 is in the electric field produced by the charge Q_2. This field has the value

$$E = k \frac{Q_2}{r^2} \hat{r} \tag{3}$$

in newtons per coulomb (N/C). (Electric field can also be expressed in volts per metre [V/m], which is the equivalent of newtons per coulomb.) The electric force on Q_1 is given by

$$F = 2.16\hat{x} - 2.88\hat{y} \tag{2}$$

in newtons. This equation can be used to define the electric field of a point charge. The electric field E produced by charge Q_2 is a vector. The magnitude of the field varies inversely as the square of the distance from Q_2; its direction is away from Q_2 when Q_2 is a positive charge and toward Q_2 when Q_2 is a negative charge. Using equations (2) and (4), the field produced by Q_2 at the position of Q_1 is

$$E = 2.16 \times 10^6 \hat{x} - 2.88 \times 10^6 \hat{y}$$

in newtons per coulomb.

When there are several charges present, the force on a given charge Q_1 may be simply calculated as the sum of the individual forces due to the other charges Q_2, Q_3, ..., etc., until all the charges are included. This sum requires that special attention be given to the direction of the individual forces since forces are vectors. The force on Q_1 can be obtained with the same amount of effort by first calculating the electric field at the position of Q_1 due to Q_2, Q_3, ..., etc. To illustrate this, a third charge is added to the example above. There are now three charges, $Q_1 = +10^{-6}$ C, $Q_2 = +10^{-6}$ C, and $Q_3 = -10^{-6}$ C. The locations of the charges, using Cartesian coordinates $[x, y, z]$ are, respectively, [0.03, 0, 0], [0, 0.04, 0], and [-0.02, 0, 0] metre. The goal is to find the force on Q_1. From the sign of the charges, it can be seen that Q_1 is repelled by Q_2 and attracted by Q_3. It is also clear that these two forces act along different directions. The electric field at the position of Q_1 due to charge Q_2 is, just as in the example above,

$$E_{1,2} = 2.16 \times 10^6 \hat{x} - 2.88 \times 10^6 \hat{y}$$

in newtons per coulomb. The electric field at the location of Q_1 due to charge Q_3 is

$$E_{1,3} = -3.6 \times 10^6 \hat{x}$$

in newtons per coulomb. Thus, the total electric field at position 1 (i.e., at [0.03, 0, 0]) is the sum of these two fields $E_{1,2} + E_{1,3}$ and is given by

$$E_1 (total) = -1.44 \times 10^6 \hat{x} - 2.88 \times 10^6 \hat{y}.$$

The fields are $E_{1,2}$ and $E_{1,3}$, as well as their sum, the total electric field at the location of Q_1, E_1 (total). The total force on Q_1 is then obtained from equation (4) by multiplying the electric field E_1 (*total*) by Q_1. In Cartesian coordinates, this force, expressed in newtons, is given by its components along the x and y axes by

$$F_1(total) = -1.44\,\hat{x} - 2.88\,\hat{y}.$$

The resulting force on Q_1 is in the direction of the total electric field at Q_1. The magnitude of the force, which is obtained as the square root of the sum of the squares of the components of the force given in the above equation, equals 3.22 newtons.

SUPERPOSITION PRINCIPLE

This calculation demonstrates an important property of the electromagnetic field known as the superposition

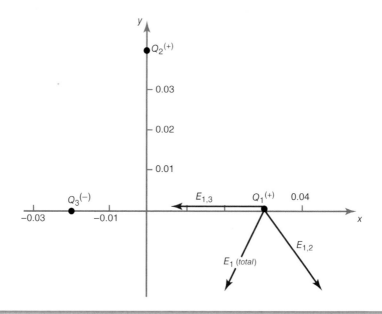

Electric field at the location of Q_1. Courtesy of the Department of Physics and Astronomy, Michigan State University; rendering for this edition by Rosen Educational Services

principle. According to this principle, a field arising from a number of sources is determined by adding the individual fields from each source. Studies of electric fields over an extremely wide range of magnitudes have established the validity of the superposition principle.

The vector nature of an electric field produced by a set of charges introduces a significant complexity. Specifying the field at each point in space requires giving both the magnitude and the direction at each location. In the Cartesian coordinate system, this necessitates knowing the magnitude of the x, y, and z components of the electric field at each point in space. It would be much simpler if the value of the electric field vector at any point in space could be derived from a scalar function with magnitude and sign.

ELECTRIC POTENTIAL

The electric potential is just such a scalar function. Electric potential is related to the work done by an external force when it transports a charge slowly from one position to another in an environment containing other charges at

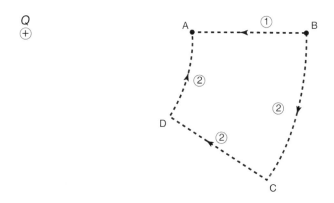

Positive charge +Q and two paths in moving a second charge, q, from B to A. Courtesy of the Department of Physics and Astronomy, Michigan State University; rendering for this edition by Rosen Educational Services

rest. The difference between the potential at point A and the potential at point B is defined by the equation

$$V_A - V_B = \frac{\text{work to move charge } q \text{ from B to A}}{q} . \qquad (5)$$

As noted, electric potential is measured in volts. Since work is measured in joules in the SI, one volt is equivalent to one joule per coulomb. The charge q is taken as a small test charge; it is assumed that the test charge does not disturb the distribution of the remaining charges during its transport from point B to point A.

To illustrate the work in equation (5), let $+Q$ be a positive charge. Consider the work involved in moving a second charge q from B to A. Along path 1, work is done to offset the electric repulsion between the two charges. If path 2 is chosen instead, no work is done in moving q from B to C, since the motion is perpendicular to the electric force; moving q from C to D, the work is, by symmetry, identical as from B to A, and no work is required from D to A. Thus, the total work done in moving q from B to A is the same for either path. It can be shown easily that the same is true for any path going from B to A. When the initial and final positions of the charge q are located on a sphere centred on the location of the $+Q$ charge, no work is done; the electric potential at the initial position has the same value as at the final position. The sphere in this example is called an equipotential surface. When equation (5), which defines the potential difference between two points, is combined with Coulomb's law, it yields the following expression for the potential difference $V_A - V_B$ between points A and B:

$$V_A - V_B = k\frac{Q}{r_a} - k\frac{Q}{r_b}, \qquad (6)$$

where r_a and r_b are the distances of points A and B from Q. Choosing B far away from the charge Q and arbitrarily setting the electric potential to be zero far from the charge results in a simple equation for the potential at A:

$$V_A = k \frac{Q}{r_a}. \qquad (7)$$

The contribution of a charge to the electric potential at some point in space is thus a scalar quantity directly proportional to the magnitude of the charge and inversely proportional to the distance between the point and the charge. For more than one charge, one simply adds the contributions of the various charges. The result is a

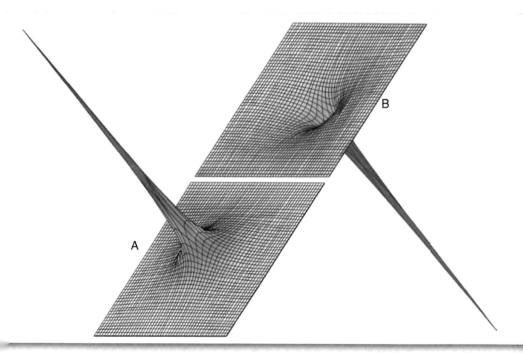

Potential energy landscape. (A) Potential energy of a positive charge near a second positive charge. (B) Potential energy of a negative charge near a positive charge. Courtesy of the Department of Physics and Astronomy, Michigan State University; rendering for this edition by Rosen Educational Services

topological map that gives a value of the electric potential for every point in space.

The potential energy of a charge q is the product qV of the charge and of the electric potential at the position of the charge. For example, the positive charge q would have to be pushed by some external agent in order to get close to the location of another positive charge $+Q$ because, as q approaches, it is subjected to an increasingly repulsive electric force. For a negative charge $-q$, the potential energy "landscape" would be, instead of a steep hill, a deep funnel. The electric potential due to $+Q$ is still positive, but the potential energy is negative, and the negative charge $-q$, in a manner quite analogous to a particle under the influence of gravity, is attracted toward the origin where charge $+Q$ is located.

The electric field is related to the variation of the electric potential in space. The potential provides a convenient tool for solving a wide variety of problems in electrostatics. In a region of space where the potential varies, a charge is subjected to an electric force. For a positive charge the direction of this force is opposite the gradient of the potential—that is to say, in the direction in which the potential decreases the most rapidly. A negative charge would be subjected to a force in the direction of the most rapid increase of the potential. In both instances, the magnitude of the force is proportional to the rate of change of the potential in the indicated directions. If the potential in a region of space is constant, there is no force on either positive or negative charge. In a 12-volt car battery, positive charges would tend to move away from the positive terminal and toward the negative terminal, while negative charges would tend to move in the opposite direction—i.e., from the negative to the positive terminal. The latter occurs when a copper wire, in which there are electrons that are free to move, is connected between the two terminals of the battery.

Deriving Electric Field from Potential

The electric field has already been described in terms of the force on a charge. If the electric potential is known at every point in a region of space, the electric field can be derived from the potential. In vector calculus notation, the electric field is given by the negative of the gradient of the electric potential, $E = -gradV$. This expression specifies how the electric field is calculated at a given point. Since the field is a vector, it has both a direction and magnitude. The direction is that in which the potential decreases most rapidly, moving away from the point. The magnitude of the field is the change in potential across a small distance in the indicated direction divided by that distance.

To become more familiar with the electric potential, a numerically determined solution is presented for a two-dimensional configuration of electrodes. A long, circular

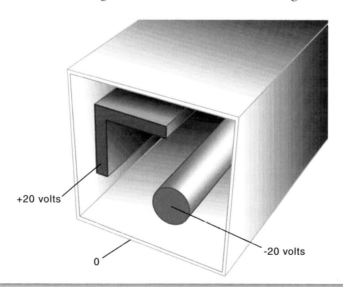

Electrode configuration. Courtesy of the Department of Physics and Astronomy, Michigan State University; rendering for this edition by Rosen Educational Services

conducting rod is maintained at an electric potential of -20 volts. Next to the rod, a long L-shaped bracket, also made of conducting material, is maintained at a potential of +20 volts. Both the rod and bracket are placed inside a long, hollow metal tube with a square cross section; this enclosure is at a potential of zero (i.e., it is at "ground" potential). Because the situation is static, there is no electric field inside the material of the conductors. If there were such a field, the charges that are free to move in a conducting material would do so until equilibrium was reached. The charges are arranged so that their individual contributions to the electric field at points inside the conducting material add up to zero. In a situation of static equilibrium, excess charges are located on the surface of conductors. Because there are no electric fields inside the conducting material, all parts of a given conductor are at the same potential; hence, a conductor is an equipotential in a static situation.

The numerical solution of the problem gives the potential at a large number of points inside the cavity. In carrying out the numerical solution of the electrostatic problem, the electrostatic potential is determined directly by means of one of its important properties: In a region where there is no charge (in this case, between the conductors), the value of the potential at a given point is the average of the values of the potential in the neighbourhood of the point. This follows from the fact that the electrostatic potential in a charge-free region obeys Laplace's equation, which in vector calculus notation is $div\ \mathbf{grad}V = 0$.

This equation is a special case of Poisson's equation div $\mathbf{grad}V = \rho$, which is applicable to electrostatic problems in regions where the volume charge density is ρ. Laplace's equation states that the divergence of the gradient of the potential is zero in regions of space with no charge. In our example, the potential on the conductors remains constant. Arbitrary values of potential are initially assigned elsewhere inside the cavity. To obtain a solution, a computer replaces the potential at each coordinate point that is not on a conductor by the average of the values of the potential around that point; it scans the entire set of points many times until the values of the potentials differ by an amount small enough to indicate a satisfactory solution. Clearly, the larger the number of points, the more accurate the solution will be. The computation time as well as the computer memory size requirement increase rapidly, however, especially in three-dimensional problems with complex geometry. This method of solution is called the "relaxation" method.

Points with the same value of electric potential can be connected to reveal a number of important properties associated with conductors in static situations. Such lines

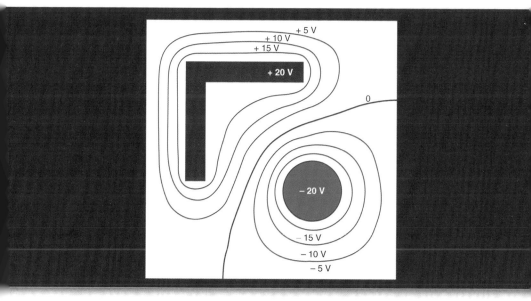

Lines that represent the distance between two equipotential surfaces. Courtesy of the Department of Physics and Astronomy, Michigan State University; rendering for this edition by Rosen Educational Services

represent equipotential surfaces. The distance between two equipotential surfaces tells how rapidly the potential changes, with the smallest distances corresponding to the location of the greatest rate of change and thus to the largest values of the electric field. Looking at the +20-volt and +15-volt equipotential surfaces, one observes immediately that they are closest to each other at the sharp external corners of the right-angle conductor. This shows that the strongest electric fields on the surface of a charged conductor are found on the sharpest external parts of the conductor; electrical breakdowns are most likely to occur there. It also should be noted that the electric field is weakest in the inside corners, both on the inside corner of the right-angle piece and on the inside corners of the square enclosure.

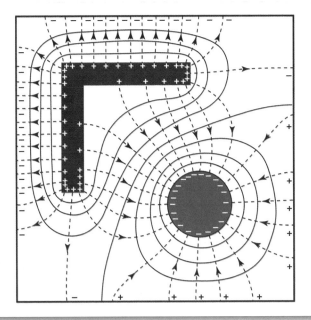

Electric field lines. The density of the dashed lines indicates the strength of the field. Courtesy of the Department of Physics and Astronomy, Michigan State University; rendering for this edition by Rosen Educational Services

In the example of the two conductors, the field is strongest on outside corners of the charged L-shaped conductor; the largest surface charge density must occur at those locations. The field is weakest in the inside corners. The signs of the charges on the conducting surfaces can be deduced from the fact that electric fields point away from positive charges and toward negative charges. The magnitude of the surface charge density σ on the conductors is measured in coulombs per metre squared and is given by

$$\sigma = \varepsilon_0 E, \tag{8}$$

where ε_0 is called the permittivity of free space and has the value of 8.854×10^{-12} coulomb squared per newton-square metre. In addition, ε_0 is related to the constant k in Coulomb's law by

$$k = \frac{1}{4\pi\varepsilon_0}. \tag{9}$$

This example also illustrates an important property of an electric field in static situations, namely that field lines are always perpendicular to equipotential surfaces. The field lines meet the surfaces of the conductors at right angles, since these surfaces also are equipotentials. Consider the potential energy landscape of a small positive charge q in the region. From the variation in potential energy, it is easy to picture how electric forces tend to drive the positive charge q from higher to lower potential—i.e., from the L-shaped bracket at +20 volts toward the square-shaped enclosure at ground (o volts) or toward the cylindrical rod maintained at a potential of -20 volts. It also graphically displays the strength of force near the sharp corners of conducting electrodes.

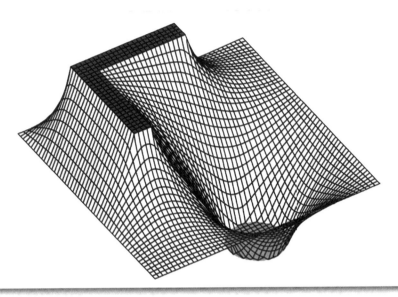

Potential energy. Courtesy of the Department of Physics and Astronomy, Michigan State University; rendering for this edition by Rosen Educational Services

Electric flux is a property of an electric field that may be thought of as the number of electric lines of force (or electric field lines) that intersect a given area. Electric field lines are considered to originate on positive electric charges and to terminate on negative charges. Field lines directed into a closed surface are considered negative, while those directed out of a closed surface are positive. If there is no net charge within a closed surface, every field line directed into the surface continues through the interior and is directed outward elsewhere on the surface. The negative flux just equals in magnitude the positive flux, so that the net, or total, electric flux is zero. If a net charge is contained inside a closed surface, the total flux through the surface is proportional to the enclosed charge, positive if it is positive, negative if it is negative.

The mathematical relation between electric flux and enclosed charge is known as Gauss's law for the electric field, one of the fundamental laws of electromagnetism. In the metre–kilogram–second system and the SI the net flux of an electric field through any closed surface is equal to the enclosed charge, in units of coulombs, divided by a constant, called the permittivity of free space; in the centimetre–gram–second system the net flux of an electric field through any closed surface is equal to the constant 4π times the enclosed charge, in electrostatic units (esu).

CAPACITANCE

A useful device for storing electrical energy consists of two conductors in close proximity and insulated from each other. A simple example of such a storage device is the parallel-plate capacitor. If positive charges with total charge $+Q$ are deposited on one of the conductors and an equal amount of negative charge $-Q$ is deposited on the second conductor, the capacitor is said to have a charge Q. Such a device consists of two flat conducting plates,

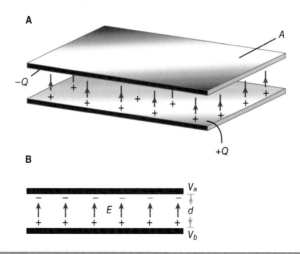

Parallel-plate capacitor. Courtesy of the Department of Physics and Astronomy, Michigan State University; rendering for this edition by Rosen Educational Services

each of area A, parallel to each other and separated by a distance d.

Principle of the Capacitor

To understand how a charged capacitor stores energy, consider the following charging process. With both plates of the capacitor initially uncharged, a small amount of negative charge is removed from the lower plate and placed on the upper plate. Thus, little work is required to make the lower plate slightly positive and the upper plate slightly negative. As the process is repeated, however, it becomes increasingly difficult to transport the same amount of negative charge, since the charge is being moved toward a plate that is already negatively charged and away from a plate that is positively charged. The negative charge on the upper plate repels the negative charge moving toward it, and the positive charge on the lower plate exerts an attractive force on the negative charge being moved away. Therefore, work has to be done to charge the capacitor.

Where and how is this energy stored? The negative charges on the upper plate are attracted toward the positive charges on the lower plate and could do work if they could leave the plate. Because they cannot leave the plate, however, the energy is stored. A mechanical analogy is the potential energy of a stretched spring. Another way to understand the energy stored in a capacitor is to compare an uncharged capacitor with a charged capacitor. In the uncharged capacitor, there is no electric field between the plates. In the charged capacitor, because of the positive and negative charges on the inside surfaces of the plates, there is an electric field between the plates with the field lines pointing from the positively charged plate to the negatively charged one. The energy stored is the energy that was required to establish the field. It is apparent that there is a nearly uniform electric field between the plates;

the field becomes more uniform as the distance between the plates decreases and the area of the plates increases. In summary, the electric field is the change in the potential across a small distance in a direction perpendicular to an equipotential surface divided by that small distance. The upper plate is assumed to be at a potential of V_a volts, and the lower plate at a potential of V_b volts. The size of the electric field is

$$E = \frac{V_b - V_a}{d} \tag{10}$$

in volts per metre, where d is the separation of the plates. If the charged capacitor has a total charge of $+Q$ on the inside surface of the lower plate (it is on the inside surface because it is attracted to the negative charges on the upper plate), the positive charge will be uniformly distributed on the surface with the value

$$\sigma = \frac{Q}{A} \tag{11}$$

in coulombs per metre squared. Equation (8) gives the electric field when the surface charge density is known as $E = \sigma/\varepsilon_0$. This, in turn, relates the potential difference to the charge on the capacitor and the geometry of the plates. The result is

$$V_b - V_a = \frac{Qd}{\varepsilon_0 A} = \frac{Q}{C}. \tag{12}$$

The quantity C is termed capacity; for the parallel-plate capacitor, C is equal to $\varepsilon_0 A/d$. The unit used for capacity is the farad (F), named in honour of the English scientist Michael Faraday; one farad equals one coulomb per volt. In terms of ordinary electric and electronic equipment, the farad is enormous, and capacitors are generally rated in microfarads (one microfarad equals 10^{-6} farad) or picofarads (10^{-12} farad). In equation (12), only the potential difference is involved. The potential of either plate can be set arbitrarily without altering the electric field between the plates. Often one of the plates is grounded—i.e., its potential is set at the Earth potential, which is referred to as zero volts. The potential difference is then denoted as ΔV, or simply as V.

Three equivalent formulas for the total energy W of a capacitor with charge Q and potential difference V are

$$W = \frac{1}{2}\frac{Q^2}{C} = \frac{1}{2}CV^2 = \frac{1}{2}QV. \tag{13}$$

All are expressed in joules. The stored energy in the parallel-plate capacitor also can be expressed in terms of the electric field; it is, in joules,

$$W = \frac{1}{2}\varepsilon_0 E^2 (Ad). \tag{14}$$

The quantity Ad, the area of each plate times the separation of the two plates, is the volume between the plates. Thus, the energy per unit volume (i.e., the energy density of the electric field) is given by $\frac{1}{2}\varepsilon_0 E^2$ in units of joules per metre cubed.

DIELECTRICS, POLARIZATION, AND ELECTRIC DIPOLE MOMENT

The amount of charge stored in a capacitor is the product of the voltage and the capacity. What limits the amount of charge that can be stored on a capacitor? The voltage can be increased, but electric breakdown will occur if the electric field inside the capacitor becomes too large. The capacity can be increased by expanding the electrode areas and by reducing the gap between the electrodes. In general, capacitors that can withstand high voltages have a relatively small capacity. If only low voltages are needed, however, compact capacitors with rather large capacities can be manufactured. One method for increasing capacity is to insert between the conductors an insulating material that reduces the voltage because of its effect on the electric field. Such materials are called dielectrics (substances with no free charges). When the molecules of a dielectric are placed in the electric field, their negatively charged electrons separate slightly from their positively charged cores. With this separation, referred to as polarization, the molecules acquire an electric dipole moment. A cluster of charges with an electric dipole moment is often called an electric dipole.

Is there an electric force between a charged object and uncharged matter, such as a piece of wood? Surprisingly, the answer is yes, and the force is attractive. The reason is that under the influence of the electric field of a charged object, the negatively charged electrons and positively charged nuclei within the atoms and molecules are subjected to forces in opposite directions. As a result, the negative and positive charges separate slightly. Such atoms and molecules are said to be polarized and to have an electric dipole moment. The molecules in the wood acquire an electric dipole moment in the direction of the external electric field. The polarized molecules are attracted toward the charged object because the field increases in the direction of the charged object. A water molecule (H_2O), in which two hydrogen atoms stick out on one side and form together with the oxygen atom a vertex with a $105°$ angle, constitutes a permanent electric dipole. The oxygen side of the molecule is always somewhat negative and the hydrogen side somewhat positive. In these materials whose molecules are permanently polarized by chemical forces some of the polarization is caused by molecules rotating into the same alignment under the influence of the electric field.

The electric dipole moment p of two charges $+q$ and $-q$ separated by a distance l is a vector of magnitude $p = ql$ with a direction from the negative to the positive charge. An electric dipole in an external electric field is subjected to a torque $\tau = pE \sin \theta$, where θ is the angle between p and E. The torque tends to align the dipole moment p in the direction of E. The potential energy of the dipole is given by $U_e = -pE \cos \theta$, or in vector notation $U_e = -p \cdot E$. In a nonuniform electric field, the potential energy of an electric dipole also varies with position, and the dipole can be subjected to a force. The force on the dipole is in the direction of increasing field when p is aligned with E, since the potential energy U_e decreases in that direction. Because electric dipole moment has dimensions of electric charge times displacement, its unit in the metre–kilogram–second system is the coulomb-metre; in the centimetre–gram–second system it is the esu-centimetre.

The polarization of a medium P gives the electric dipole moment per unit volume of the material; it is expressed in units of coulombs per metre squared. Polarization P in its quantitative meaning is the amount of dipole moment p per unit volume V of a polarized material, $P = p/V$. When a dielectric is placed in an electric field, it acquires a polarization that depends on the field. The electric susceptibility χ_e relates the polarization to the electric field as $P = \chi_e E$. In general, χ_e varies slightly depending on the strength of the electric field, but for some materials, called linear dielectrics, it is a constant.

The dielectric constant κ of a substance is related to its susceptibility as $\kappa = 1 + \chi_e/\varepsilon_0$; it is a dimensionless quantity. The dielectric constant is sometimes called relative permittivity or specific inductive capacity. The permittivity characterizes the tendency of the atomic charge in an insulating material to distort in the presence of an electric field. The larger the tendency for charge distortion (also called electric polarization), the larger the value of the permittivity. The value of the static dielectric constant of any material is always greater than one, its value for a vacuum. The value of the dielectric constant at room temperature (25 °C, or 77 °F) is 1.00059 for air, 2.25 for paraffin, 78.2 for water, and about 2,000 for barium titanate ($BaTiO_3$) when the electric field is applied perpendicularly to the principal axis of the crystal. (The table lists the dielectric constants of a few substances.) Because the value of the dielectric constant for air is nearly the same as that for a vacuum, for all practical purposes air does not increase the capacitance of a capacitor. Dielectric constants of liquids and solids may be determined by comparing the value of the capacitance when the dielectric is in place to its value when the capacitor is filled with air.

DIELECTRIC CONSTANTS OF SOME MATERIALS (AT ROOM TEMPERATURE)	
MATERIAL	DIELECTRIC CONSTANT
vacuum	1.0
air	1.0006
oil	2.2
polyethylene	2.26
beeswax	2.8
fused quartz	3.78
water	80
calcium titanate	168
barium titanate	1,250

The presence of a dielectric affects many electric quantities. A dielectric reduces by a factor K the value of the electric field and consequently also the value of the electric potential from a charge within the medium. As seen in the table, a dielectric can have a large effect. The insertion of a dielectric between the electrodes of a capacitor with a given charge reduces the potential difference between the electrodes and thus increases the capacitance of the capacitor by the factor K. For a parallel-plate capacitor filled with a dielectric, the capacity becomes $C = K\varepsilon_o A/d$. A third and important effect of a dielectric is to reduce the speed of electromagnetic waves in a medium by the factor $\sqrt{K}$.

Capacitors come in a wide variety of shapes and sizes. Not all have parallel plates; some are cylinders, for example. If two plates, each one square centimetre in area, are separated by a dielectric with $K = 2$ of 1 mm thickness, the capacity is 1.76×10^{-12} F, about 2 picofarads. Charged to 20 volts, this capacitor would store about 40 picocoulombs of charge; the electric energy stored would be 400 picojoules. Even small-sized capacitors can store enormous amounts of charge. Modern techniques and dielectric materials permit the manufacture of capacitors that occupy less than one cubic centimetre and yet store 10^{10} times more charge and electric energy than in the above example.

APPLICATIONS OF CAPACITORS

Capacitors have many important applications. They are used, for example, in digital circuits so that information stored in large computer memories is not lost during a momentary electric power failure; the electric energy stored in such capacitors maintains the information during the temporary loss of power. Capacitors play an even more important role as filters to divert spurious electric signals and thereby prevent damage to sensitive components and circuits caused by electric surges.

DIRECT ELECTRIC CURRENT

Direct current (DC) is a flow of electric charge that does not change direction. Direct current is produced by batteries, fuel cells, rectifiers, and generators with commutators. Direct current was supplanted by alternating current (AC) for common commercial power in the late 1880s because it was then uneconomical to transform it to the high voltages needed for long-distance transmission. Techniques that were developed in the 1960s overcame this obstacle, and direct current is now transmitted over very long distances, even though it must ordinarily be converted to alternating current for final distribution. For some uses, such as electroplating, direct current is essential.

Many electric phenomena occur under what is termed steady-state conditions. This means that such electric quantities as current, voltage, and charge distributions are not affected by the passage of time. For instance, because the current through a filament inside a car headlight does not change with time, the brightness of the headlight remains constant. An example of a nonsteady-state situation is the flow of charge between two conductors that are connected by a thin conducting wire and that initially have an equal but opposite charge. As current flows from the positively charged conductor to the negatively charged one, the charges on both conductors decrease with time, as does the potential difference between the conductors. The current therefore also decreases with time and eventually ceases when the conductors are discharged.

In an electric circuit under steady-state conditions, the flow of charge does not change with time and the charge distribution stays the same. Since charge flows from one location to another, there must be some mechanism to keep the charge distribution constant. In turn, the values of the electric potentials remain unaltered with time. Any device capable of keeping the potentials of electrodes unchanged as charge flows from one electrode to another is called a source of electromotive force, or simply an emf.

Consider a wire made of a conducting material such as copper. By some external means, an electric field is established inside the wire in a direction along its length. The electrons that are free to move will gain some speed. Since they have a negative charge, they move in the direction opposite that of the electric field. The current i is defined to have a positive value in the direction of flow of positive charges. If the moving charges that constitute the current i in a wire are electrons, the current is a positive number when it is in a direction opposite to the motion of the negatively charged electrons. (If the direction of motion of the electrons were also chosen to be the direction of a current, the current would have a negative value.) The current is the amount of charge crossing a plane transverse to the wire per unit time—i.e., in a period of one second. If there are n free particles of charge q per unit volume with average velocity v and the cross-sectional area of the wire is A, the current i, in elementary calculus notation, is

$$i = \frac{dQ}{dt} = nev\,A,\qquad(15)$$

where dQ is the amount of charge that crosses the plane in a time interval dt. The unit of current is the ampere (A); one ampere equals one coulomb per second. A useful quantity related to the flow of charge is current density, the flow of current per unit area. Symbolized by J, it has a magnitude of i/A and is measured in amperes per square metre.

Wires of different materials have different current densities for a given value of the electric field E; for many materials, the current density is directly proportional to the electric field. This behaviour is represented by Ohm's law:

$$J = \sigma_J E. \qquad (16)$$

The proportionality constant σ_J is the conductivity of the material. The metre–kilogram–second unit of conductivity is mho per metre, or ampere per volt-metre. In a metallic conductor, the charge carriers are electrons and, under the influence of an external electric field, they acquire some average drift velocity in the direction opposite the field. In conductors of this variety, the drift velocity is limited by collisions, which heat the conductor.

If the copper wire has a length l and area A and if an electric potential difference of V is maintained between the ends of the wire, a current i will flow in the wire. The

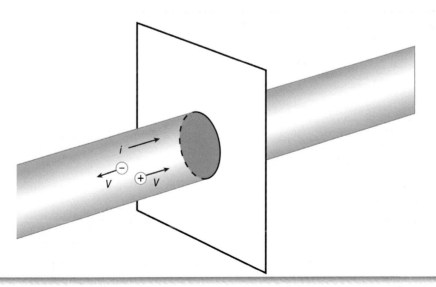

Motion of charge in electric current i. Courtesy of the Department of Physics and Astronomy, Michigan State University; rendering for this edition by Rosen Educational Services

electric field E in the wire has a magnitude V/l. The equation for the current, using Ohm's law, is

$$i = JA = \frac{\sigma_J V}{l} A \qquad (17)$$

or

$$V = i \frac{l}{\sigma_J A}. \qquad (18)$$

The quantity $l/\sigma_J A$, which depends on both the shape and material of the wire, is called the resistance R of the wire. Resistance is measured in ohms (Ω). The equation for resistance,

$$R = \frac{l}{\sigma_J A}, \qquad (19)$$

is often written as

$$R = \frac{\rho l}{A}, \qquad (20)$$

where ρ is the resistivity of the material and is simply $1/\sigma_J$. The geometric aspects of resistance in equation (20) are easy to appreciate: the longer the wire, the greater the resistance to the flow of charge. A greater cross-sectional area results in a smaller resistance to the flow.

The resistive strain gauge is an important application of equation (20). Strain, $\delta l/l$, is the fractional change in the length of a body under stress, where δl is the change of length and l is the length. The strain gauge consists of a thin wire or narrow strip of a metallic conductor such as constantan, an alloy of nickel and copper. A strain changes the resistance because the length, area, and resistivity of the conductor change. In constantan, the fractional change in resistance $\delta R/R$ is directly proportional to the strain with a proportionality constant of approximately 2.

A common form of Ohm's law is

$$V = iR, \qquad\qquad (21)$$

where V is the potential difference in volts between the two ends of an element with an electric resistance of R ohms and where i is the current through that element. That the resistance, or the ratio of voltage to current, for all or part of an electric circuit at a fixed temperature is generally constant had been established by 1827 as a result of the investigations of the German physicist Georg Simon Ohm.

In a circuit in which the potential difference, or voltage, is constant, the current may be decreased by adding more resistance or increased by removing some resistance. Ohm's law may also be expressed in terms of the electromotive force, or voltage, E, of the source of electric energy, such as a battery. For example, $I = E/R$.

The table "Electric Resistivities (At Room Temperature)" (next page) lists the resistivities of certain materials at room temperature. The resistivity of an exceedingly good electrical conductor, such as hard-drawn copper, at 20 °C (68 °F) is 1.77×10^{-8} ohm-metre, or 1.77×10^{-6} ohm-centimetre. At the other extreme, electrical insulators have resistivities in the range 10^{12} to 10^{20} ohm-metres. These values depend to some extent on temperature. Resistivity of metallic conductors generally increases with a rise in temperature; but resistivity of semiconductors, such as carbon and silicon, generally decreases with temperature rise. In applications where the temperature is very different from room temperature, the proper values of resistivities must be used to calculate the resistance. As an example, equation (20) shows that a copper wire 59 metres long and with a cross-sectional area of one square millimetre has an electric resistance of one ohm at room temperature.

ELECTRIC RESISTIVITIES (AT ROOM TEMPERATURE)	
MATERIAL	RESISTIVITY (OHM-METRE)
silver	1.6×10^{-8}
copper	1.7×10^{-8}
aluminum	2.7×10^{-8}
carbon (graphite)	1.4×10^{-5}
germanium*	4.7×10^{-1}
silicon*	2×10^{3}
carbon (diamond)	5×10^{12}
polyethylene	1×10^{17}
fused quartz	$>1 \times 10^{19}$

*Values very sensitive to purity.

CONDUCTORS, INSULATORS, AND SEMICONDUCTORS

Materials are classified as conductors, insulators, or semiconductors according to their electric conductivity. The classifications can be understood in atomic terms. Electrons in an atom can have only certain well-defined energies, and, depending on their energies, the electrons are said to occupy particular energy levels. In a typical atom with many electrons, the lower energy levels are filled, each with the number of electrons allowed by a quantum mechanical rule known as the Pauli exclusion principle. Depending on the element, the highest energy level to have electrons may or may not be completely full. If two atoms of some element are brought close enough together so that they interact, the two-atom system has two closely spaced levels for each level of the single atom. If 10 atoms interact, the 10-atom system will have a cluster of 10 levels corresponding to each single level of an individual atom. In a solid, the number of atoms and hence the number of levels is extremely large; most of the higher energy levels overlap in a continuous fashion except for certain energies in which there are no levels at all. Energy regions with levels are called energy bands, and regions that have no levels are referred to as band gaps.

The highest energy band occupied by electrons is the valence band. In a conductor, the valence band is partially filled, and since there are numerous empty levels, the electrons are free to move under the influence of an electric field; thus, in a metal the valence band is also the conduction band. In an insulator, electrons completely fill the valence band; and the gap between it and the next band, which is the conduction band, is large. The electrons cannot move under the influence of an electric field unless they are given enough energy to cross the large energy gap to the conduction band. In a semiconductor, the gap to the conduction band is smaller than in an insulator. At room temperature, the valence band is almost completely filled. A few electrons are missing from the valence band because they have acquired enough thermal energy to cross the band gap to the conduction band; as a result, they can move under the influence of an external electric field. The "holes" left behind in the valence band are mobile charge carriers but behave like positive charge carriers.

For many materials, including metals, resistance to the flow of charge tends to increase with temperature. For example, an increase of 5 °C (9 °F) increases the resistivity of copper by 2 percent. In contrast, the resistivity of insulators and especially of semiconductors such as silicon and germanium decreases rapidly with temperature; the increased thermal energy causes some of the electrons to populate levels in the conduction band where, influenced by an external electric field, they are free to move. The energy difference between the valence levels and the conduction band has a strong influence on the conductivity of these materials, with a smaller gap resulting in higher conduction at lower temperatures.

The values of electric resistivities listed in the table show an extremely large variation in the capability of different materials to conduct electricity. The principal reason for the large variation is the wide range in the availability and mobility of charge carriers within the materials. The copper wire has many extremely mobile carriers; each copper atom has approximately one free electron, which is highly mobile because of its small mass. An electrolyte, such as a saltwater solution, is not as good a conductor as copper. The sodium and chlorine ions in the solution provide the charge carriers. The large mass of each sodium and chlorine ion increases as other attracted ions cluster around them. As a result, the sodium and chlorine ions are far more difficult to move than the free electrons in copper. Pure water also is a conductor, although it is a poor one because only a very small fraction of the water molecules are dissociated into ions. The oxygen, nitrogen, and argon gases that make up the atmosphere are somewhat conductive because a few charge carriers form when the gases are ionized by radiation from radioactive elements on Earth as well as from extraterrestrial cosmic rays (i.e., high-speed atomic nuclei and electrons). Electrophoresis is an interesting application based on the mobility of particles suspended in an electrolytic solution. Different particles (proteins, for example) move in the same electric field at different speeds; the difference in speed can be utilized to separate the contents of the suspension.

A current flowing through a wire heats it. This familiar phenomenon occurs in the heating coils of an electric range or in the hot tungsten filament of an electric light bulb. This ohmic heating is the basis for the fuses used to protect electric circuits and prevent fires; if the current exceeds a certain value, a fuse, which is made of an alloy with a low melting point, melts and interrupts the flow of current. The power P dissipated in a resistance R through which current i flows is given by

$$P = iV = \frac{V^2}{R}. \tag{22}$$

where P is in watts (one watt equals one joule per second), i is in amperes, and R is in ohms. According to Ohm's law, the potential difference V between the two ends of the resistor is given by $V = iR$, and so the power P can be expressed equivalently as

$$P = i^2 R, \tag{23}$$

The English physicist James Prescott Joule discovered this relation, called Joule's law, in 1840.

In certain materials, however, the power dissipation that manifests itself as heat suddenly disappears if the conductor is cooled to a very low temperature. The disappearance of all resistance is a phenomenon known as superconductivity. As mentioned earlier, electrons acquire some average drift velocity v under the influence of an electric field in a wire. Normally the electrons, subjected to a force because of an electric field, accelerate and progressively acquire greater speed. Their velocity is, however, limited in a wire because they lose some of their acquired energy to the wire in collisions with other electrons and in collisions with atoms in the wire. The lost energy is either transferred to other electrons, which later radiate, or the wire becomes excited with tiny mechanical vibrations referred to as phonons. Both processes heat the material. The term phonon emphasizes the relationship of these vibrations to another mechanical vibration— namely, sound.

In a superconductor, a complex quantum mechanical effect prevents these small losses of energy to the medium. The effect involves interactions between electrons and also those between electrons and the rest of the material. It can be visualized by considering the coupling of the electrons in pairs with opposite momenta; the motion of the paired electrons is such that no energy is given up to the medium in inelastic collisions or phonon excitations. One can imagine that an electron about to "collide" with and lose energy to the medium could end up instead colliding with its partner so that they exchange momentum without imparting any to the medium.

A superconducting material widely used in the construction of electromagnets is an alloy of niobium and titanium. This material must be cooled to a few degrees above absolute zero temperature, -263.66 °C (-442.58 °F, or 9.49 K), in order to exhibit the superconducting property. Such cooling requires the use of liquefied helium, which is rather costly. During the late 1980s, materials that exhibit superconducting properties at much higher temperatures were discovered. These temperatures are higher than the -196 °C (-320.8 °F, or 77 K) of liquid nitrogen, making it possible to use the latter instead of liquid helium. Since liquid nitrogen is plentiful and cheap, such materials may provide great benefits in a wide variety of applications, ranging from electric power transmission to high-speed computing.

ELECTROMOTIVE FORCE

A 12-volt automobile battery can deliver current to a circuit such as that of a car radio for a considerable length of time, during which the potential difference between the terminals of the battery remains close to 12 volts. The battery must have a means of continuously replenishing the excess positive and negative charges that are located on the respective terminals and that are responsible for the 12-volt potential difference between the terminals. The charges must be transported from one terminal to the other in a direction opposite to the electric force on the charges between the terminals. Any device that accomplishes this transport of charge constitutes a source of electromotive force. A car battery, for example, uses chemical reactions to generate electromotive force. The Van de Graaff generator is a mechanical device that produces an electromotive force. Invented by the American physicist Robert J. Van de Graaff in the 1930s, this type of particle accelerator has been widely used to study subatomic particles. Because it is conceptually simpler than a chemical source of electromotive force, the Van de Graaff generator will be discussed first.

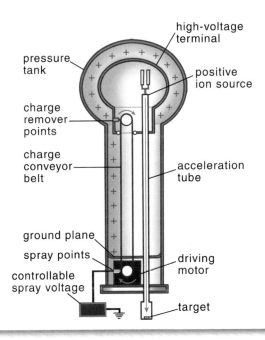

Van de Graaff accelerator. Copyright Encyclopædia Britannica; rendering for this edition by Rosen Educational Services

An insulating conveyor belt carries positive charge from the base of the Van de Graaff machine to the inside of a large conducting dome. The charge is removed from the belt by the proximity of sharp metal electrodes called charge remover points. The charge then moves rapidly to the outside of the conducting dome. The positively charged dome creates an electric field, which points away from the dome and provides a repelling action on additional positive charges transported on the belt toward the dome. Thus, work is done to keep the conveyor belt turning. If a current is allowed to flow from the dome to ground and if an equal current is provided by the transport of charge on the insulating belt, equilibrium is established and the potential of the dome remains at a constant positive value. In this example, the current from the dome to ground consists of a stream of positive ions inside the accelerating tube, moving in the direction of the electric field. The motion of the charge on the belt is in a direction opposite to the force that the electric field of the dome exerts on the charge. This motion of charge in a direction opposite the electric field is a feature common to all sources of electromotive force.

In the case of a chemically generated electromotive force, chemical reactions release energy. If these reactions take place with chemicals in close proximity to each other (e.g., if they mix), the energy released heats the mixture. To produce a voltaic cell, these reactions must occur in separate locations. A copper wire and a zinc wire poked into a lemon make up a simple voltaic cell. The potential difference between the copper and the zinc wires can be measured easily and is found to be 1.1 volts; the copper wire acts as the positive terminal. Such a "lemon battery" is a rather poor voltaic cell capable of supplying only small amounts of electric power. Another kind of 1.1-volt battery constructed with essentially the same materials can provide much more electricity. In this case, a copper wire is placed in a solution of copper sulfate and a zinc wire in a solution of zinc sulfate; the two solutions are connected electrically by a potassium chloride salt bridge. (A salt bridge is a conductor with ions as charge carriers.) In both kinds of batteries, the energy comes from the difference in the degree of binding between the electrons in copper and those in zinc. Energy is gained when copper ions from the copper sulfate solution are deposited on the copper electrode as neutral copper ions, thus removing free electrons from the copper wire. At the same time, zinc atoms from the zinc wire go into solution as positively charged zinc ions, leaving the zinc wire with excess free electrons. The result is a positively charged copper wire and a negatively charged zinc wire. The two reactions are separated physically, with the salt bridge completing the internal circuit.

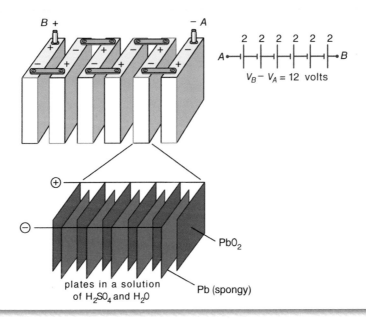

$V_B - V_A = 12$ volts

Voltaic cells and electrodes of a 12-volt lead-acid battery. Courtesy of the Department of Physics and Astronomy, Michigan State University; rendering for this edition by Rosen Educational Services

Consider a 12-volt lead-acid battery, using standard symbols for depicting batteries in a circuit. The battery consists of six voltaic cells, each with an electromotive force of approximately two volts; the cells are connected in series, so that the six individual voltages add up to about 12 volts. Each two-volt cell consists of a number of positive and negative electrodes connected electrically in parallel. The parallel connection is made to provide a large surface area of electrodes, on which chemical reactions can take place. The higher rate at which the materials of the electrodes are able to undergo chemical transformations allows the battery to deliver a larger current.

In the lead-acid battery, each voltaic cell consists of a negative electrode of pure, spongy lead (Pb) and a positive electrode of lead oxide (PbO_2). Both the lead and lead oxide are in a solution of sulfuric acid (H_2SO_4) and water (H_2O). At the positive electrode, the chemical reaction is $PbO_2 + SO_4^{--} + 4H^+ + 2e^- \rightarrow PbSO_4 + 2H_2O + (1.68\ V)$. At the negative terminal, the reaction is $Pb + SO_4^{--} \rightarrow PbSO_4 + 2e^- + (0.36\ V)$. The cell potential is $1.68 + 0.36 = 2.04$ volts. The 1.68 and 0.36 volts in the above equations are, respectively, the reduction and oxidation potentials; they are related to the binding of the electrons in the chemicals. When the battery is recharged, either by a car generator or by an external power source, the two chemical reactions are reversed.

DIRECT-CURRENT CIRCUITS

The simplest direct-current (DC) circuit consists of a resistor connected across a source of electromotive force. The symbol for a resistor is a zigzag line. The conventional symbol for a source of electromotive force, E, is two parallel lines of differing length with the terminal

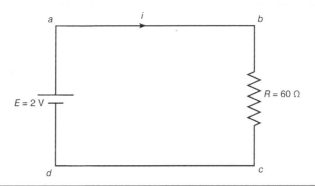

Direct-current circuit. Courtesy of the Department of Physics and Astronomy, Michigan State University; rendering for this edition by Rosen Educational Services

with the long line having a higher (i.e., more positive) potential than the terminal with the short line. Straight lines connecting various elements in a circuit are assumed to have negligible resistance, so that there is no change in potential across these connections. Consider a square circuit with a 12-volt electromotive force connected to a 60Ω resistor. The corners of the square, *a*, *b*, *c*, and *d*, are reference points.

The function of the source of electromotive force is to maintain point *a* at a potential 12 volts more positive than point *d*. Thus, the potential difference $V_a - V_d$ is 12 volts. The potential difference across the resistance is $V_b - V_c$. From Ohm's law, the current *i* flowing through the resistor is

$$i = \frac{V_b - V_c}{R} = \frac{V_b - V_c}{60}. \qquad (24)$$

Since points *a* and *b* are connected by a conductor of negligible resistance, they are at the same potential. For the same reason, *c* and *d* are at the same potential. Therefore,

THE BRITANNICA GUIDE TO ELECTRICITY AND MAGNETISM

$V_b - V_c = V_a - V_d$ = 12 volts. The current in the circuit is given by equation (24). Thus, i = 12/60 = 0.2 ampere. The power dissipated in the resistor as heat is easily calculated using equation (22):

$$P = i^2 R = (0.2)^2 \times 60 = 2.4 \text{ watts.}$$

Where does the energy that is dissipated as heat in the resistor come from? It is provided by a source of electromotive force (e.g., a lead-acid battery). Within such a source, for each amount of charge dQ moved from the lower potential at d to the higher potential at a, an amount of work is done equal to $dW = dQ(V_a - V_d)$. If this work is done in a time interval dt, the power delivered by the battery is obtained by dividing dW by dt. Thus, the power delivered by the battery (in watts) is

$$\frac{dW}{dt} = (V_a - V_d)\frac{dQ}{dt} = (V_a - V_d)i.$$

Using the values i = 0.2 ampere and $V_a - V_d$ = 12 volts makes dW/dt = 2.4 watts. As expected, the power delivered by the battery is equal to the power dissipated as heat in the resistor.

RESISTORS IN SERIES AND PARALLEL

If two resistors are connected so that all of the electric charge must traverse both resistors in succession, the equivalent resistance to the flow of current is the sum of the resistances.

Using R_1 and R_2 for the individual resistances, the resistance between a and b is given by

$$R_{ab} = R_1 + R_2. \tag{25a}$$

70

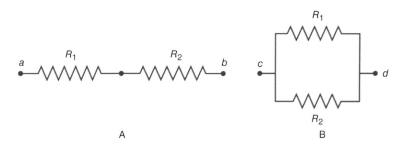

A

B

Resistors, in series (A) and in parallel (B). Courtesy of the Department of Physics and Astronomy, Michigan State University; rendering for this edition by Rosen Educational Services

This result can be appreciated by thinking of the two resistors as two pieces of the same type of thin wire. Connecting the wires in series as shown simply increases their length to equal the sum of their two lengths. As equation (20) indicates, the resistance is the same as that given by equation (25a). The resistances R_1 and R_2 can be replaced in a circuit by the equivalent resistance R_{ab}. If $R_1 = 5\Omega$ and $R_2 = 2\Omega$, then $R_{ab} = 7\Omega$. If two resistors are connected as shown in parallel, the electric charges have alternate paths for flowing from c to d. The resistance to the flow of charge from c to d is clearly less than if either R_1 or R_2 were missing. Anyone who has ever had to find a way out of a crowded theatre can appreciate how much easier it is to leave a building with several exits than one with a single exit. The value of the equivalent resistance for two resistors in parallel is given by the equation

$$\frac{1}{R_{cd}} = \frac{1}{R_1} + \frac{1}{R_2}. \qquad (25b)$$

This relationship follows directly from the definition of resistance in equation (20), where $1/R$ is proportional to the area. If the resistors R_1 and R_2 are imagined to be wires of the same length and material, they would be wires with different cross-sectional areas. Connecting them in parallel is equivalent to placing them side by side, increasing the total area available for the flow of charge. Clearly, the equivalent resistance is smaller than the resistance of either resistor individually. As a numerical example, for $R_1 = 5\Omega$ and $R_2 = 2\Omega$, $1/R_{cd} = 1/5 + 1/2 = 0.7$. Therefore, $R_{cd} = 1/0.7 = 1.43\Omega$. As expected, the equivalent resistance of 1.43 ohms is smaller than either 2 ohms or 5 ohms. It should be noted that both equations (25a) and (25b) are given in a form in which they can be extended easily to any number of resistances.

KIRCHHOFF'S LAWS OF ELECTRIC CIRCUITS

Two simple relationships can be used to determine the value of currents in circuits. They are useful even in rather complex situations such as circuits with multiple loops. The first relationship deals with currents at a junction of conductors. Simply stated, the sum of currents entering a junction equals the sum of currents leaving that junction. This statement is commonly called Kirchhoff's first law (after the German physicist Gustav Robert Kirchhoff, who formulated it). In solving a problem, the direction

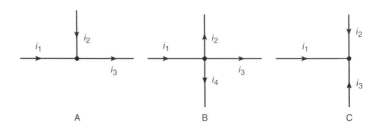

Electric currents at a junction. Courtesy of the Department of Physics and Astronomy, Michigan State University; rendering for this edition by Rosen Educational Services

chosen for the currents is arbitrary. Once the problem has been solved, some currents have a positive value, and the direction arbitrarily chosen is the one of the actual current. In the solution some currents may have a negative value, in which case the actual current flows in a direction opposite that of the arbitrary initial choice.

Kirchhoff's second law is as follows: the sum of electromotive forces in a loop equals the sum of potential drops in the loop. When electromotive forces in a circuit are symbolized as circuit components, this law can be stated quite simply: the sum of the potential differences across all the components in a closed loop equals zero. To illustrate and clarify this relation, one can consider a single circuit with two sources of electromotive forces E_1 and E_2, and two resistances R_1 and R_2. The letters a, b, c, and d are used to indicate certain locations around the circuit. Applying Kirchhoff's second law to the circuit,

$$(V_b - V_a) + (V_c - V_b) + (V_d - V_c) + (V_a - V_d) = 0. \qquad (26)$$

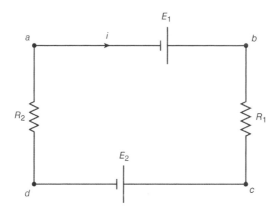

Circuit illustrating Kirchhoff's loop equation. Courtesy of the Department of Physics and Astronomy, Michigan State University; rendering for this edition by Rosen Educational Services

The potential differences maintained by the electromotive forces indicated are $V_b - V_a = E_1$, and $V_c - V_d = -E_2$. From Ohm's law, $V_b - V_c = iR_1$, and $V_d - V_a = iR_2$. Using these four relationships in equation (26), the so-called loop equation becomes $E_1 - E_2 - iR_1 - iR_2 = 0$.

Given the values of the resistances R_1 and R_2 in ohms and of the electromotive forces E_1 and E_2 in volts, the value of the current i in the circuit is obtained. If E_2 in the circuit had a greater value than E_1, the solution for the current i would be a negative value for i. This negative sign indicates that the current in the circuit would flow in the opposite direction.

Kirchhoff's laws can be applied to circuits with several connected loops. The same rules apply, though the algebra required becomes rather tedious as the circuits increase in complexity.

ALTERNATING ELECTRIC CURRENTS

An alternating current (AC) is a flow of electric charge that periodically reverses; it starts, say, from zero, grows to a maximum, decreases to zero, reverses, reaches a maximum in the opposite direction, returns again to the original value, and repeats this cycle indefinitely. The interval of time between the attainment of a definite value on two successive cycles is called the period; the number of cycles or periods per second is the frequency, and the maximum value in either direction is the amplitude of the alternating current. Low frequencies, such as 50 and 60 cycles per second (hertz), are used for domestic and commercial power, but alternating currents of frequencies around 100,000,000 cycles per second (100 megahertz) are used in television and of several thousand megahertz in radar or microwave communication.

TRANSIENT RESPONSE

Consider a circuit consisting of 50-volt battery, a switch, a capacitor, and a resistor. What will be the voltage at point b (between the resistor and the capacitor) if the voltage at a (between the switch and the resistor) is increased suddenly from $V_a = 0$ to $V_a = +50$ volts? Closing the switch produces such a voltage because it connects the positive terminal of a 50-volt battery to point a while the negative terminal is at ground.

Initially, the capacitor has no charge and does not affect the flow of charge. The initial current is obtained from Ohm's law, $V = iR$, where $V = V_a - V_b$, V_a is 50 volts and V_b is zero. Using 2,000 ohms for the value of the resistance, there is an initial current of 25 milliamperes in the circuit. This current begins to charge the capacitor, so that a positive charge accumulates on the plate of the capacitor connected to point b and a negative charge accumulates on the other plate. As a result, the potential at point b increases from zero to a positive value. As more charge accumulates on the capacitor, this positive potential continues to increase. As it does so, the value of the potential across the resistor is reduced; consequently, the current decreases with time, approaching the value of zero as the capacitor potential reaches 50 volts. The behaviour of the potential at point b is described by the equation $V_b = V_a(1 - e^{-t/RC})$ in volts. For $R = 2,000\Omega$ and capacitance $C = 2.5$ microfarads, $V_b = 50(1 - e^{-t/0.005})$ in volts. The potential V_b at b increases from zero when the capacitor is uncharged and reaches the ultimate value of V_a when equilibrium is reached.

How would the potential at point b vary if the potential at point a, instead of being maintained at +50 volts, were to remain at +50 volts for only a short time, say, one millisecond, and then return to zero? The superposition principle is used to solve the problem. The voltage at a starts at zero, goes to +50 volts at t = 0, then returns to zero at t = +0.001 second. This voltage can be viewed as the sum of two voltages, $V_{1a} + V_{2a}$, where V_{1a} becomes +50 volts at t = 0 and remains there indefinitely, and V_{2a} becomes -50 volts at t = 0.001 second and remains there indefinitely. Since the solutions for V_{1b} and V_{2b} corresponding to V_{1a} and V_{2a} are known from the previous example, their sum V_b is the answer to the problem.

The voltage at b reaches a maximum of only 9 volts. The superposition principle also shows that the shorter the duration of the positive "pulse" at a, the smaller the value of the voltage generated at b. Increasing the size of the capacitor also decreases the maximum voltage at b. This decrease in the potential of a transient explains the "guardian role" that capacitors play in protecting delicate and complex electronic circuits from damage by large transient voltages. These transients, which generally occur at high frequency, produce effects similar to those produced by pulses of short duration. They can damage equipment when they induce circuit components to break down electrically. Transient voltages are often introduced into electronic circuits through power supplies. A concise way to describe the role of the capacitor in the above example is to say that its impedance to an electric signal decreases with increasing frequency. In the example, much of the signal is shunted to ground instead of appearing at point b.

ALTERNATING-CURRENT CIRCUITS

Certain circuits include sources of alternating electromotive forces of the sinusoidal form $V = V_0 \cos(\omega t)$ or $V = V_0$

$\sin(\omega t)$. The sine and cosine functions have values that vary between +1 and -1; either of the equations for the voltage represents a potential that varies with respect to time and has values from $+V_o$ to $-V_o$. The voltage varies with time at a rate given by the numerical value of ω; ω, which is called the angular frequency, is expressed in radians per second. Consider an example with V_o = 170 volts and ω = 377 radians per second, so that V = 170 cos(377t). The time interval required for the pattern to be repeated is called the period T, given by $T = 2\pi/\omega$. The pattern is repeated every 16.7 milliseconds, which is the period. The frequency of the voltage is symbolized by f and given by $f = 1/T$. In terms of ω, $f = \omega/2\pi$, in hertz.

The root-mean-square (rms) voltage of a sinusoidal source of electromotive force (V_{rms}) is used to characterize the source. It is the square root of the time average of the voltage squared. The value of V_{rms} is $V_o/\sqrt{2}$, or, equivalently, $0.707V_o$. Thus, the 60-hertz, 120-volt alternating current, which is available from most electric outlets in U.S. homes, has V_o = 120/0.707 = 170 volts. The potential difference at the outlet varies from +170 volts to -170 volts and back to +170 volts 60 times each second. The rms values of voltage and current are especially useful in calculating average power in AC circuits.

A sinusoidal electromotive force can be generated using the principles described in Faraday's law of electromagnetic induction. Briefly, an alternating electromotive force can be induced in a loop of conducting wire by rotating the loop of wire in a uniform magnetic field.

In AC circuits, it is often necessary to find the currents as a function of time in the various parts of the circuit for a given source of sinusoidal electromotive force. While the problems can become quite complex, the solutions are based on Kirchhoff's two laws. The solution for the current in a given loop takes the form $i = i_o \cos(\omega t - \phi)$. The current has the same frequency as the applied voltage but is not necessarily "in phase" with that voltage. When the phase angle ϕ does not equal zero, the maximum of the current does not occur when the driving voltage is at its maximum.

BEHAVIOUR OF AN AC CIRCUIT

The way an AC circuit functions can be better understood by examining one that includes a source of sinusoidally varying electromotive force, a resistor, a capacitor, and an inductor, all connected in series. For this single-loop problem, only the second of Kirchhoff's laws is needed since there is only one current. The points a, b, c, and d are located between the inductor and the electromotive force, between the electromotive force and the resistor, between the resistor and the capacitor, and between the capacitor and the inductor, respectively. The letters R, L, and C represent, respectively, the values of the resistance in ohms, the inductance in henrys, and the capacitance in farads. The source of the AC electromotive force is located between a and b. For the potential between b and a,

$$V_b - V_a = V_0 \cos \omega t. \tag{27a}$$

Equation (27a) represents a potential difference that has its maximum positive value at $t = 0$.

The direction chosen for the current i in the circuit represents the direction of that current at some particular time, since AC circuits feature continuous reversals of the direction of the flow of charge. The direction chosen for the current is important, however, because the loop equation must consider all the elements at the same instant in time. The potential difference across the resistor is given by Ohm's law as

$$V_b - V_c = iR. \qquad (27b)$$

For equation (27b), the direction of the current is important. The potential difference across the capacitor, $V_c - V_d$, depends on the charge on the capacitor. When the charge on the upper plate of the capacitor has a value Q, the potential difference across the capacitor is

$$V_c - V_d = \frac{Q}{C}, \qquad (27c)$$

which is a variant of equation (12). One must be careful labeling the charge and the direction of the current, since the charge on the other plate is $-Q$. For the choices shown in the figure, the current in the circuit is given by the rate of change of the charge Q—that is, $i = dQ/dt$. Finally, the value of the potential difference $V_d - V_a$ across the inductor depends on the rate of change of the current through the inductor, di/dt. For the direction chosen for i, the value is

$$V_d - V_a = +L\frac{di}{dt}. \qquad (27d)$$

The result of combining equations (27a, b, c, d) in accordance with Kirchhoff's second law for the loop is

$$V_0\cos(\omega t) = L\frac{di}{dt} + iR + \frac{Q}{C}. \qquad (28)$$

Both the current i and the rate of change of the current di/dt can be eliminated from equation (28), since $i = dQ/dt$, and $di/dt = d^2Q/dt^2$. The result is a linear, inhomogeneous, second-order differential equation with well-known solutions for the charge Q as a function of time. The most important solution describes the current and voltages after transient effects have been dampened; the transient effects last only a short time after the circuit is completed. Once the charge is known, the current in the circuit can be obtained by taking the first derivative of the charge. The expression for the current in the circuit is

$$i = \frac{V_0}{Z} \cos(\omega t - \varphi) = i_0 \cos(\omega t - \varphi). \tag{29}$$

In equation (29), Z is the impedance of the circuit; impedance, like resistance, is measured in units of ohms. Z is a function of the frequency of the source of applied electromotive force. The equation for Z is

$$Z = \sqrt{R^2 + \left(\omega L - \frac{1}{\omega C}\right)^2}. \tag{30}$$

If the resistor were the only element in the circuit, the impedance would be $Z = R$, the resistance of the resistor. For a capacitor alone, $Z = 1/\omega C$, showing that the impedance of a capacitor decreases as the frequency increases. For an inductor alone, $Z = \omega L$; the reason why the impedance of the inductor increases with frequency stems from Faraday's law of magnetic induction. Here it is sufficient to say that an induced electromotive force in the inductor opposes the change in current, and it is directly proportional to the frequency.

With modifications, Ohm's law also applies to alternating-current circuits, in which the relation between the voltage and the current is more complicated than for direct currents. When the impedance, equivalent to the ratio of voltage to current, in an alternating current circuit is constant, a common occurrence, Ohm's law is applicable. For example, $V/I = Z$.

The phase angle ϕ in equation (29) gives the time relationship between the current in the circuit and the driving electromotive force, $V_o \cos(\omega t)$. The tangent of the angle ϕ is

$$\tan \varphi = \frac{\left(\omega L - \frac{1}{\omega C} \right)}{R}. \tag{31}$$

Depending on the values of ω, L, and C, the angle ϕ can be positive, negative, or zero. If ϕ is positive, the current "lags" the voltage, while for negative values of ϕ, the current "leads" the voltage.

The power dissipated in the circuit is the same as the power delivered by the source of electromotive force, and both are measured in watts. Using equation (23), the power is given by

$$P = iV = i_0 \cos(\omega t - \varphi) V_0 \cos(\omega t). \tag{32}$$

An expression for the average power dissipated in the circuit can be written either in terms of the peak values i_o and V_o or in terms of the rms values i_{rms} and V_{rms}. The average power is

$$P_{ave} = I_{rms} V_{rms} \cos \varphi = \frac{1}{2} i_0 V_0 \cos \varphi. \tag{33}$$

The $\cos \phi$ in equation (33) is called the power factor. It is evident that the only element that can dissipate energy is the resistance.

RESONANCE

A most interesting condition known as resonance occurs when the phase angle is zero in equation (31), or equivalently, when the angular frequency ω has the value $\omega = \omega_r = \sqrt{1/LC}$.

The impedance in equation (30) then has its minimum value and equals the resistance R. The amplitude of the current in the circuit, i_o, is at its maximum value (see equation [29]). The amplitude of the current is dependent on the angular frequency ω of the source of alternating electromotive force. Consider a circuit with the values of the electric parameters as V_o = 50 volts, R = 25 ohms, L = 4.5 millihenrys, and C = 0.2 microfarad. With these values, the resonant angular frequency ω_r of the circuit is 3.33×10^4 radians per second.

The peaking in the current constitutes a resonance. At the resonant frequency, the impedance Z of the circuit is at a minimum and the power dissipated is at a maximum. The phase angle ϕ is zero so that the current is in phase with the driving voltage, and the power factor, $\cos \phi$, is 1. The resonance in the variation of the average power with the angular frequency of the sinusoidal electromotive force is seen to be even more pronounced. The quality factor Q for the circuit is the electric energy stored in the circuit divided by the energy dissipated in one period. The Q of a circuit is an important quantity in certain applications, as in the case of electromagnetic waveguides and radio-frequency cavities where Q has values around 10,000 and where high voltages and electric fields are desired. For the present circuit, $Q = \omega_r L/R$. Q also can be obtained from the average power graph as the ratio $\omega_r/(\omega_2 - \omega_1)$, where ω_1 and ω_2 are the angular frequencies at which the average power dissipated in the circuit is one-half its maximum value. For the circuit considered here, $Q = 6$.

What is the maximum value of the potential difference across the inductor? Since it is given by Ldi/dt, it will occur when the current has the maximum rate of change. The maximum amplitude of the voltage across the inductor, 300 volts, is much greater than the 50-volt amplitude of the driving sinusoidal electromotive force. This result is typical of resonance phenomena. In a familiar mechanical system, children on swings time their kicks to attain very large swings (much larger than they could attain with a single kick). In a more spectacular, albeit costly, example, the collapse of the Tacoma Narrows Bridge (a suspension bridge across the Narrows of Puget Sound, Wash.) on Nov. 7, 1940, was the result of the large amplitudes of oscillations that the span attained as it was driven in resonance by high winds. A ubiquitous example of electric resonance occurs when a radio dial is turned to receive a broadcast. Turning the dial changes the value of the tuning capacitor of the radio. When the circuit attains a resonance frequency corresponding to the frequency of the radio wave, the voltage induced is enhanced and processed to produce sound.

REACTANCE

Reactance is the measure of the opposition that a circuit or a part of a circuit presents to electric current insofar as the current is varying or alternating. Steady electric currents flowing along conductors in one direction undergo opposition called electrical resistance, but no reactance. Reactance is present in addition to resistance when conductors carry alternating current. Reactance also occurs for short intervals when direct current is changing as it approaches or departs from steady flow, for example, when switches are closed or opened.

There are two types of reactance, inductive and capacitive. Inductive reactance is associated with the magnetic field that surrounds a wire or a coil carrying a current. An alternating current in such a conductor, or inductor, sets up an alternating magnetic field that in turn affects the current in, and the voltage (potential difference) across, that part of the circuit. An inductor essentially opposes changes in current, making changes in the current lag behind those in the voltage. The current builds up as the driving voltage is already decreasing, tends to continue on at maximum value when the voltage is reversing its direction, falls off to zero as the voltage is increasing to maximum in the opposite direction, and reverses itself and builds up in the same direction as the voltage even as the voltage is falling off again. Inductive reactance, a measure of this opposition to the current, is proportional to both the frequency f of the alternating current and the inductance (which depends on the inductor's dimensions, arrangement, and surrounding medium). Inductive reactance X_L equals 2π times the product of the frequency of the current and the inductance of the conductor, simply $X_L = 2\pi f L$. Inductive reactance is expressed in ohms.

Capacitive reactance, on the other hand, is associated with the changing electric field between two conducting surfaces (plates) separated from each other by an insulating medium. Such a set of conductors, a capacitor, essentially opposes changes in voltage, or potential difference, across its plates. A capacitor in a circuit retards current flow by causing the alternating voltage to lag behind the alternating current, a relationship in contrast to that caused by an inductor. The capacitive reactance, a measure of this opposition, is inversely proportional to the frequency f of the alternating current and to the capacitance (which depends on the capacitor's dimensions, arrangement, and insulating medium). The capacitive reactance X_C equals the reciprocal of the product of 2π, the frequency of the current, and the capacitance of that part of the circuit, simply $X_C = 1/(2\pi f C)$. Capacitive reactance has units of ohms.

Because inductive reactance X_L causes the voltage to lead the current and capacitive reactance X_C causes the voltage to lag behind the current, total reactance X is their difference—that is, $X = X_L - X_C$. The reciprocal of the reactance, $1/X$, is called the susceptance and is expressed in units of reciprocal ohm, called mho (*ohm* spelled backward).

ELECTRICAL UNITS

We encounter some of the units used to measure electrical phenomena in our everyday lives. The power of a light-bulb is measured in watts. The load of a household circuit breaker is measured in amperes. Others, such as the coulomb and the henry, measure more intangible quantities.

Ampere

The ampere is the unit of electric current in the SI, used by both scientists and technologists. Since 1948 the ampere has been defined as the constant current which, if maintained in two straight parallel conductors of infinite length of negligible circular cross section and placed one metre apart in a vacuum, would produce between these conductors a force equal to 2×10^{-7} newton per metre of length. Named for the 19th-century French physicist André-Marie Ampère, it represents a flow of one coulomb of electricity per second. A flow of one ampere is produced in a resistance of one ohm by a potential difference of one volt.

Coulomb

The coulomb is the unit of electric charge in the metre–kilogram–second-ampere system, the basis of the SI system of physical units. The coulomb is defined as the quantity of electricity transported in one second by a current of one ampere. Named for the 18th–19th-century French physicist

Charles-Augustin de Coulomb, it is approximately equivalent to 6.24×10^{18} electrons.

ELECTRON VOLT

A unit of energy commonly used in atomic and nuclear physics, the electron volt is equal to the energy gained by an electron (a charged particle carrying unit electronic charge when the electrical potential at the electron increases by one volt). The electron volt equals 1.602×10^{-12} erg. The abbreviation MeV indicates 10^6 (1,000,000) electron volts and GeV, 10^9 (1,000,000,000).

FARADAY

The faraday (also called the faraday constant) is a unit of electricity used in the study of electrochemical reactions and equal to the amount of electric charge that liberates one gram equivalent of any ion from an electrolytic solution. It was named in honour of the 19th-century English scientist Michael Faraday and equals 9.64853399×10^4 coulombs, or $6.02214179 \times 10^{23}$ electrons.

HENRY

The henry is a unit of either self-inductance or mutual inductance, abbreviated h (or hy), and named for the American physicist Joseph Henry. One henry is the value of self-inductance in a closed circuit or coil in which one volt is produced by a variation of the inducing current of one ampere per second. One henry is also the value of the mutual inductance of two coils arranged such that an electromotive force of one volt is induced in one if the current in the other is changing at a rate of one ampere per second.

OHM

The unit of electrical resistance in the metre–kilogram–
second system is the ohm (abbreviation Ω), named in
honour of the 19th-century German physicist Georg
Simon Ohm. It is equal to the resistance of a circuit
in which a potential difference of one volt produces a
current of one ampere ($1\Omega = 1\ V/A$); or, the resistance
in which one watt of power is dissipated when one
ampere flows through it. Ohm's law states that resistance equals the ratio of the potential difference to
current, and the ohm, volt, and ampere are the respective fundamental units used universally for expressing
quantities.

Impedance, the apparent resistance to an alternating
current, and reactance, the part of impedance resulting
from capacitance or inductance, are circuit characteristics that are measured in ohms. The acoustic ohm and
the mechanical ohm are analogous units sometimes
used in the study of acoustic and mechanical systems,
respectively.

SIEMENS

The siemens (S) is the unit of electrical conductance. In the
case of direct current (DC), the conductance in siemens
is the reciprocal of the resistance in ohms (S = amperes
per volts); in the case of alternating current (AC), it is the
reciprocal of the impedance in ohms. A former term for
the reciprocal of the ohm is the mho (ohm spelled backward). It is disputed whether the siemens was named after
the German-born engineer-inventor Sir William Siemens
(1823–83) or his brother, the electrical engineer Werner
von Siemens (1816–92).

VOLT

The unit of electrical potential, potential difference and electromotive force in the metre–kilogram–second system (SI) is the volt; it is equal to the difference in potential between two points in a conductor carrying one ampere current when the power dissipated between the points is one watt. An equivalent is the potential difference across a resistance of one ohm when one ampere is flowing through it. The volt is named in honour of the 18th–19th-century Italian physicist Alessandro Volta. These units are defined in accordance with Ohm's law, that resistance equals the ratio of potential to current, and the respective units of ohm, volt, and ampere are used universally for expressing electrical quantities.

WATT

The watt is the unit of power in the SI equal to one joule of work performed per second, or to $\frac{1}{746}$ horsepower. An equivalent is the power dissipated in an electrical conductor carrying one ampere current between points at one volt potential difference. It is named in honour of James Watt, British engineer and inventor. One thousand watts equal one kilowatt. Most electrical devices are rated in watts.

WEBER

The weber is the unit of magnetic flux in the SI, defined as the amount of flux that, linking an electrical circuit of one turn (one loop of wire), produces in it an electromotive force of one volt as the flux is reduced to zero at a uniform rate in one second. It was named in honour of the 19th-century German physicist Wilhelm Eduard Weber and equals 10^8 maxwells, the unit used in the centimetre–gram–second system.

Electricity is often thought of in association with metals. Metals are very good conductors; however, other materials do have electric properties. Crystals experience piezoelectricity. Inside our own bodies, bioelectricity is constantly occurring.

PIEZOELECTRICITY

Some solids, notably certain crystals, have permanent electric polarization. Other crystals become electrically polarized when subjected to stress. In electric polarization, the centre of positive charge within an atom, molecule, or crystal lattice element is separated slightly from the centre of negative charge. Piezoelectricity (literally "pressure electricity") is observed if a stress is applied to a solid, for example, by bending, twisting, or squeezing it. If a thin slice of quartz is compressed between two electrodes, a potential difference occurs; conversely, if the quartz crystal is inserted into an electric field, the resulting stress changes its dimensions. Piezoelectricity is responsible for the great precision of clocks and watches equipped with quartz oscillators. It also is used in electric guitars and various other musical instruments to transform mechanical vibrations into corresponding electric signals, which are then amplified and converted to sound by acoustical speakers.

A crystal under stress exhibits the direct piezoelectric effect; a polarization P, proportional to the stress, is produced. In the converse effect, an applied electric field produces a distortion of the crystal, represented by a strain proportional to the applied field. The basic equations of piezoelectricity are $P = d \times stress$ and $E = strain/d$. The piezoelectric coefficient d (in metres per volt) is approximately 3×10^{-12} for quartz, 5×-10^{-11} for ammonium dihydrogen phosphate, and 3×10^{-10} for lead zirconate titanate.

For an elastic body, the stress is proportional to the strain—i.e., $stress = \Upsilon_e \times strain$. The proportionality constant is the coefficient of elasticity Υ_e, also called Young's modulus for the English physicist Thomas Young. Using that relation, the induced polarization can be written as $P = d\Upsilon_e \times strain$, while the stress required to keep the strain constant when the crystal is in an electric field is $stress = -d\Upsilon_e E$. The strain in a deformed elastic body is the fractional change in the dimensions of the body in various directions; the stress is the internal pressure along the various directions. Both are second-rank tensors, and, since electric field and polarization are vectors, the detailed treatment of piezoelectricity is complex. The equations above are oversimplified but can be used for crystals in certain orientations.

The polarization effects responsible for piezoelectricity arise from small displacements of ions in the crystal lattice. Such an effect is not found in crystals with a centre of symmetry. The direct effect can be quite strong; a potential $V = \Upsilon_e d\delta/\varepsilon_o K$ is generated in a crystal compressed by an amount δ, where K is the dielectric constant. If lead zirconate titanate is placed between two electrodes and a pressure causing a reduction of only 1/20th of one millimetre is applied, a 100,000-volt potential is produced. The direct effect is used, for example, to generate an electric spark with which to ignite natural gas in a heating unit or an outdoor cooking grill.

In practice, the converse piezoelectric effect, which occurs when an external electric field changes the dimensions of a crystal, is small because the electric fields that can be generated in a laboratory are minuscule compared to those existing naturally in matter. A static electric field of 10^6 volts per metre produces a change of only about 0.001 millimetre in the length of a one-centimetre quartz crystal. The effect can be enhanced by the application of an alternating electric field of the same frequency as the natural mechanical vibration frequency of the crystal. Many of the crystals have a quality factor Q of several hundred, and, in the case of quartz, the value can be 10^6. The result is a piezoelectric coefficient a factor Q higher than for a static electric field. The very large Q of quartz is exploited in electronic oscillator circuits to make remarkably accurate timepieces. The mechanical vibrations that can be induced in a crystal by the converse piezoelectric effect are also used to generate ultrasound, which is sound with a frequency far higher than frequencies audible to the human ear—above 20 kilohertz. The reflected sound is detectable by the direct effect. Such effects form the basis of ultrasound systems used to fathom the depths of lakes and waterways and to locate fish. Ultrasound has found application in medical imaging (e.g., fetal monitoring and the detection of abnormalities such as prostate tumours). The use of ultrasound makes it possible to produce detailed pictures of organs and other internal structures because of the variation in the reflection of sound from various body tissues. Thin films of polymeric plastic with a piezoelectric coefficient of about 10^{-11} metres per volt are being developed and have numerous potential applications as pressure transducers.

Related to piezoelectricity is electrostriction, a property of all electrical nonconductors, or dielectrics, that manifests itself as a relatively slight change of shape, or mechanical deformation, under the application of an electric field. Reversal of the electric field does not reverse the direction of the deformation.

ELECTRO-OPTIC PHENOMENA

The index of refraction n of a transparent substance is related to its electric polarizability and is given by $n^2 = 1 + \chi_e/\varepsilon_0$. As discussed earlier, χ_e is the electric susceptibility of a medium, and the equation $P = \chi_e E$ relates the polarization of the medium to the applied electric field. For most matter, χ_e is not a constant independent of the value of the electric field, but rather depends to a small degree on the value of the field. Thus, the index of refraction can be changed by applying an external electric field to a medium. In liquids, glasses, and crystals that have a centre of symmetry, the change is usually very small. Called the Kerr effect (for its discoverer, the Scottish physicist John Kerr), it is proportional to the square of the applied electric field. In noncentrosymmetric crystals, the change in the index of refraction n is generally much greater; it depends linearly on the applied electric field and is known as the Pockels effect (after the German physicist F. R. Pockels).

A varying electric field applied to a medium will modulate its index of refraction. This change in the index of refraction can be used to modulate light and make it carry information. A crystal widely used for its Pockels effect is potassium dihydrogen phosphate, which has good optical properties and low dielectric losses even at microwave frequencies.

An unusually large Kerr effect is found in nitrobenzene, a liquid with highly "acentric" molecules that have large electric dipole moments. Applying an external electric field partially aligns the otherwise randomly oriented dipole moments and greatly enhances the influence of the field on the index of refraction. The length of the path of light through nitrobenzene can be adjusted easily because it is a liquid.

THERMOELECTRICITY

When two metals are placed in electric contact, electrons flow out of the one in which the electrons are less bound and into the other. The binding is measured by the location of the so-called Fermi level of electrons in the metal; the higher the level, the lower is the binding. The Fermi level represents the demarcation in energy within the conduction band of a metal between the energy levels occupied by electrons and those that are unoccupied. The energy of an electron at the Fermi level is $-W$ relative to a free electron outside the metal. The flow of electrons between the two conductors in contact continues until the change in electrostatic potential brings the Fermi levels of the two metals (W_1 and W_2) to the same value. This electrostatic potential is called the contact potential ϕ_{12} and is given by $e\phi_{12} = W_1 - W_2$, where e is 1.6×10^{-19} coulomb.

If a closed circuit is made of two different metals, there will be no net electromotive force in the circuit because the two contact potentials oppose each other and no current will flow. There will be a current if the temperature of one of the junctions is raised with respect to that of the second. There is a net electromotive force generated in the circuit, as it is unlikely that the two metals will have Fermi levels with identical temperature dependence. To maintain the temperature difference, heat must enter the hot junction and leave the cold junction; this is consistent with the fact that the current can be used to do mechanical work.

The generation of a thermal electromotive force at a junction is called the Seebeck effect (after the Estonian-born German physicist Thomas Johann Seebeck). The electromotive force is approximately linear with the temperature difference between two junctions of dissimilar metals, which are called a thermocouple. Any two different metals or metal alloys exhibit the thermoelectric effect, but only a few are used as thermocouples—e.g., antimony and bismuth, copper and iron, or copper and constantan (a copper-nickel alloy). For a thermocouple made of iron and constantan (an alloy of 60 percent copper and 40 percent nickel), the electromotive force is about five millivolts when the cold junction is at 0 °C (32 °F) and the hot junction at 100 °C (212 °F). One of the principal applications of the Seebeck effect is the measurement of temperature. The chemical properties of the medium, the temperature of which is measured, and the sensitivity required dictate the choice of components of a thermocouple. Usually platinum, either with rhodium or a platinum-rhodium alloy, is used in high-temperature thermocouples.

For a thermocouple to work, one junction is placed where the temperature is to be measured, and the other is kept at a constant lower temperature. A measuring instrument is connected in the circuit. Temperature can be read from standard tables, or the measuring instrument can be calibrated to read temperature directly.

A thermopile is a number of thermocouples connected in series; its results are comparable to the average of several temperature readings. A series circuit also gives greater sensitivity.

The absorption or release of heat at a junction in which there is an electric current is called the Peltier effect (after the French physicist Jean-Charles Peltier). Both the Seebeck and Peltier effects also occur at the junction between a metal and a semiconductor and at the junction between two semiconductors. The development of semiconductor thermocouples (e.g., those consisting of n-type and p-type bismuth telluride) has made the use of the Peltier effect practical for refrigeration. Sets of such thermocouples are connected electrically in series and thermally in parallel. When an electric current is made to flow, a temperature difference, which depends on the current, develops between the two junctions. If the temperature of the hotter junction is kept low by removing heat, the second junction can be tens of degrees colder and act as a refrigerator. Peltier refrigerators are used to cool small bodies; they are compact, have no moving mechanical parts, and can be regulated to maintain precise and stable temperatures. They are employed in numerous applications, as, for example, to keep the temperature of a sample constant while it is on a microscope stage.

THERMIONIC EMISSION

A metal contains mobile electrons in a partially filled band of energy levels—i.e., the conduction band. These electrons, though mobile within the metal, are rather tightly bound to it. The energy that is required to release a mobile electron from the metal varies from about 1.5 to approximately six electron volts, depending on the metal. In thermionic emission, some of the electrons acquire enough energy from thermal collisions to escape from the metal. The number of electrons emitted and therefore the thermionic emission current depend critically on temperature.

In a metal the conduction-band levels are filled up to the Fermi level, which lies at an energy -W relative to a free electron outside the metal. The work function of the metal, which is the energy required to remove an electron from the metal, is therefore equal to W. At a temperature of 1,000 K (700 °C, or 1,300 °F) only a small fraction of the mobile electrons have sufficient energy to escape. The electrons that can escape are moving so fast in the metal and have such high kinetic energies that they are unaffected by the periodic potential caused by atoms of the metallic lattice. They behave like electrons trapped in a region of constant potential. Because of this, when the rate at which electrons escape from the metal is calculated, the detailed structure of the metal has little influence on the final result. A formula known as Richardson's law (first proposed by the English physicist Owen W. Richardson) is roughly valid for all metals. It is usually expressed in terms of the emission current density (J) as

$$J = AT^2 \varepsilon^{-W/kT}$$

in amperes per square metre. The Boltzmann constant k has the value 8.62×10^{-5} electron volts per kelvin, and temperature T is in kelvins. The constant A is 1.2×10^6 ampere degree squared per square metre, and varies slightly for different metals. For tungsten, which has a work function W of 4.5 electron volts, the value of A is 7×10^5 amperes per square metre kelvin squared and the current density at T equaling 2,400 K is 0.14 ampere per square centimetre. J rises rapidly with temperature. If T is increased to 2,600 K, J rises to 0.9 ampere per square centimetre. Tungsten does not emit appreciably at 2,000 K (1,700 °C, or 3,100 °F) or below (less than 0.05 milliampere per square centimetre) because its work function of 4.5 electron volts is large compared to the thermal energy kT, which is only 0.16 electron volt. In vacuum tubes, the cathode usually is coated with a mixture of barium and strontium oxides. At 1,000 K the oxide has a work function of approximately 1.3 electron volts and is a reasonably good conductor. Currents of several amperes per square centimetre can be drawn from oxide cathodes, but in practice the current density is generally less than 0.2 ampere per square centimetre. The oxide layer deteriorates rapidly when higher current densities are drawn.

SECONDARY ELECTRON EMISSION

If electrons with energies of 10 to 1,000 electron volts strike a metal surface in a vacuum, their energy is lost in collisions in a region near the surface, and most of it is transferred to other electrons in the metal. Because this occurs near the surface, some of these electrons may be ejected from the metal and form a secondary emission current. The ratio of secondary electrons to incident electrons is known as the secondary emission coefficient.

For low-incident energies (below about one electron volt), the primary electrons tend to be reflected and the secondary emission coefficient is near unity. With increasing energy, the coefficient at first falls and then at about 10 electron volts begins to rise again, usually reaching a peak of value between 2 and 4 at energies of a few hundred electron volts. At higher energies, the primary electrons penetrate so far below the surface before losing energy that the excited electrons have little chance of reaching the surface and escaping. The secondary emission coefficients fall and, when the electrons have energies exceeding 20 kiloelectron volts, are usually well below unity. Secondary emission also can occur in insulators. Because many insulators have rather high secondary emission coefficients, it is often useful when high secondary emission yields are required to coat a metal electrode with a thin insulator layer a few atoms thick.

PHOTOELECTRIC CONDUCTIVITY

If light with a photon energy $h\nu$ that exceeds the work function W falls on a metal surface, some of the incident photons will transfer their energy to electrons, which then will be ejected from the metal. Since $h\nu$ is greater than W, the excess energy $h\nu - W$ transferred to the electrons will be observed as their kinetic energy outside the metal. The relation between electron kinetic energy E and the frequency ν (that is, $E = h\nu - W$) is known as the Einstein relation, and its experimental verification helped to establish the validity of quantum theory. The energy of the electrons depends on the frequency of the light, while the intensity of the light determines the rate of photoelectric emission.

In a semiconductor the valence band of energy levels is almost completely full while the conduction band is almost empty. The conductivity of the material derives from the few holes present in the valence band and the few electrons in the conduction band. Electrons can be excited from the valence to the conduction band by light photons having an energy $h\nu$ that is larger than energy gap E_g between the bands. The process is an internal photoelectric effect. The value of E_g varies from semiconductor to semiconductor. For lead sulfide, the threshold frequency occurs in the infrared, whereas for zinc oxide it is in the ultraviolet. For silicon, E_g equals 1.1 electron volts, and the threshold wavelength is in the infrared, about 1,100 nanometres. Visible radiation produces electron transitions with almost unity quantum efficiency in silicon. Each transition yields a hole–electron pair (i.e., two carriers) that contributes to electric conductivity. For example, if one milliwatt of light strikes a sample of pure silicon in the form of a thin plate one square centimetre in area and 0.03 cm thick (which is thick enough to absorb all incident light), the resistance of the plate will be decreased by a factor of about 1,000. In practice, photoconductive effects are not usually as large as this, but this example indicates that appreciable changes in conductivity can occur even with low illumination. Photoconductive devices are simple to construct and are used to detect visible, infrared, and ultraviolet radiation.

ELECTROLUMINESCENCE

Conduction electrons moving in a solid under the influence of an electric field usually lose kinetic energy in low-energy collisions as fast as they acquire it from the field. Under certain circumstances in semiconductors, however, they can acquire enough energy between collisions to excite atoms in the next collision and produce radiation as the atoms de-excite. A voltage applied across a thin layer of zinc sulfide powder causes just such an electroluminescent effect. Electroluminescent panels are of more interest as signal indicators and display devices than as a source of general illumination.

A somewhat similar effect occurs at the junction in a reverse-biased semiconductor p–n junction diode—i.e., a p–n junction diode in which the applied potential is in the direction of small current flow. Electrons in the intense field at the depleted junction easily acquire enough energy to excite atoms. Little of this energy finally emerges as light, though the effect is readily visible under a microscope.

When a junction between a heavily doped n-type material and a less doped p-type material is forward-biased so that a current will flow easily, the current consists mainly of electrons injected from the n-type material into the conduction band of the p-type material. These electrons ultimately drop into holes in the valence band and release energy equal to the energy gap of the material. In most cases, this energy E_g is dissipated as heat, but in gallium phosphide and especially in gallium arsenide, an appreciable fraction appears as radiation, the frequency v of which satisfies the relation $hv = E_g$. In gallium arsenide, though up to 30 percent of the input electric energy is available as radiation, the characteristic wavelength of 900 nanometres is in the infrared. Gallium phosphide gives off visible green light but is inefficient; other related III-V compound semiconductors emit light of different colours. Electroluminescent injection diodes of such materials, commonly known as light-emitting diodes (LEDs), are employed mainly as indicator lamps and numeric displays.

Semiconductor lasers built with layers of indium phosphide and of gallium indium arsenide phosphide have proved more useful. Unlike gas or optically pumped lasers, these semiconductor lasers can be modulated directly at high frequencies. Not only are they used in devices such as compact digital disc players but also as light sources for long-distance optical fibre communications systems.

BIOELECTRIC EFFECTS

Bioelectricity refers to the generation or action of electric currents or voltages in biological processes. Bioelectric phenomena include fast signaling in nerves and the triggering of physical processes in muscles or glands. There is some similarity among the nerves, muscles, and glands of all organisms, possibly because fairly efficient electrochemical systems evolved early. Scientific studies tend to focus on the following: nerve or muscle tissue; such organs as the heart, brain, eye, ear, stomach, and certain glands; electric organs in some fish; and potentials associated with damaged tissue.

Electric activity in living tissue is a cellular phenomenon, dependent on the cell membrane. The membrane acts like a capacitor, storing energy as electrically charged ions on opposite sides of the membrane. The stored energy is available for rapid utilization and stabilizes the membrane system so that it is not activated by small disturbances.

Cells capable of electric activity show a resting potential in which their interiors are negative by about 0.1 volt or less compared with the outside of the cell. When the cell is activated, the resting potential may reverse suddenly in sign; as a result, the outside of the cell becomes negative and the inside positive. This condition lasts for a short time, after which the cell returns to its original resting state.

This sequence, called depolarization and repolarization, is accompanied by a flow of substantial current through the active cell membrane, so that a "dipole-current source" exists for a short period. Small currents flow from this source through the aqueous medium containing the cell and are detectable at considerable distances from it. These currents, originating in active membrane, are functionally significant very close to their site of origin but must be considered incidental at any distance from it. In electric fish, however, adaptations have occurred, and this otherwise incidental electric current is actually utilized. In some species the external current is apparently used for sensing purposes, while in others it is used to stun or kill prey. In both cases, voltages from many cells add up in series, thus assuring that the specialized functions can be performed. Bioelectric potentials detected at some distance from the cells generating them may be as small as the 20 or 30 microvolts associated with certain components of the human electroencephalogram or the millivolt of the human electrocardiogram. On the other hand, electric eels can deliver electric shocks with voltages as large as 1,000 volts.

In addition to the potentials originating in nerve or muscle cells, relatively steady or slowly varying potentials (often designated dc) are known. These dc potentials occur in the following cases: in areas where cells have been damaged and where ionized potassium is leaking (as much as 50 millivolts); when one part of the brain is compared with another part (up to one millivolt); when different areas of the skin are compared (up to 10 millivolts); within pockets in active glands, e.g., follicles in the thyroid (as high as 60 millivolts); and in special structures in the inner ear (about 80 millivolts).

A small electric shock caused by static electricity during cold, dry weather is a familiar experience. While the sudden muscular reaction it engenders is sometimes unpleasant, it is usually harmless. Even though static potentials of several thousand volts are involved, a current exists for only a brief time and the total charge is very small. A steady current of two milliamperes through the body is barely noticeable. Severe electrical shock can occur above 10 milliamperes, however. Lethal current levels range from 100 to 200 milliamperes. Larger currents, which produce burns and unconsciousness, are not fatal if the victim is given prompt medical care. (Above 200 milliamperes, the heart is clamped during the shock and does not undergo ventricular fibrillation.) Prevention clearly includes avoiding contact with live electric wiring; risk of injury increases considerably if the skin is wet, as the electric resistance of wet skin may be hundreds of times smaller than that of dry skin.

PYROELECTRICITY

Pyroelectricity is the development of opposite electrical charges on different parts of a crystal that is subjected to temperature change. First observed (1824) in quartz, pyroelectricity is exhibited only in crystallized nonconducting substances having at least one axis of symmetry that is polar (that is, having no centre of symmetry, the different crystal faces occurring on opposite ends). Portions of the crystal with the same symmetry will develop charges of like sign. Opposite temperature changes produce opposite charges at the same point; i.e., if a crystal develops a positive charge on one face during heating, it will develop a negative charge there during cooling. The charges gradually dissipate if the crystal is kept at a constant temperature. A pyroelectric thermometer can determine change by measurement of the voltage induced by the separation of the charges.

SUPERCONDUCTIVITY

Superconductivity happens when electrical resistance in various solids completely disappears when they are cooled below a characteristic temperature. This temperature, called the transition temperature, varies for different materials but generally is below 20 K (-253 °C, or -424 °F).

The use of superconductors in magnets is limited by the fact that strong magnetic fields above a certain critical value, depending upon the material, cause a superconductor to revert to its normal, or nonsuperconducting, state, even though the material is kept well below the transition temperature.

Suggested uses for superconducting materials include medical magnetic-imaging devices, magnetic energy-storage systems, motors, generators, transformers, computer parts, and very sensitive devices for measuring magnetic fields, voltages, or currents. The main advantages of devices made from superconductors are low power dissipation, high-speed operation, and high sensitivity.

DISCOVERY

Superconductivity was discovered in 1911 by the Dutch physicist Heike Kamerlingh Onnes, who was awarded the Nobel Prize for Physics in 1913 for his low-temperature research. Kamerlingh Onnes found that the electrical resistivity of a mercury wire disappears suddenly when it is cooled below a temperature of about 4 K (-269 °C, or -452 °F); absolute zero is 0 K (-273 °C, or -460 °F), the temperature at which all matter loses its disorder. He soon discovered that a superconducting material can be returned to the normal (i.e., nonsuperconducting) state either by passing a sufficiently large current through it or by applying a sufficiently strong magnetic field to it.

For many years it was believed that, except for the fact that they had no electrical resistance (i.e., that they had infinite electrical conductivity), superconductors had the same properties as normal materials. This belief was shattered in 1933 by the discovery that a superconductor is highly diamagnetic; that is, it is strongly repelled by and tends to expel a magnetic field. This phenomenon, which is very strong in superconductors, is called the Meissner effect for one of the two men who discovered it. Its discovery made it possible to formulate, in 1934, a theory of the electromagnetic properties of superconductors that predicted the existence of an electromagnetic penetration depth, which was first confirmed experimentally in 1939. In 1950 it was clearly shown for the first time that a theory of superconductivity must take into account the fact that free electrons in a crystal are influenced by the vibrations of atoms that define the crystal structure, called the lattice vibrations. In 1953, in an analysis of the thermal conductivity of superconductors, it was recognized that the distribution of energies of the free electrons in a superconductor is not uniform but has a separation called the energy gap.

The theories referred to thus far served to show some of the interrelationships between observed phenomena but did not explain them as consequences of the fundamental laws of physics. For almost 50 years after Kamerlingh Onnes's discovery, theorists were unable to develop a fundamental theory of superconductivity. Finally, in 1957 such a theory was presented by the physicists John Bardeen, Leon N. Cooper, and John Robert Schrieffer of the United States; it won them the Nobel Prize for Physics in 1972. It is now called the BCS theory in their honour, and most later theoretical work is based on it. The BCS theory also provided a foundation for an earlier model that had been introduced by the Russian physicists Lev Davidovich

Landau and Vitaly Lazarevich Ginzburg (1950). This model has been useful in understanding electromagnetic properties, including the fact that any internal magnetic flux in superconductors exists only in discrete amounts (instead of in a continuous spectrum of values), an effect called the quantization of magnetic flux. This flux quantization, which had been predicted from quantum mechanical principles, was first observed experimentally in 1961.

In 1962 the British physicist Brian D. Josephson predicted that two superconducting objects placed in electric contact would display certain remarkable electromagnetic properties. These properties have since been observed in a wide variety of experiments, demonstrating quantum mechanical effects on a macroscopic scale.

The theory of superconductivity has been tested in a wide range of experiments, involving, for example, ultrasonic absorption studies, nuclear-spin phenomena, low-frequency infrared absorption, and electron-tunneling experiments. The results of these measurements have brought understanding to many of the detailed properties of various superconductors.

THERMAL PROPERTIES OF SUPERCONDUCTORS

Superconductivity is a startling departure from the properties of normal (i.e., nonsuperconducting) conductors of electricity. In materials that are electric conductors, some of the electrons are not bound to individual atoms but are free to move through the material; their motion constitutes an electric current. In normal conductors these so-called conduction electrons are scattered by impurities, dislocations, grain boundaries, and lattice vibrations (phonons). In a superconductor, however, there is an ordering among the conduction electrons that prevents this scattering. Consequently, electric current can flow with no resistance at all. The ordering of the electrons, called Cooper pairing, involves the momenta of the electrons rather than their positions. The energy per electron that is associated with this ordering is extremely small, typically about one thousandth of the amount by which the energy per electron changes when a chemical reaction takes place. One reason that superconductivity remained unexplained for so long is the smallness of the energy changes that accompany the transition between normal and superconducting states. In fact, many incorrect theories of superconductivity were advanced before the BCS theory was proposed.

Hundreds of materials are known to become superconducting at low temperatures. Twenty-seven of the chemical elements, all of them metals, are superconductors in their usual crystallographic forms at low temperatures and low (atmospheric) pressure. Among these are commonly known metals such as aluminum, tin, lead, and mercury and less common ones such as rhenium, lanthanum, and protactinium. In addition, 11 chemical elements that are metals, semimetals, or semiconductors are superconductors at low temperatures and high pressures. Among these are uranium, cerium, silicon, and selenium. Bismuth and five other elements, though not superconducting in their usual crystallographic form, can be made superconducting by preparing them in a highly disordered form, which is stable at extremely low temperatures. Superconductivity is not exhibited by any of the magnetic elements chromium, manganese, iron, cobalt, or nickel.

Most of the known superconductors are alloys or compounds. It is possible for a compound to be superconducting even if the chemical elements constituting it are not; examples are disilver fluoride (Ag_2F) and a compound of carbon and potassium (C_8K). Some semiconducting compounds, such as tin telluride (SnTe), become superconducting if they are properly doped with impurities.

Since 1986 some compounds containing copper and oxygen (called cuprates) have been found to have extraordinarily high transition temperatures, denoted T_c. This is the temperature below which a substance is superconducting. The properties of these high-T_c compounds are different in some respects from those of the types of superconductors known prior to 1986, which will be referred to as classic superconductors in this discussion.

A further classification problem is presented by the superconducting compounds of carbon (sometimes doped with other atoms) in which the carbon atoms are on the surface of a cluster with a spherical or spheroidal crystallographic structure. These compounds, discovered in the 1980s, are called fullerenes (if only carbon is present) or fullerides (if doped). They have superconducting transition temperatures higher than those of the classic superconductors.

TRANSITION TEMPERATURES

The vast majority of the known superconductors have transition temperatures that lie between 1 K (-272 °C, or -458 °F) and 10 K (-263 °C, or -442 °F). Of the chemical elements, tungsten has the lowest transition temperature, 0.015 K (-273.135 °C, or -459.643 °F), and niobium the highest, 9.2 K (-264 °C, or -443.1 °F). The transition temperature is usually very sensitive to the presence of magnetic impurities. A few parts per million of manganese in zinc, for example, lowers the transition temperature considerably.

SPECIFIC HEAT AND THERMAL CONDUCTIVITY

The thermal properties of a superconductor can be compared with those of the same material at the same temperature in the normal state. (The material can be forced into the normal state at low temperature by a large enough magnetic field.)

When a small amount of heat is put into a system, some of the energy is used to increase the lattice vibrations (an amount that is the same for a system in the normal and in the superconducting state), and the remainder is used to increase the energy of the conduction electrons. The electronic specific heat (C_e) of the electrons is defined as the ratio of that portion of the heat used by the electrons to the rise in temperature of the system. The specific heat of the electrons in a superconductor varies with the absolute temperature (T) in the normal and in the superconducting state. The electronic specific heat in the superconducting state (designated C_{es}) is smaller than in the normal state (designated C_{en}) at low enough temperatures, but C_{es}

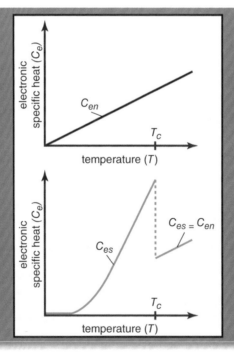

Specific heat in the normal (C_{en}) and superconducting (C_{es}) states of a classic superconductor as a function of absolute temperature. The two functions are identical at the transition temperature (T_c) and above T_c. Adapted from Zeitschrift fur Physik (1959); rendering for this edition by Rosen Educational Services

becomes larger than C_{en} as the transition temperature T_c is approached, at which point it drops abruptly to C_{en} for the classic superconductors, although the curve has a cusp shape near T_c for the high-T_c superconductors. Precise measurements have indicated that, at temperatures considerably below the transition temperature, the logarithm of the electronic specific heat is inversely proportional to the temperature. This temperature dependence, together with the principles of statistical mechanics, strongly suggests that there is a gap in the distribution of energy levels available to the electrons in a superconductor, so that a minimum energy is required for the excitation of each electron from a state below the gap to a state above the gap. Some of the high-T_c superconductors provide an additional contribution to the specific heat, which is proportional to the temperature. This behaviour indicates that there are electronic states lying at low energy; additional evidence of such states is obtained from optical properties and tunneling measurements.

The heat flow per unit area of a sample equals the product of the thermal conductivity (K) and the temperature gradient $\triangle T$: $\mathcal{J}_Q = -K\triangle T$, the minus sign indicating that heat always flows from a warmer to a colder region of a substance.

The thermal conductivity in the normal state (K_n) approaches the thermal conductivity in the superconducting state (K_s) as the temperature (T) approaches the transition temperature (T_c) for all materials, whether they are pure or impure. This suggests that the energy gap (Δ) for each electron approaches zero as the temperature (T) approaches the transition temperature (T_c). This would also account for the fact that the electronic specific heat in the superconducting state (C_{es}) is higher than in the normal state (C_{en}) near the transition temperature: as the temperature is raised toward the transition temperature

(T_c), the energy gap in the superconducting state decreases, the number of thermally excited electrons increases, and this requires the absorption of heat.

Energy Gaps

As stated above, the thermal properties of superconductors indicate that there is a gap in the distribution of energy levels available to the electrons, and so a finite amount of energy, designated as delta (Δ), must be supplied to an electron to excite it. This energy is maximum (designated Δ_o) at absolute zero and changes little with increase of temperature until the transition temperature is approached, where Δ decreases to zero, its value in the normal state. The BCS theory predicts an energy gap with just this type of temperature dependence.

According to the BCS theory, there is a type of electron pairing (electrons of opposite spin acting in unison) in the superconductor that is important in interpreting many superconducting phenomena. The electron pairs, called Cooper pairs, are broken up as the superconductor is heated. Each time a pair is broken, an amount of energy that is at least as much as the energy gap (Δ) must be supplied to each of the two electrons in the pair, so an energy at least twice as great (2Δ) must be supplied to the superconductor. The value of twice the energy gap at 0 K (which is $2\Delta_o$) might be assumed to be higher when the transition temperature of the superconductor is higher. In fact, the BCS theory predicts a relation of this type—namely, that the energy supplied to the superconductor at absolute zero would be $2\Delta_o = 3.53\ kT_c$, where k is Boltzmann's constant (1.38×10^{-23} joule per kelvin). In the high-T_c cuprate compounds, values of $2\Delta_o$ range from approximately three to eight multiplied by kT_c.

The energy gap (Δ) can be measured most precisely in a tunneling experiment (a process in quantum mechanics that allows an electron to escape from a metal without acquiring the energy required along the way according to the laws of classical physics). In this experiment, a thin insulating junction is prepared between a superconductor and another metal, assumed here to be in the normal state. In this situation, electrons can quantum mechanically tunnel from the normal metal to the superconductor if they have sufficient energy. This energy can be supplied by applying a negative voltage (V) to the normal metal, with respect to the voltage of the superconductor.

Tunneling will occur if e V—the product of the electron charge, e (-1.60 × 10^{-19} coulomb), and the voltage—is at least as large as the energy gap Δ. The current flowing between the two sides of the junction is small up to a voltage equal to $V = \Delta/e$, but then it rises sharply. This provides an experimental determination of the energy gap (Δ). In describing this experiment it is assumed here that the tunneling electrons must get their energy from the applied voltage rather than from thermal excitation.

MAGNETIC AND ELECTROMAGNETIC PROPERTIES OF SUPERCONDUCTORS

Superconducting materials have interesting electromagnetic properties. In the Meissner effect, a superconducting material expels magnetic flux. With Josephson currents, current can flow in the absence of a voltage.

CRITICAL FIELD

One of the ways in which a superconductor can be forced into the normal state is by applying a magnetic field. The weakest magnetic field that will cause this transition is called the critical field (H_c) if the sample is in the form of a long, thin cylinder or ellipsoid and the field is oriented parallel to the long axis of the sample. (In other configurations the sample goes from the superconducting state into an intermediate state, in which some regions are normal and others are superconducting, and finally into the normal state.) The critical field increases with decreasing temperature. For the superconducting elements, its values (H_0) at absolute zero range from 1.1 oersted for tungsten to 830 oersteds for tantalum.

These remarks about the critical field apply to ordinary (so-called type I) superconductors. In the following section the behaviour of other (type II) superconductors is examined.

The Meissner Effect

As stated, a type I superconductor in the form of a long, thin cylinder or ellipsoid remains superconducting at a fixed temperature as an axially oriented magnetic field is applied, provided the applied field does not exceed a critical value (H_c). Under these conditions, superconductors exclude the magnetic field from their interior, as could be predicted from the laws of electromagnetism and the fact that the superconductor has no electric resistance. A more astonishing effect occurs if the magnetic field is applied in the same way to the same type of sample at a temperature above the transition temperature and is then held at a fixed value while the sample is cooled. It is found that the sample expels the magnetic flux as it becomes superconducting. This is called the Meissner effect. Complete expulsion of the magnetic flux (a complete Meissner effect) occurs in this way for certain superconductors, called type I superconductors, but only for samples that have the described geometry. For samples of other shapes, including hollow structures, some of the magnetic flux can be trapped, producing an incomplete or partial Meissner effect.

Type II superconductors have a different magnetic behaviour. Examples of materials of this type are niobium and vanadium (the only type II superconductors among the chemical elements) and some alloys and compounds, including the high-T_c compounds. As a sample of this type, in the form of a long, thin cylinder or ellipsoid, is exposed to a decreasing magnetic field that is axially oriented with the sample, the increase of magnetization, instead of occurring suddenly at the critical field (H_c), sets in gradually. Beginning at the upper critical field (H_{c2}), it is completed at a lower critical field (H_{c1}. If the sample is of some other shape, is hollow, or is inhomogeneous or strained, some magnetic flux remains trapped, and some magnetization of the sample remains after the applied field is completely removed. Known values of the upper critical field extend up to 6×10^5 oersteds, the value for the compound of lead, molybdenum, and sulfur with formula $PbMo_6S_8$.

The expulsion of magnetic flux by type I superconductors in fields below the critical field (H_c) or by type II superconductors in fields below H_{c1} is never quite as complete as has been stated in this simplified presentation,

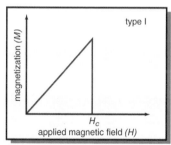

For a type I superconductor, magnetic flux is expelled, producing a magnetization (M) that increases with magnetic field (H) until a critical field (H_c) is reached, at which it falls to zero as with a normal conductor.

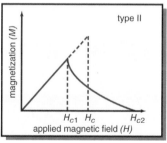

A type II superconductor has two critical magnetic fields (H_{c1} and H_{c2}); below H_{c1} type II behaves as type I, and above H_{c2} it becomes normal.

Magnetization as a function of magnetic field for a type I superconductor and a type II superconductor. Copyright Encyclopædia Britannica; rendering for this edition by Rosen Educational Services

because the field always penetrates into a sample for a small distance, known as the electromagnetic penetration depth. Values of the penetration depth for the superconducting elements at low temperature lie in the range from about 390 to 1,300 angstroms. As the temperature approaches the critical temperature, the penetration depth becomes extremely large.

HIGH-FREQUENCY ELECTROMAGNETIC PROPERTIES

The foregoing descriptions have pertained to the behaviour of superconductors in the absence of electromagnetic fields or in the presence of steady or slowly varying fields; the properties of superconductors in the presence of high-frequency electromagnetic fields, however, have also been studied.

The energy gap in a superconductor has a direct effect on the absorption of electromagnetic radiation. At low temperatures, at which a negligible fraction of the electrons are thermally excited to states above the gap, the superconductor can absorb energy only in a quantized amount that is at least twice the gap energy (at absolute zero, $2\Delta_o$). In the absorption process, a photon (a quantum of electromagnetic energy) is absorbed, and a Cooper pair is broken; both electrons in the pair become excited. The photon's energy (E) is related to its frequency (v) by the Planck relation, $E = hv$, in which h is Planck's constant (6.63×10^{-34} joule second). Hence the superconductor can absorb electromagnetic energy only for frequencies at least as large as $2\Delta_o/h$.

MAGNETIC-FLUX QUANTIZATION

The laws of quantum mechanics dictate that electrons have wave properties and that the properties of an electron can be summed up in what is called a wave function. If several wave functions are in phase (i.e., act in unison), they are said to be coherent. The theory of superconductivity indicates that there is a single, coherent, quantum mechanical wave function that determines the behaviour of all the superconducting electrons. As a consequence, a direct relationship can be shown to exist between the velocity of these electrons and the magnetic flux (Φ) enclosed within any closed path inside the superconductor. Indeed, inasmuch as the magnetic flux arises because of the motion of the electrons, the magnetic flux can be shown to be quantized; i.e., the intensity of this trapped flux can change only by units of Planck's constant divided by twice the electron charge.

When a magnetic field enters a type II superconductor (in an applied field between the lower and upper critical fields, H_{c1} and H_{c2}), it does so in the form of quantized fluxoids, each carrying one quantum of flux. These fluxoids tend to arrange themselves in regular patterns that have been detected by electron microscopy and by neutron diffraction. If a large enough current is passed through the superconductor, the fluxoids move. This motion leads to energy dissipation that can heat the superconductor and drive it into the normal state. The maximum current per unit area that a superconductor can carry without being forced into the normal state is called the critical current density (J_c). In making wire for superconducting high-field magnets, manufacturers try to fix the positions of the fluxoids by making the wire inhomogeneous in composition.

Josephson Currents

If two superconductors are separated by an insulating film that forms a low-resistance junction between them, it is found that Cooper pairs can tunnel from one side of the junction to the other. (This process occurs in addition to the single-particle tunneling already described.) Thus, a flow of electrons, called the Josephson current, is generated and is intimately related to the phases of the coherent quantum mechanical wave function for all the superconducting electrons on the two sides of the junction. It was predicted that several novel phenomena should be observable, and experiments have demonstrated them. These are collectively called the Josephson effect or effects.

The first of these phenomena is the passage of current through the junction in the absence of a voltage across the junction. The maximum current that can flow at zero voltage depends on the magnetic flux (Φ) passing through the junction as a result of the magnetic field generated by currents in the junction and elsewhere.

A second type of Josephson effect is an oscillating current resulting from a relation between the voltage across

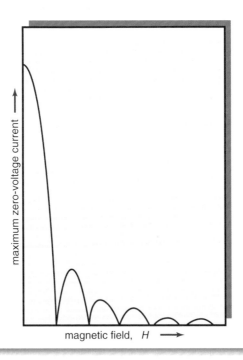

Maximum zero-voltage (Josephson) current passing through a junction by Cooper-pair tunneling as a function of magnetic field. Copyright Encyclopædia Britannica; rendering for this edition by Rosen Educational Services

the junction and the frequency (v) of the currents associated with Cooper pairs passing through the junction. The frequency (v) of this Josephson current is given by $v = 2eV/h$, where e is the charge of the electron. Thus, the frequency increases by 4.84×10^{14} hertz (cycles per second) for each additional volt applied to the junction. This effect can be demonstrated in various ways. The voltage can be established with a source of direct-current (DC) power, for instance, and the oscillating current can be detected by the electromagnetic radiation of frequency (v) that it generates. Another method is to expose the junction to radiation of another frequency (v') generated externally. It is found that a graph of the DC current versus voltage has current steps at values of the voltage corresponding to Josephson frequencies that are integral multiples (n) of the external frequency ($v = nv'$); that is, $V = nhv'/2e$. The observation of current steps of this type has made it possible to measure h/e with far greater precision than by any other method and has therefore contributed to a knowledge of the fundamental constants of nature. The Josephson effect has been used in the invention of novel devices for extremely high-sensitivity measurements of currents, voltages, and magnetic fields.

Higher-Temperature Superconductivity

Ever since Kamerlingh Onnes discovered that mercury becomes superconducting at temperatures less than 4 K (-269 °C, or -452 °F), scientists have been searching for superconducting materials with higher transition temperatures. Until 1986 a compound of niobium and germanium (Nb_3Ge) had the highest known transition temperature, 23 K (-250 °C, or -418 °F), less than a 20-degree increase in 75 years. Most researchers expected that the next increase in transition temperature would be found in a similar metallic alloy and that the rise would be only one or two degrees.

DISCOVERY AND COMPOSITION OF HIGH-TEMPERATURE SUPERCONDUCTORS

In 1986, however, the Swiss physicist Karl Alex Müller and his West German associate, Johannes Georg Bednorz, discovered, after a three-year search among metal oxides, a material that had an unprecedentedly high transition temperature of about 30 K (-243 °C, or -406 °F). They were awarded the Nobel Prize for Physics in 1987, and their discovery immediately stimulated groups of investigators in China, Japan, and the United States to produce superconducting oxides with even higher transition temperatures.

These high-temperature superconductors are ceramics. They contain lanthanum, yttrium or another of the rare-earth elements, bismuth or thallium; usually barium or strontium (both alkaline-earth elements); copper; and oxygen. Other atomic species can sometimes be introduced by chemical substitution while retaining the high-T_c properties. The value 254 K (-19 °C, or -2 °F) is the highest known T_c value. Within each family of high-T_c materials, only the subscripts (i.e., stoichiometry) vary from one compound to another. Samples in the families containing bismuth or thallium always exhibit a great deal of atomic disorder, with atoms in the "wrong" crystallographic sites and with impurity phases. It is possible that such disorder is required to make these compounds thermodynamically stable.

STRUCTURES AND PROPERTIES

The compounds have crystal structures containing planes of Cu and O atoms, and some also have chains of Cu and O atoms. The roles played by these planes and chains have come under intense investigation. Varying the oxygen content or the heat treatment of the materials dramatically changes their transition temperatures, critical magnetic fields, and other properties. Single crystals of the high-temperature superconductors are very anisotropic— i.e., their properties associated with a direction, such as the critical fields or the critical current density, are highly dependent on the angle between that direction and the rows of atoms in the crystal.

If the number of superconducting electrons per unit volume is locally disturbed by an applied force (typically electric or magnetic), this disturbance propagates for a certain distance in the material; the distance is called the superconducting coherence length (or Ginzburg-Landau coherence length), ξ. If a material has a superconducting region and a normal region, many of the superconducting properties disappear gradually—over a distance ξ—upon traveling from the former to the latter region. In the pure (i.e., undoped) classic superconductors ξ is on the order of a few thousand angstroms, but in the high-T_c superconductors it is on the order of 1 to 10 angstroms. The small size of ξ affects the thermodynamic and electromagnetic properties of the high-T_c superconductors. For example, it is responsible for the cusp shape of the specific heat curve near T_c that was mentioned above. It is also responsible for the ability of the high-T_c superconductors to remain superconducting in extraordinarily large fields—on the order of 1,000,000 gauss (100 teslas)—at low temperatures.

The high-T_c superconductors are type II superconductors. They exhibit zero resistance, strong diamagnetism, the Meissner effect, magnetic flux quantization, the Josephson effects, an electromagnetic penetration depth, an energy gap for the superconducting electrons, and the characteristic temperature dependencies of the specific heat and the thermal conductivity that are described above. Therefore, it is clear that the conduction electrons in these materials form the Cooper pairs used to explain superconductivity in the BCS theory. Thus, the central conclusions of the BCS theory are demonstrated. Indeed, that theory guided Bednorz and Müller in their search for high-temperature superconductors. It is not known, however, why the transition temperatures of these oxides are so high. It was generally believed that the members of a Cooper pair are bound together because of interactions between the electrons and the lattice vibrations (phonons), but it is unlikely that these interactions are strong enough to explain transition temperatures as high as 90 K (-183 °C, or -298 °F).

Most experts believe that interactions among the electrons generate high-temperature superconductivity. The details of this interaction are difficult to treat theoretically because the motions of the electrons are strongly correlated with each other and because magnetic phenomena play an important part in determining the microscopic properties of these materials. These strong correlations and magnetic properties may be responsible for unusual temperature dependencies of the electric resistivity ρ and Hall coefficient R_H in the normal state (i.e., above T_c). It is observed that at temperatures above T_c the electric resistivity, although higher for superconductors than for typical metals in the normal state, is roughly proportional to the temperature T, an unusually weak temperature dependence. Measurements of R_H show it to be significantly temperature-dependent in the normal state (sometimes proportional to $1/T$) rather than being roughly independent of T, which is the case for ordinary materials.

APPLICATIONS

Films of the new materials can carry currents in the superconducting state that are large enough to be of importance in making many devices. Possible applications of the high-temperature superconductors in thin-film or bulk form include the construction of computer parts (logic devices, memory elements, switches, and interconnects), oscillators, amplifiers, particle accelerators, highly sensitive devices for measuring magnetic fields, voltages, or currents, magnets for medical magnetic-imaging devices, magnetic energy-storage systems, levitated passenger trains for high-speed travel, motors, generators, transformers, and transmission lines. The principal advantages of these superconducting devices would be their low power dissipation, high operating speed, and extreme sensitivity.

Equipment made with the high-temperature superconductors would also be more economical to operate because such materials can be cooled with inexpensive liquid nitrogen (boiling point, 77 K [-196 °C, or -321 °F]) rather than with costly liquid helium (boiling point, 4.2 K [-269 °C, or -452.1 °F]). The ceramics have problems, however, which must be overcome before useful devices can be made from them. These problems include brittleness, instabilities of the materials in some chemical environments, and a tendency for impurities to segregate at surfaces and grain boundaries, where they interfere with the flow of high currents in the superconducting state.

CHAPTER 4
MAGNETISM

M agnetism is a phenomenon associated with the motion of electric charges. This motion can take many forms. It can be an electric current in a conductor or charged particles moving through space, or it can be the motion of an electron in atomic orbit. Magnetism is also associated with elementary particles, such as the electron, that have a property called spin.

FUNDAMENTALS

Basic to magnetism are magnetic fields and their effects on matter, as, for instance, the deflection of moving charges and torques on other magnetic objects. Evidence for the presence of a magnetic field is the magnetic force on charges moving in that field; the force is at right angles to both the field and the velocity of the charge. This force deflects the particles without changing their speed. The deflection can be observed in the electron beam of a television tube when a permanent magnet is brought near the tube. A more familiar example is the torque on a compass needle that acts to align the needle with the magnetic field of Earth. The needle is a thin piece of iron that has been magnetized—i.e., a small bar magnet. One end of the magnet is called a north pole and the other end a south pole. The force between a north and a south pole is attractive, whereas the force between like poles is repulsive. The magnetic field is sometimes referred to as magnetic induction or magnetic flux density; it is always symbolized by B. Magnetic fields are measured in units of tesla (T). (Another unit of measure commonly used for B is the gauss, though it is no longer considered a standard unit. One gauss equals 10^{-4} tesla.)

A fundamental property of a magnetic field is that its flux through any closed surface vanishes. (A closed surface is one that completely surrounds a volume.) This is expressed mathematically by div B = 0 and can be understood physically in terms of the field lines representing B. These lines always close on themselves, so that if they enter a certain volume at some point, they must also leave that volume. In this respect, a magnetic field is quite different from an electric field. Electric field lines can begin and end on a charge, but no equivalent magnetic charge has been found in spite of many searches for so-called magnetic monopoles.

The most common source of magnetic fields is the electric current loop. It may be an electric current in a circular conductor or the motion of an orbiting electron in an atom. Associated with both these types of current loops is a magnetic dipole moment, the value of which is iA, the product of the current and the area of the loop. The direction of the dipole moment, which may be represented mathematically as a vector, is perpendicularly away from the side of the surface enclosed by the counterclockwise path of positive charge flow. Considering the current loop as a tiny magnet, this vector corresponds to the direction from the south to the north pole. In addition, electrons, protons, and neutrons in atoms have a magnetic dipole moment associated with their intrinsic spin; such magnetic dipole moments represent another important source of magnetic fields.

A particle with a magnetic dipole moment is often referred to as a magnetic dipole. (A magnetic dipole may be thought of as a tiny bar magnet. It has the same magnetic field as such a magnet and behaves the same way in external magnetic fields.) When placed in an external magnetic field, a magnetic dipole can be subjected to a torque that tends to align it with the field; if the external field is not uniform, the dipole also can be subjected to a force.

Electrons circulating around atomic nuclei, electrons spinning on their axes, and rotating positively charged atomic nuclei all are magnetic dipoles. The sum of these effects may cancel so that a given type of atom may not be a magnetic dipole. If they do not fully cancel, the atom is a permanent magnetic dipole, as are iron atoms. Many millions of iron atoms spontaneously locked into the same alignment to form a ferromagnetic domain also constitute a magnetic dipole. Magnetic compass needles and bar magnets are examples of macroscopic magnetic dipoles.

The magnetic dipole moment may be thought of as a measure of a dipole's ability to turn itself into alignment with a given external magnetic field. In a uniform magnetic field, the magnitude of the dipole moment is proportional to the maximum amount of torque on the dipole, which occurs when the dipole is at right angles to the magnetic field. The magnetic dipole moment, often simply called the magnetic moment, may be defined then as the maximum amount of torque caused by magnetic force on a dipole that arises per unit value of surrounding magnetic field in vacuum.

Magnetic dipole moments have dimensions of current times area or energy divided by magnetic flux density. In the metre–kilogram–second–ampere and SI systems, the specific unit for dipole moment is ampere-square metre. In the centimetre–gram–second electromagnetic system, the unit is the erg (unit of energy) per gauss (unit of magnetic flux density). One thousand ergs per gauss equal one ampere-square metre. A convenient unit for the magnetic dipole moment of electrons is the Bohr magneton (equivalent to 9.273×10^{-24} ampere–square metre). A similar unit for magnetic moments of nuclei, protons, and neutrons is the nuclear magneton (equivalent to 5.051×10^{-27} ampere-square metre).

All matter exhibits magnetic properties to some degree. When placed in an inhomogeneous field, matter is either attracted or repelled in the direction of the gradient of the field. This property is described by the magnetic susceptibility of the matter and depends on the degree of magnetization of the matter in the field. Magnetization depends on the size of the dipole moments of the atoms in a substance and the degree to which the dipole moments are aligned with respect to each other. Certain materials, such as iron, exhibit very strong magnetic properties because of the alignment of the magnetic moments of their atoms within certain small regions called domains. Under normal conditions, the various domains have fields that cancel, but they can be aligned with each other to produce extremely large magnetic fields. Various alloys, such as NdFeB (an alloy of neodymium, iron, and boron), keep their domains aligned and are used to make permanent magnets. The strong magnetic field produced by a typical three-millimetre-thick magnet of this material is comparable to an electromagnet made of a copper loop carrying a current of several thousand amperes. In comparison, the current in a typical light bulb is 0.5 ampere. Since aligning the domains of a material produces a magnet, disorganizing the orderly alignment destroys the magnetic properties of the material. Thermal agitation that results from heating a magnet to a high temperature destroys its magnetic properties.

Magnetic fields vary widely in strength. Some representative values are given in the table.

TYPICAL MAGNETIC FIELDS	
inside atomic nuclei	10^{11} T
in superconducting solenoids	20 T
in a superconducting coil cyclotron	5 T
near a small ceramic magnet	0.1 T
Earth's field at the equator	$4(10^{-5})$ T
in interstellar space	$2(10^{-10})$ T

MAGNETIC FIELD OF STEADY CURRENTS

Magnetic fields produced by electric currents can be calculated for any shape of circuit using the law of Biot and Savart, named for the early 19th-century French physicists Jean-Baptiste Biot and Félix Savart. Magnetic field lines are produced by a current in a loop, and these lines of B form loops around the current. The Biot–Savart law expresses the partial contribution dB from a small segment of conductor to the total B field of a current in the conductor. For a segment of length and orientation dl that carries a current i,

$$dB = \frac{\mu_0}{4\pi} \frac{i dl \times \hat{r}}{r^2}. \qquad (34)$$

In this equation, μ_0 is the permeability of free space and has the value of $4\pi \times 10^{-7}$ newton per square ampere. Consider a small segment of a wire that carries a current

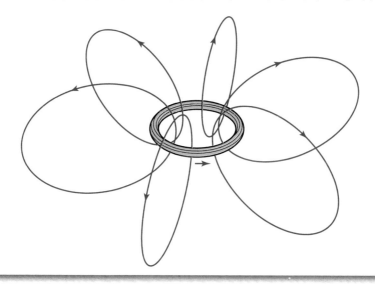

Lines of the magnetic field **B** *for an electric current* i *in a loop.* Courtesy of the Department of Physics and Astronomy, Michigan State University; rendering for this edition by Rosen Educational Services

so that, at the origin of the coordinate system, the small segment of length dl of the wire lies along the x axis.

The magnitude of $d\mathbf{B}$ varies as the sine of the angle between dl and $\hat{r}$, where $\hat{r}$ is in the direction from dl to the point. It is strongest at 90° to dl and decreases to zero for locations directly in line with dl. The magnetic field of a current in a loop or coil is obtained by summing the individual partial contributions of all the segments of the circuits, taking into account the vector nature of the field. While simple mathematical expressions for the magnetic field can be derived for a few current configurations, most of the practical applications require the use of high-speed computers.

The expression for the magnetic field $\mathbf{B}$ a distance r from a long straight wire with current i is

$$B = \frac{\mu_0 i}{2 \pi r} \hat{\theta}, \qquad (35)$$

where $\boldsymbol{\theta}$ is a unit vector pointing in a circle around the wire. The magnetic field at a distance r from a magnetic dipole with moment $\boldsymbol{m}$ is given by

$$B = \frac{\mu_0 m}{4\pi r^3} (2 \cos \theta \,\hat{r} + \sin \theta \,\hat{\boldsymbol{\theta}}) . \qquad (36)$$

The size of the magnetic dipole moment is m in ampere times square metre (A · m²), and the angle between the direction of $\boldsymbol{m}$ and of r is θ. Both $\hat{r}$ and $\boldsymbol{\theta}$ are unit vectors in the direction of r and θ. It is apparent that the magnetic field decreases rapidly as the cube of the distance from the dipole. Equation (36) is also valid for a small current loop with current i, when the distance r is much greater than the size of the current loop. A loop of area A has a magnetic

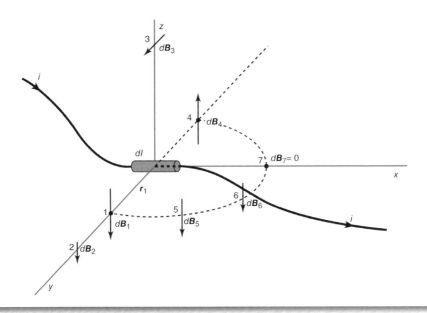

A magnetic field produced by a small section of wire with electric current i. Courtesy of the Department of Physics and Astronomy, Michigan State University; rendering for this edition by Rosen Educational Services

dipole moment with a magnitude $m = iA$; its direction is perpendicular to the plane of the loop, along the direction of B inside the loop. If the fingers of the right hand are curled and held in the direction of the current in the loop, the extended thumb points in the direction of m.

The magnetic field of the current loop at points far from the loop has the same shape as the electric field of an electric dipole; the latter consists of two equal charges of opposite sign separated by a small distance. Magnetic dipoles, like electric dipoles, occur in a variety of situations. Electrons in atoms have a magnetic dipole moment that corresponds to the current of their orbital motion around the nucleus. In addition, the electrons have a magnetic dipole moment associated with their spin.

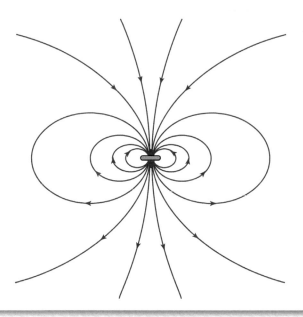

Lines of B *from the small current loop in the centre. The current in the loop flows in a clockwise direction when viewed from above.* Courtesy of the Department of Physics and Astronomy, Michigan State University ; rendering for this edition by Rosen Educational Services

Earth's magnetic field is thought to be the result of currents related to the planet's rotation. The magnetic field far from a small bar magnet is well represented by the field of a magnetic dipole. In most of these cases, moving charge produces a magnetic field B. Inside a long solenoid with current i and away from its ends, the magnetic field is uniform and directed along the axis of the solenoid. A solenoid of this kind can be made by wrapping some conducting wire tightly around a long hollow cylinder. The value of the field is

$$B = \mu_0 n i, \tag{37}$$

where n is the number of turns per unit length of the solenoid.

The parameter μ measures the relative increase or decrease in the resultant magnetic field inside a material compared with the magnetizing field in which the given material is located; it is the property of a material that is equal to the magnetic flux density B established within the material by a magnetizing field divided by the magnetic field strength H of the magnetizing field. Magnetic permeability μ is thus defined as $\mu = B/H$. Magnetic flux density B is a measure of the actual magnetic field within a material considered as a concentration of magnetic field lines, or flux, per unit cross-sectional area. Magnetic field strength H is a measure of the magnetizing field produced by electric current flow in a coil of wire.

In empty, or free, space the magnetic flux density is the same as the magnetizing field because there is no matter to modify the field. In centimetre–gram–second (cgs) units, the permeability B/H of space is dimensionless and has a value of 1. In metre–kilogram–second (mks) and SI units, B and H have different dimensions, and the permeability of free space (symbolized μ_o) is defined as equal to $4\pi \times 10^{-7}$ weber per ampere-metre so that the mks unit of electric current may be the same as the practical unit, the ampere. In these systems the permeability, B/H, is called the absolute permeability μ of the medium. The relative permeability μ_r is then defined as the ratio μ/μ_o, which is dimensionless and has the same numerical value as the permeability in the cgs system. Thus, the relative permeability of free space, or vacuum, is 1.

Materials may be classified magnetically on the basis of their permeabilities. A diamagnetic material has a constant relative permeability slightly less than 1. When a diamagnetic material, such as bismuth, is placed in a magnetic field, the external field is partly expelled, and the magnetic flux density within it is slightly reduced. A paramagnetic material has a constant relative permeability slightly more than 1. When a paramagnetic material, such as platinum, is placed in a magnetic field, it becomes slightly magnetized in the direction of the external field. A ferromagnetic material, such as iron, does not have a constant relative permeability. As the magnetizing field increases, the relative permeability increases, reaches a maximum, and then decreases. Purified iron and many magnetic alloys have maximum relative permeabilities of 100,000 or more.

MAGNETIC FORCES

Magnetic forces are observed as an attraction or repulsion that arises between electrically charged particles because of their motion. The magnetic force is the basic force responsible for the action of electric motors and the attraction of magnets for iron.

LORENTZ FORCE

A magnetic field **B** imparts a force on moving charged particles. The entire electromagnetic force on a charged particle with charge q and velocity v is called the Lorentz force (after the Dutch physicist Hendrik A. Lorentz) and is given by

$$F = q\mathbf{E} + q\mathbf{v} \times \mathbf{B}. \tag{38}$$

The first term is contributed by the electric field. The second term is the magnetic force and has a direction perpendicular to both the velocity v and the magnetic field **B**. The magnetic force is proportional to q and to the magnitude of $v \times \mathbf{B}$. In terms of the angle ϕ between v and **B**, the magnitude of the force equals $qvB \sin \phi$. An interesting result of the Lorentz force is the motion of a charged particle in a uniform magnetic field. If v is perpendicular to **B** (i.e., with the angle ϕ between v and **B** of 90°), the particle will follow a circular trajectory with a radius of $r = mv/qB$. If the angle ϕ is less than 90°, the particle orbit will be a helix with an axis parallel to the field lines. If ϕ is zero, there will be no magnetic force on the particle, which will continue to move undeflected along the field lines. Charged particle accelerators like cyclotrons make use of the fact that particles move in a circular orbit when v and **B** are at right angles. For each revolution, a carefully timed electric field gives the particles additional kinetic energy, which makes them travel in increasingly larger orbits. When the particles have acquired the desired energy, they are extracted and used in a number of different ways, from fundamental studies of the properties of matter to the medical treatment of cancer.

The magnetic force on a moving charge reveals the sign of the charge carriers in a conductor. A current flowing

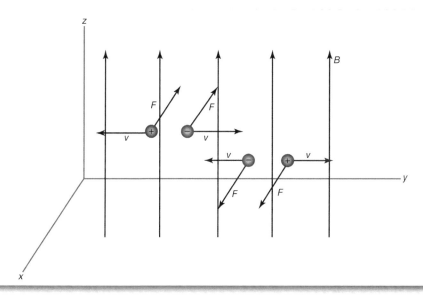

*Magnetic force on moving charges. The magnetic force **F** is proportional to the charge and to the magnitude of velocity* v *times the magnetic field* **B**. Courtesy of the Department of Physics and Astronomy, Michigan State University; rendering for this edition by Rosen Educational Services

from right to left in a conductor can be the result of positive charge carriers moving from right to left or negative charges moving from left to right, or some combination of each. When a conductor is placed in a *B* field perpendicular to the current, the magnetic force on both types of charge carriers is in the same direction. This force gives rise to a small potential difference between the sides of the conductor. Known as the Hall effect, this phenomenon (discovered by the American physicist Edwin Herbert Hall in 1879) results when an electric field is aligned with the direction of the magnetic force. The sign of the potential differs according to the sign of the charge carrier because, in one case, positive charges are pushed toward the reader and, in the other, negative charges are pushed in that direction.

In metals, such as copper, the Hall voltages are generally negative, indicating that the electric current is composed of moving negative charges, or electrons. The Hall voltage is positive, however, for a few metals such as beryllium, zinc, and cadmium, indicating that these metals conduct electric currents by the movement of positively charged carriers called holes. Electrons in zinc that are excited from the valence band leave holes, which are vacancies (i.e., unfilled levels) that behave like positive charge carriers. In semiconductors, in which the current consists of a movement of positive holes in one direction and electrons in the opposite direction, the sign of the Hall voltage shows which type of charge carrier predominates. The Hall effect can be used also to measure the density of current carriers, their freedom of movement, or mobility, as well as to detect the presence of a current on a magnetic field.

The Hall voltage that develops across a conductor is directly proportional to the current, to the magnetic field, and to the nature of the particular conducting material itself; the Hall voltage is inversely proportional to the thickness of the material in the direction of the magnetic field. Because various materials have different Hall coefficients, they develop different Hall voltages under the same conditions of size, electric current, and magnetic field. Hall coefficients may be determined experimentally and may vary with temperature.

If a wire with a current i is placed in an external magnetic field B, how will the force on the wire depend on the orientation of the wire? Since a current represents a movement of charges in the wire, the Lorentz force given in equation (38) acts on the moving charges. Because these charges are bound to the conductor, the magnetic forces on the moving charges are transferred to the wire.

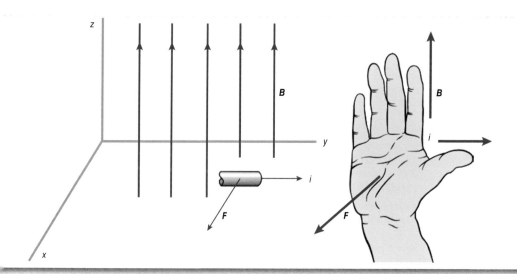

Right-hand rules for the magnetic force on an electric current. Courtesy of the Department of Physics and Astronomy, Michigan State University; rendering for this edition by Rosen Educational Services

The force on a small length *dl* of the wire depends on the orientation of the wire with respect to the field. The magnitude of the force is given by *idlB* sin ϕ, where ϕ is the angle between **B** and *dl*. There is no force when ϕ = 0 or 180°, both of which correspond to a current along a direction parallel to the field. The force is at a maximum when the current and field are perpendicular to each other. The force is obtained from equation (38) and is given by

$$d\textbf{F} = i d\textbf{l} \times \textbf{B}. \tag{39}$$

Again, the cross product denotes a direction perpendicular to both *dl* and **B**. The direction of *dF* is given by the right-hand rule. If the fingers of the right hand are in the direction of **B**, the current (or in the case of a positive moving point charge, the velocity) is in the direction of the thumb, and the force is perpendicular to the palm.

REPULSION OR ATTRACTION BETWEEN TWO MAGNETIC DIPOLES

The force between two wires, each of which carries a current, can be understood from the interaction of one of the currents with the magnetic field produced by the other current. For example, the force between two parallel wires carrying currents in the same direction is attractive. It is repulsive if the currents are in opposite directions. Two circular current loops, located one above the other and with their planes parallel, will attract if the currents are in the same directions and will repel if the currents are in opposite directions. When the loops are side by side, the situation is reversed. For two currents flowing in the same direction, whether clockwise or counterclockwise, the force is repulsive, while for opposite directions, it is attractive.

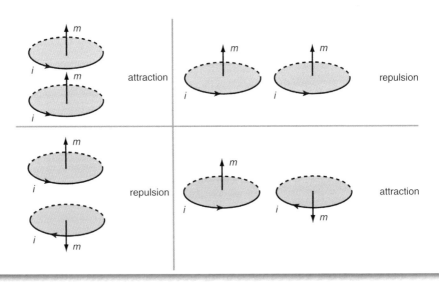

Magnetic force between current loops. In each case shown, the arrow indicates the direction of the current i and the magnetic dipole moment m of a loop. Courtesy of the Department of Physics and Astronomy, Michigan State University; rendering for this edition by Rosen Educational Services

The nature of the force for the loops can be obtained by considering the direction of the currents in the parts of the loops that are closest to each other: same current direction, attraction; opposite current direction, repulsion. This seemingly complicated force between current loops can be understood more simply by treating the fields as though they originated from magnetic dipoles. The *B* field of a small current loop is well represented by the field of a magnetic dipole at distances that are large compared to the size of the loop. In another way of looking at the interaction of current loops, the loops are replaced by small permanent magnets, with the direction of the magnets from south to north corresponding to the direction of the magnetic moment of the loop *m*. Outside the magnets, the magnetic field lines point away from the north pole and toward the south pole.

It is easy to understand the nature of the forces with the rule that two north poles repulse each other and two south poles repulse each other, while unlike poles attract. Coulomb established an inverse square law of force for

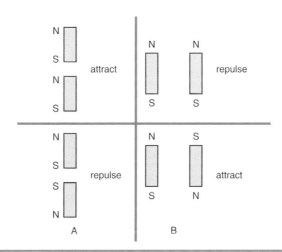

Force between small permanent bar magnets. Courtesy of the Department of Physics and Astronomy, Michigan State University; rendering for this edition by Rosen Educational Services

magnetic poles and electric charges. According to his law, unlike poles attract and like poles repel, just as unlike charges attract and like charges repel. Today, Coulomb's law refers only to charges, but historically it provided the foundation for a magnetic potential analogous to the electric potential.

The alignment of a magnetic compass needle with the direction of an external magnetic field is a good example of the torque to which a magnetic dipole is subjected. The torque has a magnitude $\tau = mB \sin \vartheta$. Here, ϑ is the angle between m and B. The torque τ tends to align m with B. It has its maximum value when ϑ is 90°, and it is zero when the dipole is in line with the external field. Rotating a magnetic dipole from a position where $\vartheta = 0$ to a position where $\vartheta = 180°$ requires work. Thus, the potential energy of the dipole depends on its orientation with respect to the field and is given in units of joules by

$$U_m = -mB\cos\vartheta. \qquad (40)$$

This equation represents the basis for an important medical application—namely, magnetic resonance imaging (MRI), also known as nuclear magnetic resonance imaging. MRI involves measuring the concentration of certain atoms, most commonly those of hydrogen, in body tissue and processing this measurement data to produce high-resolution images of organs and other anatomical structures. When hydrogen atoms are placed in a magnetic field, their nuclei (protons) tend to have their magnetic moments preferentially aligned in the direction of the field. The magnetic potential energy of the nuclei is calculated according to equation (40) as $-mB$. Inverting the direction of the dipole moment requires an energy of $2mB$, since the potential energy in the new orientation is $+mB$. A high-frequency oscillator provides energy in the form of electromagnetic radiation of frequency v, with each quantum of radiation having an energy hv, where h is Planck's constant. The electromagnetic radiation from the oscillator consists of high-frequency radio waves, which are beamed into the patient's body while it is subjected to a strong magnetic field. When the resonance condition $hv = 2mB$ is satisfied, the hydrogen nuclei in the body tissue absorb the energy and reverse their orientation. The resonance condition is met in only a small region of the body at any given time, and measurement of the energy absorption reveals the concentration of hydrogen atoms in that region alone. The magnetic field in an MRI scanner is usually provided by a large solenoid with B of one to three teslas. A number of "gradient coils" insures that the resonance condition is satisfied solely in the limited region inside the solenoid at any particular time; the coils are used to move this small target region, thereby making it possible to scan the patient's body throughout. The frequency of the radiation v is determined by the value of B and is typically 40 to 130 megahertz. The MRI technique does not harm the patient because the energy of the quanta of the electromagnetic radiation is much smaller than the thermal energy of a molecule in the human body.

The direction of the magnetic moment m of a compass needle is from the end marked S for south to the one marked N for north. The lowest energy occurs for $\vartheta = 0$, when m and B are aligned. In a typical situation, the compass needle comes to rest after a few oscillations and points along the B field in the direction called north. It must be concluded from this that Earth's North Pole is really a magnetic south pole, with the field lines pointing toward that pole, while its South Pole is a magnetic north pole. Put another way, the dipole moment of Earth currently points north to south. Short-term changes in Earth's magnetic field are ascribed to electric currents in the ionosphere. There are also longer-term fluctuations in the locations of the poles. The angle between the compass needle and geographic north is called the magnetic declination.

The repulsion or attraction between two magnetic dipoles can be viewed as the interaction of one dipole with the magnetic field produced by the other dipole. The magnetic field is not constant, but varies with the distance from the dipole. When a magnetic dipole with moment m is in a B field that varies with position, it is subjected to a force proportional to that variation—i.e., to the gradient of B. The direction of the force is understood best by considering the potential energy of a dipole in an external B field, as given by equation (40). The force on the dipole is in the direction in which that energy decreases most rapidly. For example, if the magnetic dipole m is aligned with B, then the energy is $-mB$, and the force is in the direction of increasing B. If m is directed opposite to B, then the potential energy given by equation (40) is $+mB$, and in this case the force is in the direction of decreasing B. Both types of forces are observed when various samples of matter are placed in a nonuniform magnetic field.

MAGNETIZATION EFFECTS IN MATTER

Regardless of the direction of a nonuniform magnetic field, a sample of copper is magnetically attracted toward the low field region. This behaviour is termed diamagnetism. A sample of aluminum, however, is attracted toward the high field region in an effect called paramagnetism. A magnetic dipole moment is induced when matter is subjected to an external field. For copper, the induced dipole moment is opposite to the direction of the external field; for aluminum, it is aligned with that field.

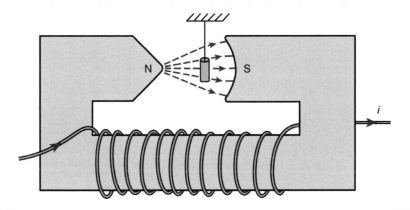

A small sample of copper in an inhomogeneous magnetic field. Courtesy of the Department of Physics and Astronomy, Michigan State University; rendering for this edition by Rosen Educational Services

The magnetization M of a small volume of matter is the sum (a vector sum) of the magnetic dipole moments in the small volume divided by that volume. M is measured in units of amperes per metre. The degree of induced magnetization is given by the magnetic susceptibility of the material χ_m, which is commonly defined by the equation

$$M = \chi_m H. \qquad (41)$$

The field H is called the magnetic intensity and, like M, is measured in units of amperes per metre. (It is sometimes also called the magnetic field, but the symbol H is unambiguous.) The definition of H is

$$H = \frac{B}{\mu_0} - M. \qquad (42)$$

The permeability μ is often used for ferromagnetic materials such as iron that have a large magnetic susceptibility dependent on the field and the previous magnetic state of the sample; permeability is defined by the equation $B = \mu H$. From equations (41) and (42), it follows that $\mu = \mu_0 (1 + \chi_m)$.

The effect of ferromagnetic materials in increasing the magnetic field produced by current loops is quite large. Consider a toroidal winding of conducting wire around a ring of iron that has a small gap. The magnetic field inside such a toroidal winding but without the iron ring is given by $B = \mu_0 Ni/2\pi r$, where r is the distance from the axis of the toroid, N is the number of turns, and i is the current in the wire. The value of B for $r = 0.1$ metre, $N = 100$, and $i = 10$ amperes is only 0.002 tesla—about 50 times the magnetic field at Earth's surface. If the same toroid is wound around an iron ring with no gap, the magnetic field inside the iron is larger by a factor equal to μ/μ_0, where μ is the magnetic permeability of the iron. For low-carbon iron in these conditions, $\mu = 8,000\mu_0$. The magnetic field in the

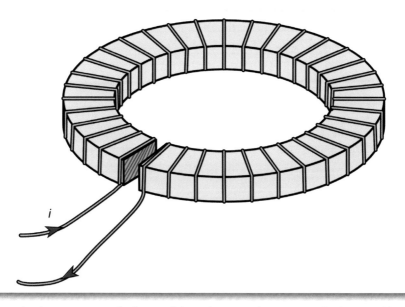

An electromagnet made of a toroidal winding around an iron ring that has a small gap. Courtesy of the Department of Physics and Astronomy, Michigan State University; rendering for this edition by Rosen Educational Services

iron is then 1.6 tesla. In a typical electromagnet, iron is used to increase the field in a small region, such as the narrow gap in an iron ring. If the gap is one centimetre wide, the field in that gap is about 0.12 tesla, a 60-fold increase relative to the 0.002-tesla field in the toroid when no iron is used. This factor is typically given by the ratio of the circumference of the toroid to the gap in the ferromagnetic material. The maximum value of B as the gap becomes very small is of course the 1.6 tesla obtained above when there is no gap.

The energy density in a magnetic field is given in the absence of matter by $\frac{1}{2}B^2/\mu_0$; it is measured in units of joules per cubic metre. The total magnetic energy can be obtained by integrating the energy density over all space.

Magnetic field **B** *of two current loops with currents in opposite directions.* Courtesy of the Department of Physics and Astronomy, Michigan State University; rendering for this edition by Rosen Educational Services

The direction of the magnetic force can be deduced in many situations by studying distribution of the magnetic field lines; motion is favoured in the direction that tends to decrease the volume of space where the magnetic field is strong. This can be understood because the magnitude of **B** is squared in the energy density. Consider some lines of the **B** field for two circular current loops with currents in opposite directions.

The high values of **B** between the two loops show that there is a large energy density in that region and separating the loops would reduce the energy. This is one more way of looking at the source of repulsion between these two loops. For two loops with currents in the same direction, the force between the loops is attractive, and the distance

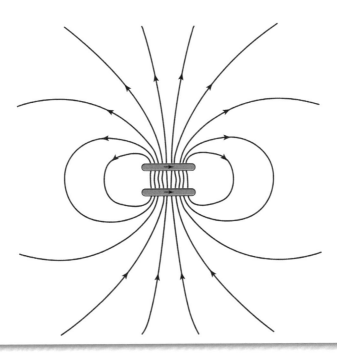

Magnetic field **B** *of two current loops with currents in the same direction.* Courtesy of the Department of Physics and Astronomy, Michigan State University; rendering for this edition by Rosen Educational Services

separating them is equal to the loop radius. The result is that the B field in the central region between the two loops is homogeneous to a remarkably high degree. Such a configuration is called a Helmholtz coil. By carefully orienting and adjusting the current in a large Helmholtz coil, it is often possible to cancel an external magnetic field (such as the magnetic field of Earth) in a region of space where experiments require the absence of all external magnetic fields.

Another magnetization effect in matter is magnetostriction, which is a change in the dimensions of a ferromagnetic material, such as iron or nickel, produced by a change in the direction and extent of its magnetization. An iron rod placed in a magnetic field directed along its length stretches slightly in a weak magnetic field and contracts slightly in a strong magnetic field. Mechanically stretching and compressing a magnetized iron rod inversely produces fluctuations in the magnetization of the rod. This effect is utilized in nickel magnetostriction transducers that transmit and receive high-frequency sound vibrations. A bent iron rod will straighten a bit in a longitudinally directed magnetic field, and a straight rod carrying an electric current will twist slightly in a magnetic field.

MAGNETOHYDRODYNAMICS

Magnetohydrodynamics (MHD) is the description of the behaviour of a plasma or, in general, any electrically conducting fluid in the presence of electric and magnetic fields. A plasma can be defined in terms of its constituents, using equations to describe the behaviour of the electrons, ions, neutral particles, etc. It is often more convenient, however, to treat it as a single fluid, even though it differs from fluids that are not ionized in that it is strongly influenced by electric and magnetic fields, both of which can be imposed on the plasma or generated by the plasma; the equations describing the behaviour of the plasma, therefore, must involve the close relationship between the plasma and the associated fields.

The inclusion of magnetic effects gives rise to a number of quantities that have counterparts in ordinary fluid mechanics—for example, magnetic viscosity, pressure, Reynolds number, and diffusion.

The magnetic Reynolds number is the combination of quantities that indicates the dynamic behaviour of a plasma. This number is analogous to the Reynolds number of ordinary fluid mechanics, which is used to determine whether or not a fluid flow will smooth out or become turbulent. If the magnetic permeability of free space is represented by μ_o (a constant of proportionality used in expressing the force between two electric charges), the electrical conductivity of the plasma is represented by σ, the plasma velocity by V, and a length characteristic of the plasma structure is L, then the magnetic Reynolds number equals their product, or $R_m = \mu_o \sigma V L$.

According to the magnetohydrodynamic description of the plasma, there are two general types of behaviour for the magnetic field depending upon the value of R_m. If R_m is much smaller than 1, the magnetic field will diffuse away, and inhomogeneities in the field will be smoothed out, as in the flow of a fluid smoothing out. If R_m is very large, the magnetic-field lines tend to remain "frozen" into the plasma, moving along with the plasma flow.

MAGNETIC PROPERTIES OF MATTER

All matter exhibits magnetic properties when placed in an external magnetic field. Even substances like copper and aluminum that are not normally thought of as having magnetic properties are affected by the presence of a magnetic field such as that produced by either pole of a bar magnet. Depending on whether there is an attraction or repulsion by the pole of a magnet, matter is classified as being either paramagnetic or diamagnetic, respectively. A few materials, notably iron, show a very large attraction toward the pole of a permanent bar magnet; materials of this kind are called ferromagnetic.

In 1845 Faraday became the first to classify substances as either diamagnetic or paramagnetic. He based this classification on his observation of the force exerted on substances in an inhomogeneous magnetic field. At moderate field strengths, the magnetization M of a substance is linearly proportional to the strength of the applied field H. The magnetization is specified by the magnetic susceptibility χ (previously labeled χ_m), defined by the relation $M = \chi H$. A sample of volume V placed in a field H directed in the x-direction and increasing in that direction at a rate dH/dx will experience a force in the x-direction of $F = \chi\mu_0 VH(dH/dx)$. If the magnetic susceptibility χ is positive, the force is in the direction of increasing field strength, whereas if χ is negative, it is in the direction of decreasing field strength. Measurement of the force F in a known field H with a known gradient dH/dx is the basis of a number of accurate methods of determining χ.

Substances for which the magnetic susceptibility is negative (e.g., copper and silver) are classified as diamagnetic. The susceptibility is small, on the order of -10^{-5} for solids and liquids and -10^{-8} for gases. A characteristic feature of diamagnetism is that the magnetic moment per unit mass in a given field is virtually constant for a given substance over a very wide range of temperatures.

It changes little between solid, liquid, and gas; the variation in the susceptibility between solid or liquid and gas is almost entirely due to the change in the number of molecules per unit volume. This indicates that the magnetic moment induced in each molecule by a given field is primarily a property characteristic of the molecule.

Substances for which the magnetic susceptibility is positive are classed as paramagnetic. In a few cases (including most metals), the susceptibility is independent of temperature, but in most compounds it is strongly temperature dependent, increasing as the temperature is lowered. Measurements by the French physicist Pierre Curie in 1895 showed that for many substances the susceptibility is inversely proportional to the absolute temperature T; that is, $\chi = C/T$. This approximate relationship is known as Curie's law and the constant C as the Curie constant. A more accurate equation is obtained in many cases by modifying the above equation to $\chi = C/(T - \theta)$, where θ is a constant called the Curie point. This equation is called the Curie–Weiss law (after Curie and Pierre-Ernest Weiss, another French physicist). From the form of this last equation, it is clear that at the temperature $T = \theta$, the value of the susceptibility becomes infinite.

Below the Curie point—for example, 770 °C (1,418 °F) for iron—atoms that behave as tiny magnets spontaneously align themselves in certain magnetic materials. In ferromagnetic materials, such as pure iron, the atomic magnets are oriented within each microscopic region (domain) in the same direction, so that their magnetic fields reinforce each other. In antiferromagnetic materials, atomic magnets alternate in opposite directions, so that their magnetic fields cancel each other. In ferrimagnetic materials, the spontaneous arrangement is a combination of both patterns, usually involving two different magnetic atoms, so that only partial reinforcement of magnetic fields occurs.

Raising the temperature to the Curie point for any of the materials in these three classes entirely disrupts the various spontaneous arrangements, and only a weak kind of more general magnetic behaviour, called paramagnetism, remains. One of the highest Curie points is 1,121 °C (2,050 °F) for cobalt. Temperature increases above the Curie point produce roughly similar patterns of decreasing paramagnetism in all three classes of materials. When these materials are cooled below their Curie points, magnetic atoms spontaneously realign so that the ferromagnetism, antiferromagnetism, or ferrimagnetism revives.

Induced and Permanent Atomic Magnetic Dipoles

Whether a substance is paramagnetic or diamagnetic is determined primarily by the presence or absence of free magnetic dipole moments (i.e., those free to rotate) in its constituent atoms. When there are no free moments, the magnetization is produced by currents of the electrons in their atomic orbits. The substance is then diamagnetic, with a negative susceptibility independent of both field strength and temperature.

In matter with free magnetic dipole moments, the orientation of the moments is normally random and, as a result, the substance has no net magnetization. When a magnetic field is applied, the dipoles are no longer completely randomly oriented; more dipoles point with the field than against the field. When this results in a net positive magnetization in the direction of the field, the substance has a positive susceptibility and is classified as paramagnetic.

The forces opposing alignment of the dipoles with the external magnetic field are thermal in origin and thus weaker at low temperatures. The excess number of dipoles pointing with the field is determined by (mB/kT), where mB represents the magnetic energy and kT the thermal energy. When the magnetic energy is small compared to the thermal energy, the excess number of dipoles pointing with the field is proportional to the field and inversely proportional to the absolute temperature, corresponding to Curie's law. When the value of (mB/kT) is large enough to align nearly all the dipoles with the field, the magnetization approaches a saturation value.

There is a third category of matter in which intrinsic moments are not normally present but appear under the influence of an external magnetic field. The intrinsic moments of conduction electrons in metals behave this

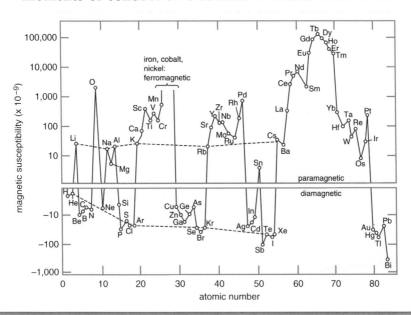

The susceptibility of a kilogram mole of the elements. Broken lines connect the alkali metals (paramagnetic) and the rare gases of the atmosphere (diamagnetic). Copyright Encyclopædia Britannica; rendering for this edition by Rosen Educational Services

way. One finds a small positive susceptibility independent of temperature comparable with the diamagnetic contribution, so that the overall susceptibility of a metal may be positive or negative.

In addition to the forces exerted on atomic dipoles by an external magnetic field, mutual forces exist between the dipoles. Such forces vary widely for different substances. Below a certain transition temperature depending on the substance, they produce an ordered arrangement of the orientations of the atomic dipoles even in the absence of an external field. The mutual forces tend to align neighbouring dipoles either parallel or antiparallel to one another. Parallel alignment of atomic dipoles throughout large volumes of the substance results in ferromagnetism, with a permanent magnetization on a macroscopic scale. On the other hand, if equal numbers of atomic dipoles are aligned in opposite directions and the dipoles are of the same size, there is no permanent macroscopic magnetization, and this is known as antiferromagnetism. If the atomic dipoles are of different magnitudes and those pointing in one direction are all different in size from those pointing in the opposite direction, there exists permanent magnetization on a macroscopic scale in an effect known as ferrimagnetism.

In all cases, the material behaves as a paramagnet above the characteristic transition temperature; it acquires a macroscopic magnetic moment only when an external field is applied.

DIAMAGNETISM

When an electron moving in an atomic orbit is in a magnetic field B, the force exerted on the electron produces a small change in the orbital motion; the electron orbit precesses about the direction of B. As a result, each electron acquires an additional angular momentum that contributes to the magnetization of the sample. The susceptibility χ is given by

$$\chi = -\mu_0 N \left(\frac{e^2}{6m}\right) \Sigma \langle r^2 \rangle,$$

where $\Sigma \langle r^2 \rangle$ is the sum of the mean square radii of all electron orbits in each atom, e and m are the charge and mass of the electron, and N is the number of atoms per unit volume. The negative sign of this susceptibility is a direct consequence of Lenz's law. When B is switched on, the change in motion of each orbit is equivalent to an induced circulating electric current in such a direction that its own magnetic flux opposes the change in magnetic flux through the orbit; i.e., the induced magnetic moment is directed opposite to B.

Since the magnetization M is proportional to the number N of atoms per unit volume, it is sometimes useful to give the susceptibility per mole, χ_{mole}. For a kilogram mole (the molecular weight in kilograms), the numerical value of the molar susceptibility is

$$\chi_{mole} = -3.55 \times 10^{12} \, \Sigma \langle r^2 \rangle.$$

For an atom, the mean value of $\Sigma \langle r^2 \rangle$ is about 10^{-21} square metre and χ_{mole} has values of 10^{-9} to 10^{-10}; the atomic number Z equals the number of electrons in each atom. The quantity $\Sigma \langle r^2 \rangle$ for each atom, and therefore the diamagnetic susceptibility, is essentially independent of temperature. It is also not affected by the surroundings of the atom.

A different kind of diamagnetism occurs in superconductors. The conduction electrons are spread out over the entire metal, and so the induced magnetic moment is governed by the size of the superconducting sample rather than by the size of the individual constituent atoms (a very large effective $< r^2 >$). The diamagnetism is so strong that the magnetic field is kept out of the superconductor.

PARAMAGNETISM

Paramagnetism occurs primarily in substances in which some or all of the individual atoms, ions, or molecules possess a permanent magnetic dipole moment. The magnetization of such matter depends on the ratio of the magnetic energy of the individual dipoles to the thermal energy. This dependence can be calculated in quantum theory and is given by the Brillouin function, which depends only on the ratio (B/T). At low magnetic fields, the magnetization is linearly proportional to the field and reaches its maximum saturation value when the magnetic energy is much greater than the thermal energy.

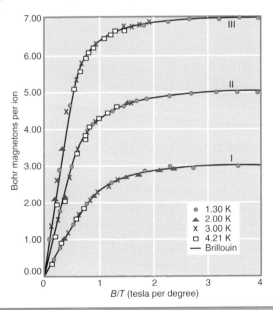

The approach to saturation in the magnetization of a paramagnetic substance following a Brillouin curve. The curves I, II, and III refer to ions of chromium, potassium alum, iron ammonium alum, and gadolinium sulfate octahydrate for which g = 2 and j = 3/2, 5/2, and 7/2, respectively. Copyright Encyclopædia Britannica; rendering for this edition by Rosen Educational Services

In substances that have a nuclear magnetic dipole moment, there is a further contribution to susceptibility. The size of the nuclear magnetic moment is only about one-thousandth that of an atom. Per kilogram mole, χ_n is on the order of $10^{-8}/T$; in solid hydrogen this just exceeds the electronic diamagnetism of 1 K.

Curie's law should hold when mB is much smaller than kT, provided that no other forces act on the atomic dipoles. In many solids, the presence of internal forces may cause the susceptibility to vary in a complicated way. If the forces orient the dipoles parallel to each other, the behaviour is ferromagnetic. The forces may orient the dipoles so that the normal state has no free moment. If the force is sufficiently weak, a small magnetic field can reorient the dipoles, resulting in a net magnetization. This type of paramagnetism occurs for conduction electrons in a metal. In normal metals, each occupied electron state has two electrons with opposite spin orientation. This is a consequence of the Pauli principle of quantum mechanics, which permits no greater occupancy of the energetically favoured states. In the presence of a magnetic field, however, it is energetically more favourable for some of the electrons to move to higher states. With only single electrons in these states, the electron moments can be oriented along the field. The resulting paramagnetic susceptibility is independent of temperature. The net susceptibility is independent of temperature. The net susceptibility of a metal can be of either sign, since the diamagnetic and paramagnetic contributions are of comparable magnitudes.

Ferromagnetism

A ferromagnetic substance contains permanent atomic magnetic dipoles that are spontaneously oriented parallel to one another even in the absence of an external field. The magnetic repulsion between two dipoles aligned side by side with their moments in the same direction makes it difficult to understand the phenomenon of ferromagnetism. It is known that within a ferromagnetic material, there is a spontaneous alignment of atoms in large clusters. A new type of interaction, a quantum mechanical effect known as the exchange interaction, is involved. A highly simplified description of how the exchange interaction aligns electrons in ferromagnetic materials is given here.

ROLE OF EXCHANGE INTERACTION

The magnetic properties of iron are thought to be the result of the magnetic moment associated with the spin of an electron in an outer atomic shell—specifically, the third d shell. Such electrons are referred to as magnetization electrons. The Pauli exclusion principle prohibits two electrons from having identical properties; for example, no two electrons can be in the same location and have spins in the same direction. This exclusion can be viewed as a "repulsive" mechanism for spins in the same direction; its effect is opposite that required to align the electrons responsible for the magnetization in the iron domains. However, other electrons with spins in the opposite direction, primarily in the fourth s atomic shell, interact at close range with the magnetization electrons, and this interaction is attractive. Because of the attractive effect of their opposite spins, these s-shell electrons influence the magnetization electrons of a number of the iron atoms and align them with each other.

A simple empirical representation of the effect of such exchange forces invokes the idea of an effective internal, or molecular, field H_{int}, which is proportional in size to the magnetization M; that is, $H_{int} = \lambda M$ in which λ is an empirical parameter. The resulting magnetization M equals

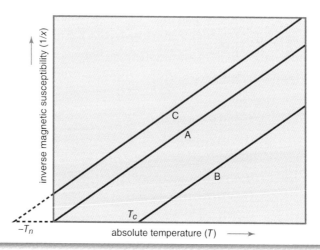

Plot of $1/\chi$. (A) Curie's law. (B) Curie–Weiss law for a ferromagnet with Curie temperature T_c. *(C) Curie–Weiss law for an antiferromagnetic substance.* Copyright Encyclopædia Britannica; rendering for this edition by Rosen Educational Services

$\chi_p(H + \lambda M)$, in which χ_p is the susceptibility that the substance would have in the absence of the internal field. Assuming that $\chi_p = C/T$, corresponding to Curie's law, the equation $M = C(H + \lambda M)/T$ has the solution $\chi = M/H = C/(T - C\lambda) = C/(T - Tc)$. This result, the Curie–Weiss law, is valid at temperatures greater than the Curie temperature T_c; at such temperatures the substance is still paramagnetic because the magnetization is zero when the field is zero. The internal field, however, makes the susceptibility larger than that given by the Curie law. A plot of $1/\chi$ against T still gives a straight line, but $1/\chi$ becomes zero when the temperature reaches the Curie temperature.

Since $1/\chi = H/M$, M at this temperature must be finite even when the magnetic field is zero. Thus, below the Curie temperature, the substance exhibits a spontaneous magnetization M in the absence of an external field, the essential property of a ferromagnet. The table gives Curie temperature values for various ferromagnetic substances.

CURIE TEMPERATURES FOR SOME FERROMAGNETIC SUBSTANCES	
iron (Fe)	1,043 K
cobalt (Co)	1,394 K
nickel (Ni)	631 K
gadolinium (Gd)	293 K
manganese arsenide (MnAs)	318 K

In the ferromagnetic phase below the Curie temperature, the spontaneous alignment is still resisted by random thermal energy, and the spontaneous magnetization M is a function of temperature. The magnitude of M can be found from the paramagnetic equation for the reduced magnetization $M/M_s = f(mB/kT)$ by replacing B

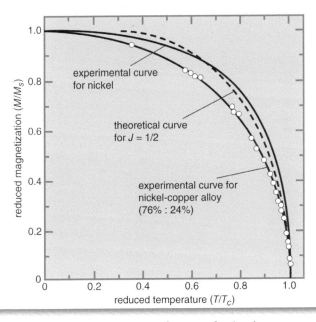

The reduced magnetization M/M_s *as a function of reduced temperature* T/T_c *for a magnet.* Copyright Encyclopædia Britannica; rendering for this edition by Rosen Educational Services

with $\mu(H + \lambda M)$. This gives an equation that can be solved numerically if the function f is known. When H equals zero, the curve of (M/M_s) should be a unique function of the ratio (T/T_c) for all substances that have the same function f.

The molecular field theory explains the existence of a ferromagnetic phase and the presence of spontaneous magnetization below the Curie temperature. The dependence of the magnetization on the external field is, however, more complex than the Curie–Weiss theory predicts. For example, for iron the variation is nonlinear, and B reaches its saturation value S in small fields. The relative permeability $B/\mu_o H$ attains values of 10^3 to 10^4 in contrast to an ordinary paramagnet, for which μ is about 1.001 at room temperature. On reducing the external field H, the field B does not return along the magnetization curve. Even at $H = 0$, its value is not far below the saturation value.

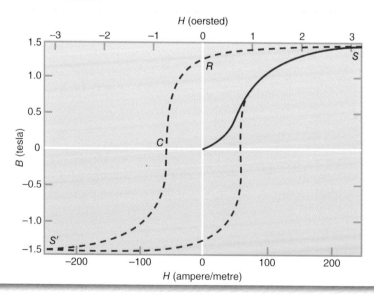

The magnetization curve (solid curve) and hysteresis loop (broken curve) for a ferromagnet. Copyright Encyclopædia Britannica; rendering for this edition by Rosen Educational Services

Remanence

When $H = 0$ (labeled R in the figure), the magnetic field constitutes what is termed the residual flux density, and the retention of magnetization in zero field is called remanence. When the external field is reversed, the value of B falls and passes through zero (point C) at a field strength known as the coercive force. Further increase in the reverse field H sets up a reverse field B that again quickly reaches a saturation value S'. Finally, as the reverse field is removed and a positive field applied, B traces out the lower broken line back to a positive saturation value. Further cycles of H retrace the broken curve, which is known as the hysteresis curve, because the change in B always lags behind the change in H. The hysteresis curve is not unique unless saturation is attained in each direction; interruption and reversal of the cycle at an intermediate field strength results in a hysteresis curve of smaller size.

To explain ferromagnetic phenomena, Weiss suggested that a ferromagnetic substance contains many small regions (called domains), in each of which the substance is magnetized locally to saturations in some direction. In the unmagnetized state, such directions are distributed at random or in such a way that the net magnetization of the whole sample is zero. Application of an external field changes the direction of magnetization of part or all of the domains, setting up a net magnetization parallel to the field. In a paramagnetic substance, atomic dipoles are oriented on a microscopic scale. In contrast, the magnetization of a ferromagnetic substance involves the reorientation of the magnetization of the domains on a macroscopic scale; large changes occur in the net magnetization even when very small fields are applied. Such macroscopic changes are not immediately reversed when the size of the field is reduced or when its direction is changed. This accounts for the presence of hysteresis and for the finite remanent magnetization.

The technological applications of ferromagnetic substances are extensive, and the size and shape of the hysteresis curve are of great importance. A good permanent magnet must have a large spontaneous magnetization in zero field (i.e., a high retentivity) and a high coercive force to prevent its being easily demagnetized by an external field. Both of these imply a "fat," almost rectangular hysteresis loop, typical of a hard magnetic material. On the other hand, ferromagnetic substances subjected to alternating fields, as in a transformer, must have a "thin" hysteresis loop because of an energy loss per cycle that is determined by the area enclosed by the hysteresis loop. Such substances are easily magnetized and demagnetized and are known as soft magnetic materials.

ANTIFERROMAGNETISM

In substances known asantiferromagnets, the mutual forces between pairs of adjacent atomic dipoles are caused by exchange interactions, but the forces between adjacent atomic dipoles have signs opposite those in ferromagnets. As a result, adjacent dipoles tend to line up antiparallel to each other instead of parallel. At high temperatures the material is paramagnetic, but below a certain characteristic temperature the dipoles are aligned in an ordered and antiparallel manner. The transition temperature T_n is known as the Néel temperature, after the French physicist Louis-Eugène-Félix Néel, who proposed this explanation of the magnetic behaviour of such materials in 1936. Values of the Néel temperature for some typical antiferromagnetic substances are given in the table.

NÉEL TEMPERATURE OF ANTIFERROMAGNETIC SUBSTANCES	
chromium	311 K
manganese fluoride	67 K
nickel fluoride	73 K
manganese oxide	116 K
ferrous oxide	198 K

The ordered antiferromagnetic state is naturally more complicated than the ordered ferromagnetic state, since there must be at least two sets of dipoles pointing in opposite directions. With an equal number of dipoles of the same size on each set, there is no net spontaneous magnetization on a macroscopic scale. For this reason, antiferromagnetic substances have few commercial applications. In most insulating chemical compounds, the exchange forces between the magnetic ions are of an antiferromagnetic nature.

FERRIMAGNETISM

Lodestone, or magnetite (Fe_3O_4), belongs to a class of substances known as ferrites. Ferrites and some other classes of magnetic substances discovered more recently possess many of the properties of ferromagnetic materials, including spontaneous magnetization and remanence. Unlike the ferromagnetic metals, they have low electric conductivity, however. In alternating magnetic fields, this greatly reduces the energy loss resulting from eddy currents. Since these losses rise with the frequency of the alternating field, such substances are of much importance in the electronics industry.

A notable property of ferrites and associated materials is that the bulk spontaneous magnetization, even at complete magnetic saturation, does not correspond to the value expected if all the atomic dipoles are aligned parallel to each other. The explanation was put forward in 1948 by Néel, who suggested that the exchange forces responsible for the spontaneous magnetization were basically antiferromagnetic in nature and that in the ordered state they contained two (or more) sublattices spontaneously magnetized in opposite directions. In contrast to the simple antiferromagnetic substances considered above, however, the sizes of the magnetization on the two sublattices are unequal, giving a resultant net magnetization parallel to that of the sublattice with the larger moment. For this phenomenon Néel coined the name ferrimagnetism, and substances that exhibit it are called ferrimagnetic materials.

MAGNETS

A magnet is any material capable of attracting iron and producing a magnetic field outside itself. By the end of the 19th century all the known elements and many compounds had been tested for magnetism, and all were found to have some magnetic property. The most common was the property of diamagnetism, the name given to materials exhibiting a weak repulsion by both poles of a magnet. Some materials, such as chromium, showed paramagnetism, being capable of weak induced magnetization when brought near a magnet. This magnetization disappears when the magnet is removed. Only three elements, iron, nickel, and cobalt, showed the property of ferromagnetism (i.e., the capability of remaining permanently magnetized).

Magnetization Process

The quantities now used in characterizing magnetization were defined and named by William Thomson (Lord Kelvin) in 1850. The symbol B denotes the magnitude of magnetic flux density inside a magnetized body, and the symbol H denotes the magnitude of magnetizing force, or magnetic field, producing it. The two are represented by the equation $B = \mu H$, in which μ symbolizes the permeability of the material and is a measure of the intensity of magnetization that can be produced in it by a given magnetic field. The modern units of the SI system for B are teslas (T) or webers per square metre (Wb/m²) and for H are amperes per metre (A/m). The units were formerly called, respectively, gauss and oersted. The units of μ are henrys per metre.

All ferromagnetic materials exhibit the phenomenon of hysteresis, a lag in response to changing forces based on energy losses resulting from internal friction. If B is measured for various values of H and the results are plotted

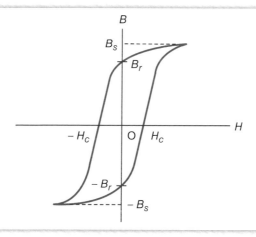

Magnetization process. Copyright Encyclopædia Britannica; rendering for this edition by Rosen Educational Services

in graphic form, the result is a loop called a hysteresis loop. The name describes the situation in which the path followed by the values of B while H is increasing differs from that followed as H is decreasing. With the aid of this diagram, the characteristics needed to describe the performance of a material to be used as a magnet can be defined. B_s is the saturation flux density and is a measure of how strongly the material can be magnetized. B_r is the remanent flux density and is the residual, permanent magnetization left after the magnetizing field is removed; this latter is obviously a measure of quality for a permanent magnet. It is usually measured in webers per square metre. In order to demagnetize the specimen from its remanent state, it is necessary to apply a reversed magnetizing field, opposing the magnetization in the specimen. The magnitude of field necessary to reduce the magnetization to zero is H_c, the coercive force, measured in amperes per metre. For a permanent magnet to retain its magnetization without loss over a long period of time, H_c should be as large as possible. The combination of large B_r and large H_c will generally be found in a material with a large saturation flux density that requires a large field to magnetize it. Thus, permanent-magnet materials are often characterized by quoting the maximum value of the product of B and H, $(BH)_{max}$, which the material can achieve. This product $(BH)_{max}$ is a measure of the minimum volume of permanent-magnet material required to produce a required flux density in a given gap and is sometimes referred to as the energy product.

It was suggested in 1907 that a ferromagnetic material is composed of a large number of small volumes called domains, each of which is magnetized to saturation. In 1931 the existence of such domains was first demonstrated by direct experiment. The ferromagnetic body as a whole appears unmagnetized when the directions of the individual domain magnetizations are distributed at random. Each domain is separated from its neighbours by a domain wall. In the wall region, the direction of magnetization turns from that of one domain to that of its neighbour. The process of magnetization, starting from a perfect unmagnetized state, comprises three stages: (1) *Low magnetizing field.* Reversible movements of the domain walls occur such that domains oriented in the general direction of the magnetizing field grow at the expense of those unfavourably oriented; the walls return to their original position on removal of the magnetizing field, and there is no remanent magnetization. (2) *Medium magnetizing field.* Larger movements of domain walls occur, many of which are irreversible, and the volume of favourably oriented domains is much increased. On removal of the field, all the walls do not return to their original positions, and there is a remanent magnetization. (3) *High magnetizing field.* Large movements of domain walls occur such that many are swept out of the specimen completely. The directions of magnetization in the remaining domains gradually rotate, as the field is increased, until the magnetization is everywhere parallel to the field and the material is magnetized to saturation. On removal of the field, domain walls reappear and the domain magnetizations may rotate away from the original field direction. The remanent magnetization has its maximum value.

The values of B_r, H_c, and $(BH)_{max}$ will depend on the ease with which domain walls can move through the material and domain magnetization can rotate. Discontinuities or imperfections in the material provide obstacles to domain wall movement. Thus, once the magnetizing field has driven the wall past an obstacle, the wall will not be able to return to its original position unless a reversed field is applied to drive it back again. The effect of these obstacles is, therefore, to increase the remanence. Conversely, in a pure, homogeneous material, in which there are few imperfections, it will be easy to magnetize the material to saturation with relatively low fields, and the remanent magnetization will be small.

Demagnetization and magnetic anisotropy. As far as domain rotation is concerned, there are two important factors to be considered, demagnetization and magnetic anisotropy (exhibition of different magnetic properties when measured along axes in different directions). The first of these concerns the shape of a magnetized specimen. Any magnet generates a magnetic field in the space surrounding it. The direction of the lines of force of this field, defined by the direction of the force exerted by the field on a (hypothetical) single magnetic north pole, is opposite to the direction of field used to magnetize it originally. Thus, every magnet exists in a self-generated field that has a direction such as to tend to demagnetize the specimen. This phenomenon is described by the demagnetizing factor. If the magnetic lines of force can be confined to the magnet and not allowed to escape into the surrounding medium, the demagnetizing effect will be absent. Thus a toroidal (ring-shaped) magnet, magnetized around its perimeter so that all the lines of force are closed loops within the material, will not try to demagnetize itself. For bar magnets, demagnetization can be minimized by keeping them in pairs, laid parallel with north and south poles adjacent and with a soft-iron keeper laid across each end.

The relevance of demagnetization to domain rotation arises from the fact that the demagnetizing field may be looked upon as a store of magnetic energy. Like all natural systems, the magnet, in the absence of constraints, will try to maintain its magnetization in a direction such as to minimize stored energy; i.e., to make the demagnetizing field as small as possible. To rotate the magnetization away from this minimum-energy position requires work to be done to provide the increase in energy stored in the increased demagnetizing field. Thus, if an attempt is made to rotate the magnetization of a domain away from its natural minimum-energy position, the rotation can be said to be hindered in the sense that work must be done by an applied field to promote the rotation against the demagnetizing forces. This phenomenon is often called shape anisotropy because it arises from the domain's geometry which may, in turn, be determined by the overall shape of the specimen.

Similar minimum-energy considerations are involved in the second mechanism hindering domain rotation, namely magnetocrystalline anisotropy. It was first observed in 1847 that in crystals of magnetic material there appeared to exist preferred directions for the magnetization. This phenomenon has to do with the symmetry of the atomic arrangements in the crystal. For example, in iron, which has a cubic crystalline form, it is easier to magnetize the crystal along the directions of the edges of the cube than in any other direction. Thus the six cube-edge directions are easy directions of magnetization, and the magnetization of the crystal is termed anisotropic.

Magnetic anisotropy can also be induced by strain in a material. The magnetization tends to align itself in accordance with or perpendicular to the direction of the in-built strain. Some magnetic alloys also exhibit the phenomenon of induced magnetic anisotropy. If an external magnetic field is applied to the material while it is annealed at a high temperature, an easy direction for magnetization is found to be induced in a direction coinciding with that of the applied field.

The above description explains why steel makes a better permanent magnet than does soft iron. The carbon in steel causes the precipitation of tiny crystallites of iron carbide in the iron that form what is called a second phase. The phase boundaries between the precipitate particles and the host iron form obstacles to domain wall movement, and thus the coercive force and remanence are raised compared with pure iron.

The best permanent magnet, however, would be one in which the domain walls were all locked permanently in position and the magnetizations of all the domains were aligned parallel to each other. This situation can be visualized as the result of assembling the magnet from a large number of particles having a high value of saturation magnetization, each of which is a single domain, each having a uniaxial anisotropy in the desired direction, and each aligned with its magnetization parallel to all the others.

Powder Magnets

The problem of producing magnets composed of compacted powders is essentially that of controlling particle sizes so that they are small enough to comprise a single domain and yet not so small as to lose their ferromagnetic properties altogether. The advantage of such magnets is that they can readily be molded and machined into desired shapes. The disadvantage of powder magnets is that when single-domain particles are packed together they are subject to strong magnetic interactions that reduce the coercive force and, to a lesser extent, the remanent magnetization. The nature of the interaction is essentially a reduction of a given particle's demagnetizing field caused by the presence of its neighbours, and the interaction limits the maximum values of H_c and $(BH)_{max}$ that can be achieved. More success has attended the development of magnetic alloys.

HIGH ANISOTROPY AND ALNICO ALLOYS

The materials described above depend on shape for their large uniaxial anisotropy. Much work has also been done on materials having a large uniaxial magnetocrystalline anisotropy. Of these, the most successful have been cobalt–platinum (CoPt) and manganese–bismuth (MnBi) alloys.

High coercive force will be obtained where domain wall motion can be inhibited. This condition can occur in an alloy in which two phases coexist, especially if one phase is a finely divided precipitate in a matrix of the other. Alloys containing the three elements iron, nickel, and aluminum show just such behaviour; and permanent magnet materials based on this system, with various additives, such as cobalt, copper, or titanium, are generally referred to as Alnico alloys.

RARE-EARTH

Isolated atoms of many elements have finite magnetic moments (i.e., the atoms are themselves tiny magnets). When the atoms are brought together in the solid form of the element, however, most interact in such a way that their magnetism cancels out and the solid is not ferromagnetic. Only in iron, nickel, and cobalt, of the common elements, does the cancelling-out process leave an effective net magnetic moment per atom in the vicinity of room temperature and above. Unfortunately, however, it loses its ferromagnetism at temperatures above 16 °C (60 °F) so that it is not of practical importance. Several of the rare-earth elements show ferromagnetic behaviour at extremely low temperatures, and many of them have large atomic moments. They are not, however, of great practical value.

BARIUM FERRITES

Barium ferrite, essentially BaO:$6Fe_2O_3$, is a variation of the basic magnetic iron-oxide magnetite but has a hexagonal crystalline form. This configuration gives it a very high uniaxial magnetic anisotropy capable of producing high values of H_c. The powdered material can be magnetically aligned and then compacted and sintered. The temperature and duration of the sintering process determines the size of the crystallites and provides a means of tailoring the properties of the magnet. For very small crystallites the coercive force is high and the remanence is in the region of half the saturation flux density. Larger crystallites give higher B_r but lower H_c. This material has been widely used in the television industry for focussing magnets for television tubes.

A further development of commercial importance is to bond the powdered ferrite by a synthetic resin or rubber to give either individual moldings or extruded strips, or sheets, that are semiflexible and can be cut with knives. This material has been used as a combination gasket (to make airtight) and magnetic closure for refrigerator doors.

PERMEABLE MATERIALS

A wide range of magnetic devices utilizing magnetic fields, such as motors, generators, transformers, and electromagnets, require magnetic materials with properties quite contrary to those required for good permanent magnets. Such materials must be capable of being magnetized to a high value of flux density in relatively small magnetic fields and then must lose this magnetization completely on removal of the field.

Because iron has the highest value of magnetic moment per atom of the three ferromagnetic metals, it remains the best material for applications where a high-saturation flux density is required. Extensive investigations have been undertaken to determine how to produce iron as free from imperfections as possible, in order to attain the easiest possible domain wall motion. The presence of such elements as carbon, sulfur, oxygen, and nitrogen, even in small amounts, is particularly harmful; and thus sheet materials used in electrical equipment have a total impurity content of less than 0.4 percent.

Important advantages are obtained by alloying iron with a small amount (about 4 percent) of silicon. The added silicon reduces the magnetocrystalline anisotropy of the iron and hence its coercive force and hysteresis loss. Although there is a reduction in the saturation flux density, this loss is outweighed by the other advantages, which include increased electrical resistivity. The latter is important in applications where the magnetic flux alternates because this induces eddy currents in the magnetic material. The lower the resistivity and the higher the frequency of the alternations, the higher are these currents. They produce a loss of energy by causing heating of the material and will be minimized, at a given frequency, by raising the resistivity of the material.

By a suitable manufacturing process, silicon-iron sheet material can be produced with a high degree of preferred orientation of the crystallites. The material then has a preferred direction of magnetization, and in this direction high permeability and low loss are attained. Commercially produced material has about 3.2 percent silicon and is known as cold-reduced, grain-oriented silicon steel.

Alloys of nickel and iron in various proportions are given the general name Permalloy. As the proportion of nickel varies downward, the saturation magnetization increases, reaching a maximum at about 50 percent, falling to zero at 27 percent nickel, then rising again toward the value for pure iron. The magnetocrystalline anisotropy also falls from the value for pure nickel to a very low value in the region of 80 percent nickel, rising only slowly thereafter. Highest value of permeability is at 78.5 percent nickel, which is called Permalloy A. The maximum relative permeability, which can reach a value in the region of 1,000,000 in carefully prepared Permalloy A, makes the alloy useful and superior to iron and silicon iron at low flux densities.

In addition to barium ferrite, which has a hexagonal crystal form, most of the ferrites of the general formula $MeO·Fe_2O_3$, in which Me is a metal, are useful magnetically. They have a different crystalline form called spinel after the mineral spinel ($MgAl_2O_4$), which crystallizes in the cubic system. All the spinel ferrites are soft magnetic materials; that is, they exhibit low coercive force and narrow hysteresis loops. Furthermore, they all have a high electrical resistivity and high relative permeabilities, thus making them suitable for use in high-frequency electronic equipment. Their saturation magnetization, however, is low compared with the alloys, and this property limits their use in high-field, high-power transformers. They are hard, brittle, ceramic-like materials and are difficult to machine. Nevertheless, they are widely used, most importantly in computer memories.

MAGNETIC UNITS

As with electricity, magnetism has its own specialized units. The phenomenon of magnetic induction even has two units, the gauss and the tesla.

GAUSS

The gauss is the unit of magnetic induction in the centimetre–gram–second system of physical units. One gauss corresponds to the magnetic flux density that will induce an electromotive force of one abvolt (10^{-8} volt) in each linear centimetre of a wire moving laterally at one centimetre per second at right angles to a magnetic flux. One gauss corresponds to 10^{-4} tesla (T), the SI unit. The gauss is equal to 1 maxwell per square centimetre, or 10^{-4} weber per square metre. Magnets are rated in gauss. The gauss was named for the German scientist Carl Friedrich Gauss. Before 1932 the name was applied to the unit of magnetic-field strength now called the oersted, and it is sometimes still used in this sense (e.g., Earth may be said to have a magnetic-field strength of about one gauss).

OERSTED

The oersted is the unit of magnetic-field strength, in the centimetre–gram–second system of physical units. Named for the 19th-century Danish physicist Hans Christian Ørsted, it is defined as the intensity of a magnetic field in a vacuum in which a unit magnetic pole (one that repels a similar pole at a distance of one centimetre with a force of one dyne) experiences a mechanical force of one dyne in the direction of the field. Before 1932 the ocrsted was known as the gauss, a name sometimes still applied, though now more properly used for the unit of magnetic induction.

TESLA

The tesla is the unit of magnetic induction or magnetic flux density in the metre–kilogram–second system (SI) of physical units. One tesla equals one weber per square metre, corresponding to 10^4 gauss. It is named for Nikola Tesla. It is used in all work involving strong magnetic fields, while the gauss is more useful with small magnets.

CHAPTER 5
THE FUNDAMENTALS OF
ELECTROMAGNETISM

Electromagnetism encompasses charge and the forces and fields associated with charge. Electricity and magnetism are two aspects of electromagnetism.

Electricity and magnetism had been known for millennia, but it was not until the 19th century that they were understood to be related. In 1864, James Clerk Maxwell formulated a theory that related the two, and in 1905, Albert Einstein's special theory of relativity showed that they were two facets of the same phenomenon. Realization of the unity of electricity and magnetism was so long in coming because electric and magnetic forces behave very differently and can be described with different equations. One great difference between the two is that electric forces arise from charges that can be either stationary or moving, but magnetic forces come from and act upon moving charges only.

Electric phenomena take place throughout the universe. Even in matter that has no net positive or negative charge, electric effects are present because of the forces between the individual charges. The electric force is much stronger than that of gravity. For two electrons, the repulsive Coulomb force between them is 1042 times stronger than the attractive gravitational force.

The regions in which electric and magnetic forces can exert their effects are called electric and magnetic fields. Electric and magnetic forces do not have a distance limit, so the fields can be measured far from the original charges that generate them. A magnetic field can give rise to an electric field, and an electric field can give rise to a magnetic field. A changing magnetic field produces an electric field, as the English physicist Michael Faraday discovered in work that forms the basis of electric power generation. Conversely, a changing electric field produces a magnetic field, as the Scottish physicist James Clerk Maxwell deduced. The mathematical equations formulated by Maxwell incorporated light and wave phenomena into electromagnetism. He showed that electric and magnetic fields travel together through space as waves of electromagnetic radiation, with the changing fields mutually sustaining each other. Examples of electromagnetic waves traveling through space independent of matter are radio and television waves, microwaves, infrared rays, visible light, ultraviolet light, X-rays, and gamma rays. All of these waves travel at the same speed—namely, the velocity of light (roughly 300,000 kilometres, or 186,000 miles, per second). They differ from each other only in the frequency at which their electric and magnetic fields oscillate.

An important aspect of electromagnetism is the science of electricity, which is concerned with the behaviour of aggregates of charge, including the distribution of charge within matter and the motion of charge from place to place. Different types of materials are classified as either conductors or insulators on the basis of whether charges can move freely through their constituent matter. Electric current is the measure of the flow of charges; the laws governing currents in matter are important in technology, particularly in the production, distribution, and control of energy.

The concept of voltage, like those of charge and current, is fundamental to the science of electricity. Voltage is a measure of the propensity of charge to flow from one place to another; positive charges generally tend to move from a region of high voltage to a region of lower voltage. A common problem in electricity is determining the relationship between voltage and current or charge in a given physical situation.

Everyday modern life is pervaded by electromagnetic phenomena. When a light bulb is switched on, a current flows through a thin filament in the bulb; the current heats the filament to such a high temperature that it glows, illuminating its surroundings. Electric clocks and connections link simple devices of this kind into complex systems such as traffic lights that are timed and synchronized with the speed of vehicular flow. Radio and television sets receive information carried by electromagnetic waves traveling through space at the speed of light. To start an automobile, currents in an electric starter motor generate magnetic fields that rotate the motor shaft and drive engine pistons to compress an explosive mixture of gasoline and air; the spark initiating the combustion is an electric discharge, which makes up a momentary current flow.

COULOMB'S LAW

Many of these devices and phenomena are complex, but they derive from the same fundamental laws of electromagnetism. One of the most important of these is Coulomb's law, which describes the electric force between charged objects. Formulated by the 18th-century French physicist Charles-Augustin de Coulomb, it is analogous to Newton's law for the gravitational force. Both gravitational and electric forces decrease with the square of the distance between the objects, and both forces act along a line between them. In Coulomb's law, however, the magnitude and sign of the electric force are determined by the charge, rather than the mass, of an object. Thus, charge determines how electromagnetism influences the motion of charged objects. (Charge is a basic property of matter. Every constituent of matter has an electric charge with a value that can be positive, negative, or zero. For example, electrons are negatively charged, and atomic nuclei are positively charged. Most bulk matter has an equal amount of positive and negative charge and thus has zero net charge.)

According to Coulomb, the electric force for charges at rest has the following properties:

(1) Like charges repel each other; unlike charges attract. Thus, two negative charges repel one another, while a positive charge attracts a negative charge.

(2) The attraction or repulsion acts along the line between the two charges.

(3) The size of the force varies inversely as the square of the distance between the two charges. Therefore, if the distance between the two charges is doubled, the attraction or repulsion becomes weaker, decreasing to one-fourth of the original value. If the charges come 10 times closer, the size of the force increases by a factor of 100.

(4) The size of the force is proportional to the value of each charge. The unit used to measure charge is the coulomb (C). If there were two positive charges, one of 0.1 coulomb and the second of 0.2 coulomb, they would repel each other with a force that depends on the product 0.2×0.1. If each of the charges were reduced by one-half, the repulsion would be reduced to one-quarter of its former value.

The electric force is operative between charges down to distances of at least 10^{-16} metre, or approximately one-tenth of the diameter of atomic nuclei. Because of their positive charge, protons within nuclei repel each other, but nuclei hold together because of another basic physical force, the strong interaction, or nuclear force, which is stronger than the electric force. Massive, but electrically neutral, astronomical bodies such as planets and stars are bound together in solar systems and galaxies by still another basic physical force, gravitation, which though much weaker than the electric force, is always attractive and is the dominant force at great distances. At distances between these extremes, including the distances of everyday life, the only significant physical force is the electric force in its many varieties along with the related magnetic force.

Static cling is a practical example of the Coulomb force. In static cling, garments made of synthetic material collect a charge, especially in dry winter air. A plastic or rubber comb passed quickly through hair also becomes charged and will pick up bits of paper. The synthetic fabric and the comb are insulators; charge on these objects cannot move easily from one part of the object to another. Similarly, an office copy machine uses electric force to attract particles of ink to paper.

PRINCIPLE OF CHARGE CONSERVATION

Like Coulomb's law, the principle of charge conservation is a fundamental law of nature. According to this principle, the charge of an isolated system cannot change. If an additional positively charged particle appears within a system, a particle with a negative charge of the same magnitude will be created at the same time; thus, the principle of conservation of charge is maintained. In nature, a pair of oppositely charged particles is created when high-energy radiation interacts with matter; an electron and a positron are created in a process known as pair production.

The smallest subdivision of the amount of charge that a particle can have is the charge of one proton, $+1.602 \times 10^{-19}$ coulomb. The electron has a charge of the same magnitude but opposite sign—i.e., -1.602×10^{-19} coulomb. An ordinary flashlight battery delivers a current that provides a total charge flow of approximately 5,000 coulomb, which corresponds to more than 10^{22} electrons, before it is exhausted.

Electric current is a measure of the flow of charge, as, for example, charge flowing through a wire. The size of the current is measured in amperes and symbolized by i. An ampere of current represents the passage of one coulomb of charge per second, or 6.2 billion billion electrons (6.2×10^{18} electrons) per second. A current is positive when it is in the direction of the flow of positive charges; its direction is opposite to the flow of negative charges.

ELECTRIC FIELDS AND FORCES

The force and conservation laws are only two aspects of electromagnetism, however. Electric and magnetic forces are caused by electromagnetic fields. The term field denotes a property of space, so that the field quantity has a numerical value at each point of space. These values may also vary with time. The value of the electric or magnetic field is a vector—i.e., a quantity having both magnitude and direction. The value of the electric field at a point in space, for example, equals the force that would be exerted on a unit charge at that position in space.

Instead of considering the electric force as a direct interaction of two electric charges at a distance from each other, one charge is considered the source of an electric field that extends outward into the surrounding space, and the force exerted on a second charge in this space is considered as a direct interaction between the electric field and the second charge. The strength of an electric field E at any point may be defined as the electric force F exerted per unit positive electric charge q at that point, or simply $E = F/q$. If the second, or test, charge is twice as great, the resultant force is doubled; but their quotient, the measure of the electric field E, remains the same at any given point. The strength of the electric field depends on the source charge, not on the test charge. Strictly speaking, the introduction of a small test charge, which itself has an electric field, slightly modifies the existing field. The electric field may be thought of as the force per unit positive charge that would be exerted before the field is disturbed by the presence of the test charge.

The direction of the force that is exerted on a negative charge is opposite that which is exerted on a positive charge. Because an electric field has both magnitude and direction, the direction of the force on a positive charge

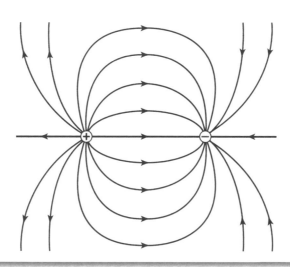

Electric field lines near equal but opposite charges. Copyright Encyclopædia Britannica; rendering for this edition by Rosen Educational Services

is chosen arbitrarily as the direction of the electric field. Because positive charges repel each other, the electric field around an isolated positive charge is oriented radially outward. When they are represented by lines of force, or field lines, electric fields are depicted as starting on positive charges and terminating on negative charges. The lines indicate the path that a small positive test charge would take if it were placed in the field. A line tangent to a field line indicates the direction of the electric field at that point. Where the field lines are close together, the electric field is stronger than where they are farther apart. The magnitude of the electric field around an electric charge, considered as source of the electric field, depends on how the charge is distributed in space. For a charge concentrated nearly at a point, the electric field is directly proportional to the amount of charge; it is inversely proportional to the square of the distance radially away from the centre of the source charge and depends also upon the nature of the medium. The presence of a material medium always diminishes the electric field below the value it has in a vacuum.

Thus, each point in space has an electric property associated with it, the magnitude and direction of which are expressed by the value of E, called electric field strength, or electric field intensity, or simply the electric field. Knowledge of the value of the electric field at a point without any specific knowledge of what produced the field is all that is needed to determine what will happen to electric charges close to that particular point.

At times the electric field itself may become detached from the source charge, as in the case of charges accelerating up and down the transmitting antenna of a television station. The electric field with an accompanying magnetic field is propagated through space as a radiated wave at the same speed as that of light. Such electromagnetic waves indicate that electric fields are generated not only from electric charges but also from changing magnetic fields.

The value of the electric field has dimensions of force per unit charge. In the metre–kilogram–second and SI systems, the appropriate units are newtons per coulomb, equivalent to volts per metre. In the centimetre–gram–second system, the electric field is expressed in units of dynes per electrostatic unit (esu), equivalent to statvolts per centimetre.

The electric potential is another useful field. It provides an alternative to the electric field in electrostatics problems. The potential is easier to use, however, because it is a single number, a scalar, instead of a vector. The difference in potential between two places measures the degree to which charges are influenced to move from one place to another. If the potential is the same at two places (i.e., if the places have the same voltage), charges will not be influenced to move from one place to the other. The potential on an object or at some point in space is measured in volts; it equals the electrostatic energy that a unit charge would have at that position. In a typical 12-volt car battery, the battery terminal that is marked with a + sign is at a potential 12 volts greater than the potential of the terminal marked with the - sign. When a wire, such as the filament of a car headlight, is connected between the + and the - terminals of the battery, charges move through the filament as an electric current and heat the filament; the hot filament radiates light.

A property of an electric conductor, or set of conductors, related to the electric potential is the capacitance, which is measured by the amount of separated electric charge that can be stored on it per unit change in electrical potential. Capacitance also implies an associated storage of electrical energy. If electric charge is transferred between two initially uncharged conductors, both become equally charged, one positively, the other negatively, and a potential difference is established between them. The capacitance C is the ratio of the amount of charge q on either conductor to the potential difference V between the conductors, or simply $C = q/V$.

In both the practical and the metre–kilogram–second scientific systems, the unit of electric charge is the coulomb and the unit of potential difference is the volt, so that the unit of capacitance—named the farad (symbolized F)—is one coulomb per volt. One farad is an extremely large capacitance. Convenient subdivisions in common use are one-millionth of a farad, called a microfarad (μF), and one-millionth of a microfarad, called a picofarad (pF; older term, micromicrofarad, $\mu\mu$F). In the electrostatic system of units, capacitance has dimensions of distance.

Capacitance in electric circuits is deliberately introduced by a device called a capacitor. It was discovered by the Prussian scientist Ewald Georg von Kleist in 1745 and independently by the Dutch physicist Pieter van Musschenbroek at about the same time, while in the process of investigating electrostatic phenomena. They discovered that electricity obtained from an electrostatic machine could be stored for a period of time and then released. The device, which came to be known as the Leyden jar, consisted of a stoppered glass vial or jar filled with water, with a nail piercing the stopper and dipping into the water. By holding the jar in the hand and touching the nail to the conductor of an electrostatic machine, they found that a shock could be obtained from the nail after disconnecting it, by touching it with the free hand. This reaction showed that some of the electricity from the machine had been stored.

A simple but fundamental step in the evolution of the capacitor was taken by the English astronomer John Bevis in 1747 when he replaced the water by metal foil forming a lining on the inside surface of the glass and another covering the outside surface. This form of the capacitor with a conductor projecting from the mouth of the jar and touching the lining had, as its principal physical features, two conductors of extended area kept nearly equally separated by an insulating, or dielectric, layer made as thin as practicable. These features have been retained in every modern form of capacitor.

A capacitor, also called a condenser, is thus essentially a sandwich of two plates of conducting material separated by an insulating material, or dielectric. Its primary function is to store electrical energy. Capacitors differ in the size and geometrical arrangement of the plates and in the kind of dielectric material used. Hence, they have such names as mica, paper, ceramic, air, and electrolytic capacitors. Their capacitance may be fixed or adjustable over a range of values for use in tuning circuits.

The energy stored by a capacitor corresponds to the work performed (by a battery, for example) in creating opposite charges on the two plates at the applied voltage. The amount of charge that can be stored depends on the area of the plates, the spacing between them, the dielectric material in the space, and the applied voltage.

A capacitor incorporated in an alternating-current (AC) circuit is alternately charged and discharged each half cycle. The time available for charging or discharging thus depends on the frequency of the current, and if the time required is greater than the length of the half cycle, the polarization (separation of charge) is not complete. Under such conditions, the dielectric constant appears to be less than that observed in a direct-current circuit and to vary with frequency, becoming lower at higher frequencies. During the alternation of polarity of the plates, the charges must be displaced through the dielectric first in one direction and then in the other, and overcoming the opposition that they encounter leads to a production of heat known as dielectric loss, a characteristic that must be considered when applying capacitors to electrical circuits, such as those in radio and television receivers. Dielectric losses depend on frequency and the dielectric material.

Except for the leakage (usually small) through the dielectric, no current flows through a capacitor when it is subject to a constant voltage. Alternating current will pass readily, however, and is called a displacement current.

MAGNETIC FIELDS AND FORCES

The magnetic force influences only those charges that are already in motion. It is transmitted by the magnetic field. Both magnetic fields and magnetic forces are more complicated than electric fields and electric forces. The magnetic field does not point along the direction of the source of the field; instead, it points in a perpendicular direction. In addition, the magnetic force acts in a direction that is perpendicular to the direction of the field. In comparison, both the electric force and the electric field point directly toward or away from the charge.

The present discussion will deal with simple situations in which the magnetic field is produced by a current of charge in a wire. Certain materials, such as copper, silver, and aluminum, are conductors that allow charge to flow freely from place to place. If an external influence establishes a current in a conductor, the current generates a magnetic field. For a long straight wire, the magnetic field has a direction that encircles the wire on a plane perpendicular to the wire. The strength of the magnetic field decreases with distance from the wire.

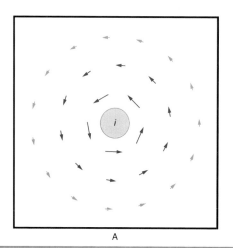 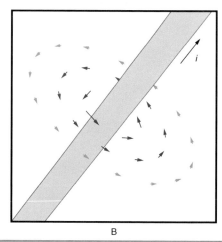

A   B

Magnetic field of a long wire. (A) An end view, with the current flow-ing toward the reader. (B) A three-dimensional view. Courtesy of the Department of Physics and Astronomy, Michigan State University; rendering for this edition by Rosen Educational Services

Electric fields begin on positive charges and end on neg-ative charges, while magnetic fields do not have beginnings or ends and close on themselves. Highly complex and use-ful magnetic fields can be generated by the proper choice of conductors to carry electric currents. Under develop-ment are thermonuclear fusion reactors for obtaining energy from the fusion of light nuclei in the form of very hot plasmas of hydrogen isotopes. The plasmas have to be confined by magnetic fields (dubbed "magnetic bottles") as no material container can withstand such high tempera-tures. Charged particles are also confined by magnetic fields in nature. Large numbers of charged particles, mostly protons and electrons, are trapped in huge bands around Earth by its magnetic field. These bands are known as the Van Allen radiation belts. Disturbance of Earth's confining magnetic field produces spectacular displays, the so-called northern lights, in which trapped charged particles are freed and crash through the atmosphere to Earth.

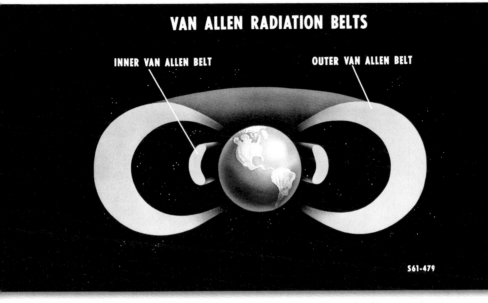

The Van Allen belts provide a grand-scale, natural example of how an electric current generates a magnetic field, which then traps charged particles. NASA Langley Research Center (NASA-LaRC)

INTERACTION OF A MAGNETIC FIELD WITH A CHARGE

How does the magnetic field interact with a charged object? If the charge is at rest, there is no interaction. If the charge moves, however, it is subjected to a force, the size of which increases in direct proportion with the velocity of the charge. The force has a direction that is perpendicular both to the direction of motion of the charge and to the direction of the magnetic field. There are two possible precisely opposite directions for such a force for a given direction of motion. This apparent ambiguity is resolved by the fact that one of the two directions applies to the force on a moving positive charge while the other direction applies to the force on a moving negative charge.

Depending on the initial orientation of the particle velocity to the magnetic field, charges having a constant speed in a uniform magnetic field will follow a circular or helical path.

Electric currents in wires are not the only source of magnetic fields. Naturally occurring minerals exhibit magnetic properties and have magnetic fields. These magnetic fields result from the motion of electrons in the atoms of the material. They also result from a property of electrons called the magnetic dipole moment, which is related to the intrinsic spin of individual electrons. In most materials, little or no field is observed outside the matter because of the random orientation of the various constituent atoms. In some materials such as iron, however, atoms within certain distances tend to become aligned in one particular direction.

Magnets have numerous applications, ranging from use as toys and paper holders on home refrigerators to essential components in electric generators and machines that can accelerate particles to speeds approaching that of light. The practical application of magnetism in technology is greatly enhanced by using iron and other ferromagnetic materials with electric currents in devices like motors. These materials amplify the magnetic field produced by the currents and thereby create more powerful fields.

While electric and magnetic effects are well separated in many phenomena and applications, they are coupled closely together when there are rapid time fluctuations. Faraday's law of induction describes how a time-varying magnetic field produces an electric field. Important practical applications include the electric generator and transformer. In a generator, the physical motion of a magnetic field produces electricity for power. In a transformer, electric power is converted from one voltage level to another by the magnetic field of one circuit inducing an electric current in another circuit.

The existence of electromagnetic waves depends on the interaction between electric and magnetic fields. Maxwell postulated that a time-varying electric field produces a magnetic field. His theory predicted the existence of electromagnetic waves in which each time-varying field produces the other field. For example, radio waves are generated by electronic circuits known as oscillators that cause rapidly oscillating currents to flow in antennas; the rapidly varying magnetic field has an associated varying electric field. The result is the emission of radio waves into space.

Many electromagnetic devices can be described by circuits consisting of conductors and other elements. These circuits may operate with a steady flow of current, as in a flashlight, or with time-varying currents. Important elements in circuits include sources of power called electromotive forces; resistors, which control the flow of current for a given voltage; capacitors, which store charge and energy temporarily; and inductors, which also store electrical energy for a limited time. Circuits with these elements can be described entirely with algebra.

Two mathematical quantities associated with vector fields, like the electric field E and the magnetic field B, are useful for describing electromagnetic phenomena. They are the flux of such a field through a surface and the line integral of the field along a path. The flux of a field through a surface measures how much of the field penetrates through the surface; for every small section of the surface, the flux is proportional to the area of that section and depends also on the relative orientation of the section and the field. The line integral of a field along a path measures the degree to which the field is aligned with the path; for every small section of path, it is proportional to the length of that section and is also dependent on the alignment of the field with that section of path. When the field is perpendicular to the path, there is no contribution to the line integral. The fluxes of E and B through a surface and the line integrals of these fields along a path play an important role in electromagnetic theory. As examples, the flux of the electric field E through a closed surface measures the amount of charge contained within the surface; the flux of the magnetic field B through a closed surface is always zero because there are no magnetic monopoles (magnetic charges consisting of a single pole) to act as sources of the magnetic field in the way that charge is a source of the electric field.

EFFECTS OF VARYING MAGNETIC FIELDS

The merger of electricity and magnetism from distinct phenomena into electromagnetism is tied to three closely related events. The first was Hans Christian Ørsted's accidental discovery of the influence of an electric current on a magnetic needle—namely, that magnetic fields are produced by electric currents. Ørsted's 1820 report of his observation spurred an intense effort by scientists to prove that magnetic fields can induce currents. The second event was Faraday's experimental proof that a changing magnetic field can induce a current in a circuit. The third was Maxwell's prediction that a changing electric field has an associated magnetic field. The technological revolution attributed to the development of electric power and radio communications can be traced to these three landmarks.

FARADAY'S LAW OF INDUCTION

Faraday's discovery in 1831 of the phenomenon of magnetic induction is one of the great milestones in the quest toward understanding and exploiting nature. Stated simply, Faraday found that (1) a changing magnetic field in a circuit induces an electromotive force in the circuit; and (2) the magnitude of the electromotive force equals the rate at which the flux of the magnetic field through the circuit changes. The flux is a measure of how much field penetrates through the circuit. The electromotive force is measured in volts and is represented by the equation

$$\text{emf} = -\frac{d\Phi}{dt}. \qquad (43)$$

Here, Φ, the flux of the vector field **B** through the circuit, measures how much of the field passes through the circuit. To illustrate the meaning of flux, imagine how much water from a steady rain will pass through a circular ring of area A. When the ring is placed parallel to the path of the water drops, no water passes through the ring. The maximum rate at which drops of rain pass through the ring occurs when the surface is perpendicular to the motion of the drops. The rate of water drops crossing the surface is the flux of the vector field ρv through that surface, where ρ is the density of water drops and v represents the velocity of the water. Clearly, the angle between v and the surface is essential in determining the flux. To specify the orientation of the surface, a vector A is defined so that its magnitude is the surface area A in units of square metres and its direction is perpendicular to the surface. The rate at which raindrops pass through the surface is $\rho v \cos \theta A$, where θ is the angle between v and A. Using vector notation, the flux is $\rho v \cdot A$. For the magnetic field, the amount of flux through a small area represented by the vector dA is given by $B \cdot dA$. For a circuit consisting of a single turn of wire, adding the contributions from the entire surface that is surrounded by the wire gives the magnetic flux Φ of equation (43). The rate of change of this flux is the induced electromotive force. The units of magnetic flux are webers, with one weber equaling one tesla per square metre. Finally, the minus sign in equation (43) indicates the direction of the induced electromotive force and hence of any induced current. The magnetic flux through the circuit generated by the induced current is in whatever direction will keep the total flux in the circuit from changing. The minus sign in equation (43) is an example of Lenz's law for magnetic systems. This law, deduced by the Russian-born physicist Heinrich Friedrich Emil Lenz, states that "what happens is that which opposes any change in the system."

A small amount of work, therefore, is done in pushing the magnet into the coil and in pulling it out against the magnetic effect of the induced current. The small amount of energy represented by this work manifests itself as a slight heating effect, the result of the induced current encountering resistance in the material of the coil. Lenz's law upholds the general principle of the conservation of energy. If the current were induced in the opposite direction, its action would spontaneously draw the bar magnet into the coil in addition to the heating effect, which would violate conservation of energy.

Faraday's law is valid regardless of the process that causes the magnetic flux to change. It may be that a magnet is moved closer to a circuit or that a circuit is moved

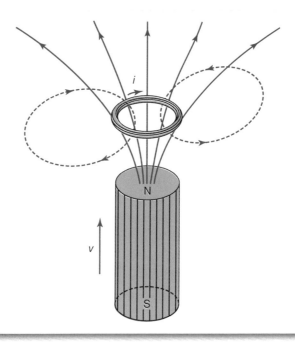

Demonstration of Faraday's and Lenz's laws. The dashed field lines represent the magnetic field inside the ring. Courtesy of the Department of Physics and Astronomy, Michigan State University; rendering for this edition by Rosen Educational Services

closer to a magnet. Another alternative is that the circuit may change in size in a fixed external magnetic field or, as in the case of alternating-current generation, that the circuit may be a coil of conducting wire rotating in a magnetic field so that the flux Φ varies sinusoidally in time.

The magnetic flux Φ through a circuit has to be considered carefully in the application of Faraday's law given in equation (43). For example, if a circuit consists of a coil with five closely spaced turns and if ϕ is the magnetic flux through a single turn, then the value of Φ for the five-turn circuit that must be used in Faraday's law is $\Phi = 5\phi$. If the five turns are not the same size and closely spaced, the problem of determining Φ can be quite complex.

SELF-INDUCTANCE AND MUTUAL INDUCTANCE

The self-inductance of a circuit is used to describe the reaction of the circuit to a changing current in the circuit, while the mutual inductance with respect to a second circuit describes the reaction to a changing current in the second circuit. When a current i_1 flows in circuit 1, i_1 produces a magnetic field $\boldsymbol{B}_1$; the magnetic flux through circuit 1 due to current i_1 is Φ_{11}. Since $\boldsymbol{B}_1$ is proportional to i_1, Φ_{11} is as well. The constant of proportionality is the self-inductance L_1 of the circuit. It is defined by the equation

$$\Phi_{11} = L_1 i_1. \tag{44}$$

As indicated earlier, the units of inductance are henrys. If a second circuit is present, some of the field $\boldsymbol{B}_1$ will pass through circuit 2 and there will be a magnetic flux Φ_{21} in circuit 2 due to the current i_1. The mutual inductance M_{21} is given by

$$\Phi_{21} = M_{21} i_1. \tag{45}$$

The magnetic flux in circuit 1 due to a current in circuit 2 is given by $\Phi_{12} = M_{12} i_2$. An important property of the mutual inductance is that $M_{21} = M_{12}$. It is therefore sufficient to use the label M without subscripts for the mutual inductance of two circuits.

The value of the mutual inductance of two circuits can range from $+\sqrt{L_1 L_2}$ to $-\sqrt{L_1 L_2}$, depending on the flux linkage between the circuits. If the two circuits are very far apart or if the field of one circuit provides no magnetic flux through the other circuit, the mutual inductance is zero. The maximum possible value of the mutual inductance of two circuits is approached as the two circuits produce $\boldsymbol{B}$ fields with increasingly similar spatial configurations.

If the rate of change with respect to time is taken for the terms on both sides of equation (44), the result is $d\Phi_{\scriptscriptstyle\mathrm{II}}/dt = L_1 di_1/dt$. According to Faraday's law, $d\Phi_{\scriptscriptstyle\mathrm{II}}/dt$ is the negative of the induced electromotive force. The result is the equation frequently used for a single inductor in an AC circuit—i.e.,

$$\mathrm{emf} = -L\frac{di}{dt}. \tag{46}$$

The phenomenon of self-induction was first recognized by the American scientist Joseph Henry. He was able to generate large and spectacular electric arcs by interrupting the current in a large copper coil with many turns. While a steady current is flowing in a coil, the energy in the magnetic field is given by $\frac{1}{2}Li^2$. If both the inductance L and the current i are large, the amount of energy is also large. If the current is interrupted, as, for example, by opening a knife-blade switch, the current and therefore the magnetic flux through the coil drop quickly. Equation (46) describes the resulting electromotive force induced in the coil, and a large potential difference is developed between the two poles of the switch. The energy stored in the magnetic field of the coil is dissipated as heat and

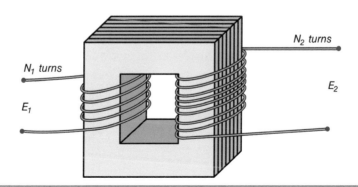

Representation of an AC transformer. Courtesy of the Department of Physics and Astronomy, Michigan State University; rendering for this edition by Rosen Educational Services

radiation in an electric arc across the space between the terminals of the switch. Due to advances in superconducting wires for electromagnets, it is possible to use large magnets with magnetic fields of several teslas for temporarily storing electric energy as energy in the magnetic field. This is done to accommodate short-term fluctuations in the consumption of electric power.

A transformer is an example of a device that uses circuits with maximum mutual induction. Here, coils of insulated conducting wire are wound around a ring of iron constructed of thin isolated laminations or sheets. The laminations minimize eddy currents in the iron. Eddy currents are circulatory currents induced in the metal by the changing magnetic field. These currents produce an undesirable by-product—heat in the iron. Energy loss in a transformer can be reduced by using thinner laminations, very "soft" (low-carbon) iron and wire with a larger cross section, or by winding the primary and secondary circuits with conductors that have very low resistance. Unfortunately, reducing the heat loss increases the cost of transformers. Transformers used to transmit and distribute power are commonly 98 to 99 percent efficient. While eddy currents are a problem in transformers, they are useful for heating objects in a vacuum. Eddy currents are induced in the object to be heated by surrounding a relatively nonconducting vacuum enclosure with a coil carrying a high-frequency alternating current.

In a transformer, the iron ensures that nearly all the lines of B passing through one circuit also pass through the second circuit and that, in fact, essentially all the magnetic flux is confined to the iron. Each turn of the conducting coils has the same magnetic flux; thus, the total flux for each coil is proportional to the number of turns in the coil. As a result, if a source of sinusoidally varying electromotive force is connected to one coil, the electromotive force in the second coil is given by

$$\text{emf}_2 = \text{emf}_1 \frac{N_2}{N_1}. \qquad (47)$$

Thus, depending on the ratio of N_2 to N_1, the transformer can be either a step-up or a step-down device for alternating voltages. For many reasons, including safety, generation and consumption of electric power occur at relatively low voltages. Step-up transformers are used to obtain high voltages before electric power is transmitted, since for a given amount of power, the current in the transmission lines is much smaller. This minimizes energy lost by resistive heating of the conductors.

Faraday's law constitutes the basis for the power industry and for the transformation of mechanical energy into electric energy. In 1821, a decade before his discovery of magnetic induction, Faraday conducted experiments with electric wires rotating around compass needles. This earlier work, in which a wire carrying a current rotated around a magnetized needle and a magnetic needle was made to rotate around a wire carrying an electric current, provided the groundwork for the development of the electric motor.

EFFECTS OF VARYING ELECTRIC FIELDS

Maxwell's prediction that a changing electric field generates a magnetic field was a masterstroke of pure theory. The Maxwell equations for the electromagnetic field unified all that was hitherto known about electricity and magnetism and predicted the existence of an electromagnetic phenomenon that can travel as waves with the velocity of $1/\sqrt{\varepsilon_o \mu_o}$ in a vacuum. That velocity, which is based on constants obtained from purely electric measurements, corresponds to the speed of light. Consequently, Maxwell concluded that light itself was an electromagnetic phenomenon. Later, Einstein's special relativity theory postulated that the value of the speed of light is independent of the motion of the source of the light. Since then, the speed of light has been measured with increasing accuracy. In 1983 it was defined to be exactly 299,792,458 metres per second. Together with the cesium clock, which has been used to define the second, the speed of light serves as the new standard for length.

Consider a circuit that is an example of a magnetic field generated by a changing electric field. A capacitor with parallel plates is charged at a constant rate by a steady current flowing through a wire. The objective is to apply Ampère's circuital law for magnetic fields to the path P, which goes around the wire. This law (named in honour of the French physicist André-Marie Ampère) can be derived

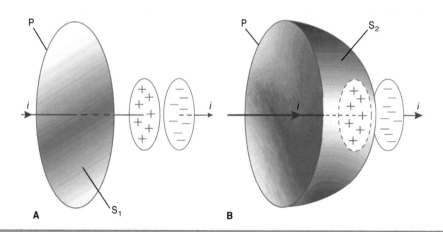

Current i charging a capacitor as an illustration of Maxwell's displacement current. Courtesy of the Department of Physics and Astronomy, Michigan State University; rendering for this edition by Rosen Educational Services

from the Biot and Savart equation for the magnetic field produced by a current (equation [34]). Using vector calculus notation, Ampère's law states that the integral $\oint \boldsymbol{B} \cdot d\boldsymbol{l}$ along a closed path surrounding the current i is equal to $\mu_o i$. (An integral is essentially a sum, and, in this case, $\oint \boldsymbol{B} \cdot d\boldsymbol{l}$ is the sum of $B \cos \theta dl$ taken for a small length of the path until the complete loop is included. At each segment of the path dl, θ is the angle between the field $\boldsymbol{B}$ and $d\boldsymbol{l}$.) The current i in Ampère's law is the total flux of the current density $\boldsymbol{J}$ through any surface surrounded by the closed path. The closed path is labeled P, and a surface S_1 is surrounded by path P. All the current density through S_1 lies within the conducting wire. The total flux of the current density is the current i flowing through the wire. The result for surface S_1 reflects the value of the magnetic field around the wire in the region of the path P. Now consider the situation in which path P is the same but the surface S_2 passes between the two plates of the capacitor. The value of the total flux of the current density through the surface should also be i. There is, however, clearly no motion of charge at all through the surface S_2. The dilemma is that the value of the integral $\oint \boldsymbol{B} \cdot d\boldsymbol{l}$ for the path P cannot be both $\mu_o i$ and zero.

Maxwell's resolution of this dilemma was his conclusion that there must be some other kind of current density, called the displacement current $\boldsymbol{J}_d$, for which the total flux through the surface S_2 would be the same as the current i through the surface S_1. $\boldsymbol{J}_d$ would take, for the surface S_2, the place of the current density $\boldsymbol{J}$ associated with the movement of charge, since $\boldsymbol{J}$ is clearly zero due to the lack of charges between the plates of the capacitor. What happens between the plates while the current i is flowing? Because the amount of charge on the capacitor increases with time, the electric field between the plates increases with time too. If the current stops, there is an electric field between the plates as long as the plates are charged, but there is no magnetic field around the wire. Maxwell decided that the new type of current density was associated with the changing of the electric field. He found that

$$J_d = \frac{dD}{dt}, \tag{48}$$

where $D = \varepsilon_0 E$ and E is the electric field between the plates. In situations where matter is present, the field D in equation (48) is modified to include polarization effects; the result is $D = \varepsilon_0 E + P$. The field D is measured in coulombs per square metre. Adding the displacement current to Ampère's law represented Maxwell's prediction that a changing electric field also could be a source of the magnetic field B. Following Maxwell's predictions of electromagnetic waves, the German physicist Heinrich Hertz initiated the era of radio communications in 1887 by generating and detecting electromagnetic waves.

Using vector calculus notation, the four equations of Maxwell's theory of electromagnetism are

$$\text{I. div } D = \rho, \tag{49}$$

$$\text{II. div } B = 0, \tag{50}$$

$$\text{III. } \mathbf{curl}\, E = -\frac{dB}{dt}, \tag{51}$$

$$\text{IV. } \mathbf{curl}\, H = J + \frac{dD}{dt}, \tag{52}$$

where $D = \varepsilon_0 E + P$, and $H = B/\mu_0 - M$. The first equation is based on Coulomb's inverse square law for the force between two charges; it is a form of Gauss's law, which relates the flux of the electric field through a closed surface to the total charge enclosed by the surface. The second equation is based on the fact that apparently no magnetic monopoles exist in nature; if they did, they would be point sources of magnetic field. The third is a statement of Faraday's law of magnetic induction, which reveals that a changing magnetic field generates an electric field. The fourth is Ampère's law as extended by Maxwell to include the displacement current discussed above; it associates a magnetic field to a changing electric field as well as to an electric current.

Maxwell's four equations represent a complete description of the classical theory of electromagnetism. His discovery that light is an electromagnetic wave meant that optics could be understood as part of electromagnetism. Only in microscopic situations is it necessary to modify Maxwell's equations to include quantum effects. That modification, known as quantum electrodynamics (QED), accounts for certain atomic properties to a degree of precision exceeding one part in 100 million.

Sometimes it is necessary to shield apparatus from external electromagnetic fields. For a static electric field, this is a simple matter; the apparatus is surrounded by a shield made of a good conductor (e.g., copper). Shielding apparatus from a steady magnetic field is more difficult because materials with infinite magnetic permeability μ do not exist; for example, a hollow shield made of soft iron will reduce the magnetic field inside to a considerable extent but not completely. As discussed earlier, it is sometimes possible to superpose a field in the opposite direction to produce a very low field region and then to use additional material with a high μ for shielding. In the case of electromagnetic waves, the penetration of the waves in matter varies, depending on the frequency of the radiation and the electric conductivity of the medium. The skin depth δ

(which is the distance in the conducting medium traversed for an amplitude decrease of $1/e$, about $1/3$) is given by

$$\delta = \sqrt{\frac{2}{\omega \mu_0 \sigma_J}}\ .$$

At high frequency, the skin depth is small. Therefore, to transmit electronic messages through seawater, for example, a very low frequency must be used to get a reasonable fraction of the signal far below the surface.

A metal shield can have some holes in it and still be effective. For instance, a typical microwave oven has a frequency of 2.5 gigahertz, which corresponds to a wavelength of about 12 centimetres for the electromagnetic wave inside the oven. The metal shield on the door has small holes about two millimetres in diameter; the shield works because the wavelength of the microwave radiation is much greater than the size of the holes. On the other hand, the same shield is not effective with radiation of a much shorter wavelength. Visible light passes through the holes in the shield, as evidenced by the fact that it is possible to see inside a microwave oven when the door is closed.

ELECTROMAGNETS

An electromagnet is a device consisting of a core of magnetic material surrounded by a coil through which an electric current is passed to magnetize the core. An electromagnet is used wherever controllable magnets are required, as in contrivances in which the magnetic flux is to be varied, reversed, or switched on and off.

A magnetic circuit is a closed path to which a magnetic field, represented as lines of magnetic flux, is confined. In contrast to an electric circuit through which electric charge flows, nothing actually flows in a magnetic circuit.

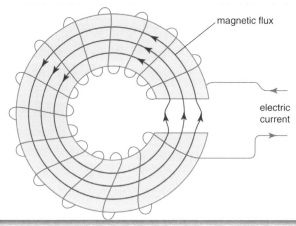

magnetic flux

electric
current

Magnetic circuit. Copyright Encyclopædia Britannica; rendering for this edition by Rosen Educational Services

In a ring-shaped electromagnet with a small air gap, the magnetic field or flux is almost entirely confined to the metal core and the air gap, which together form the magnetic circuit. In an electric motor, the magnetic field is largely confined to the magnetic pole pieces, the rotor, the air gaps between the rotor and the pole pieces, and the metal frame. Each magnetic field line makes a complete unbroken loop. All the lines together constitute the total flux. If the flux is divided, so that part of it is confined to a portion of the device and part to another, the magnetic circuit is called parallel. If all the flux is confined to a single closed loop, as in a ring-shaped electromagnet, the circuit is called a series magnetic circuit.

In analogy to an electric circuit in which the current, the electromotive force (voltage), and the resistance are related by Ohm's law (current equals electromotive force divided by resistance), a similar relation has been developed to describe a magnetic circuit.

The magnetic flux is analogous to the electric current. The magnetomotive force, mmf, is analogous to the electromotive force and may be considered the factor that sets up the flux. The mmf is equivalent to a number of turns of wire carrying an electric current and has units of ampere-turns. If either the current through a coil (as in an electromagnet) or the number of turns of wire in the coil is increased, the mmf is greater; and if the rest of the magnetic circuit remains the same, the magnetic flux increases proportionally.

The reluctance of a magnetic circuit is analogous to the resistance of an electric circuit. Reluctance depends on the geometrical and material properties of the circuit that offer opposition to the presence of magnetic flux. Reluctance of a given part of a magnetic circuit is proportional to its length and inversely proportional to its cross-sectional area and a magnetic property of the given material called its permeability. Iron, for example, has an extremely high permeability as compared to air so that it has a comparatively small reluctance, or it offers relatively little opposition to the presence of magnetic flux. In a series magnetic circuit, the total reluctance equals the sum of the individual reluctances encountered around the closed flux path. In a magnetic circuit, in summary, the magnetic flux is quantitatively equal to the magnetomotive force divided by the reluctance. These concepts of magnetic flux and reluctance can be employed to calculate the reluctance of a magnetic circuit and thus the current required through a coil to force the desired flux through this circuit.

Several assumptions involved in this type of calculation, however, make it at best only an approximate guide to design. The effect of a permeable medium on a magnetic field can be visualized as being to crowd the magnetic lines of force into itself. Conversely, the lines of force passing from a region of high to one of low permeability tend to spread out, and this occurrence will take place at an air gap. Thus the flux density, which is proportional to the number of lines of force per unit area, will be reduced in the air gap by the lines bulging out, or fringing, at the sides of the gap. This effect will increase for longer gaps; rough corrections can be made for taking the fringing effect into account.

It has also been assumed that the magnetic field is entirely confined within the coil. In fact, there is always a certain amount of leakage flux, represented by magnetic lines of force around the outside of the coil, which does not contribute to the magnetization of the core. The leakage flux is generally small if the permeability of the magnetic core is relatively high.

In practice, the permeability of a magnetic material is a function of the flux density in it. Thus, the calculation can only be done for a real material if the actual magnetization curve, or, more usefully, a graph of μ against B, is available.

Finally, the design assumes that the magnetic core is not magnetized to saturation. If it were, the flux density could not be increased in the air gap in this design, no matter how much current were passed through the coil. These concepts are expanded further in following sections on specific devices.

SOLENOIDS

A solenoid is generally a long coil through which current is flowing, establishing a magnetic field. More narrowly, the name has come to refer to an electromechanical device that produces a mechanical motion on being energized with an electric current. In its simplest form it consists of an iron frame enclosing the coil and a cylindrical plunger moving inside the coil. For an alternating current supply, the iron losses in a solid frame restrict the efficiency and a laminated frame is used, which is made up of a pile of thin sheets of iron cut to the appropriate shape and stacked with a layer of insulating varnish between each sheet. When the coil is energized, the plunger moves into the coil by virtue of the magnetic attraction between it and the frame until it makes contact with the frame.

Alternating-current solenoids tend to be more powerful in the fully open position than direct-current units. This occurs because the initial current, high because of the inductance of the coil, is lowered by the air gap between the plunger and frame. As the solenoid closes, this air gap decreases, the inductance of the coil increases, and the alternating current through it falls. If an alternating-current solenoid sticks in the open position the coil is likely to burn out.

When a solenoid is fully opened, it has a large air gap, and the high reluctance of this gap keeps the flux in the magnetic circuit low for a given magnetomotive force, and the force on the plunger is correspondingly low. As the plunger closes, the reluctance falls and the flux increases so that the force increases progressively. Manufacturers of solenoids provide force-stroke curves so that users can select the proper unit for their purpose. The curve can be

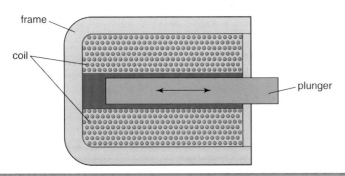

Elements of a solenoid. Copyright Encyclopædia Britannica; rendering for this edition by Rosen Educational Services

modified by spring loading the plunger so that the force provided throughout the stroke may be matched to the particular mechanical load.

RELAYS

A relay is a device in which the solenoid principle is applied to opening and closing light-current electrical circuits. The same device applied in heavy-current circuits is called a contactor, or circuit breaker.

Because the amount of mechanical movement required is generally small, the solenoid plunger is usually stationary, and part of the frame is hinged to give the necessary movement. When the coil is energized, the hinged part of the frame is attracted to the solid iron core in the coil; this attraction pushes the contacts together. When the energizing current is removed, the hinged part is forced back to the open position by the springiness of the contact.

With the appearance of transistorized switching circuits, which use remarkably low power, a need arose for a relay that would operate reliably with a power of 100 to 300 milliwatts, compared with 4 watts for the

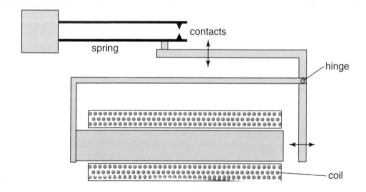

Elements of a relay. Copyright Encyclopædia Britannica; rendering for this edition by Rosen Educational Services

conventional relay. This need was met by the reed relay, or reed switch. It consists of two flat blades of 50–50 nickel–iron alloy that overlap with a gap between them. When a magnetic field is applied along the length of the blades, opposite magnetic poles are induced in the overlapping parts, and they are attracted together, making electrical contact. On removal of the field, the springiness of the contact blade opens the contact. The overlap region is plated on each blade with gold to ensure good electrical contact, and the enclosing glass capsule is filled with dry nitrogen to prevent corrosion. The field required to operate the device is a function of the amount of overlap, and there is an optimum overlap corresponding to minimum required operating current.

Present reed switches used in telephone equipment are operated by up to 50 volts direct current. Typically, the reed closes at 58 ampere-turns and releases at 15 ampere-turns, the hold current being 27 ampere-turns. The contact closes to give a stable contact resistance in 2 milliseconds, releases in 100 microseconds, and has a lifetime of more than 50,000,000 operations. Using a 35,000 turn coil the coil resistance is typically 18,600 ohms so that the current at 50 volts is 2.7 milliamperes. The minimum operating condition requires only about 1.7 milliamperes, so that the relay can be worked satisfactorily at lower voltage.

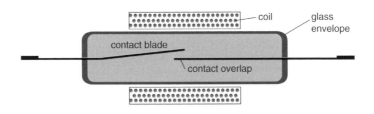

Elements of a reed relay. Copyright Encyclopædia Britannica; rendering for this edition by Rosen Educational Services

By the use of small, external, permanent magnets, reed switches can be made into latching relays that remain closed when the energizing field is removed. They can also be designed with three blades to give changeover contacts.

DESIGN OF LARGE ELECTROMAGNETS

Sooner or later almost every scientific research laboratory finds that it requires a facility for producing large magnetic fields. A number of advanced technologies likewise require large electromagnets. A cyclotron, for example, is a device used for scientific research in which subatomic charged particles are accelerated by an alternating electric field in a constant magnetic field. It uses a large magnet to produce moderate fields but with a pole diameter that may be several metres. Some industries make use of huge, high-powered electromagnets for lifting purposes.

The basic design principles of large electromagnets are those discussed earlier. The difficulties arise in trying to estimate the magnitude of the fringing flux across the air gap and the leakage flux around the coils. Their effects are minimized by using a tapered shape for the cores and pole cap. Because soft iron saturates at 2.16 webers per square metre, flux densities in the air gap are generally limited to the region of 2.1 webers per square metre with iron magnets.

When designed for lifting or load-carrying purposes, an electromagnet may be required to have a single exposed pole face to which the load to be carried will attach itself, and it will therefore have the shape of a bar magnet. The design is then dominated by the demagnetizing field. Suitably designed magnets can lift many times their own weight and are in general use in steelworks and scrapyards.

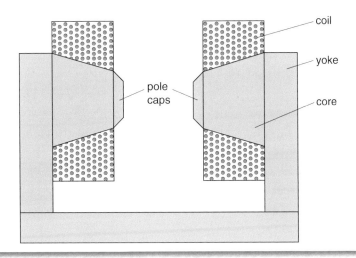

Elements of a typical electromagnet. Copyright Encyclopædia Britannica; rendering for this edition by Rosen Educational Services

PRINCIPAL APPLICATIONS

Electromagnets have a wide variety of uses. Modern telephone systems are based on the reed relay, together with solid-state circuits for complex routing of connections. The telephone receiver is basically an electromagnet with a U-shaped yoke having coils wound on each leg of the U. Passage of the electrical signal through the coils causes magnetic attraction of a soft-iron diaphragm supported a small distance from the ends of the U. The diaphragm is deflected by an amount proportional to the magnitude of the current in the coil and generates sound waves as it moves back and forth. Improvement in magnetic materials has increased the sensitivity of the telephone receiver, but the basic design has remained unchanged.

The loudspeaker performs the same function as the earphone of the telephone receiver but is required to displace a larger volume of air. The diaphragm comprises a flexible cone of large area carrying a coil of fine wire on a small ring located at its apex. The ring lies between the poles of a powerful cylindrically shaped permanent magnet. Audio-frequency current through the coil causes deflection of the diaphragm, as in the earphone. Modern loudspeakers are much more sensitive and efficient than their predecessors because of the improvement in permanent-magnet materials. The higher the flux density in the gap, the greater the sensitivity and the potential for fidelity of reproduction; modern loudspeakers use flux densities of up to one weber per square metre. Alloy magnets are usually used.

Magnetic fields supply a powerful research tool without which modern physics could scarcely have grown to its present extent. A major area of application is in the interaction of magnetic fields and charged subatomic particles. A moving particle that carries a charge, such as an electron, can be regarded as an electric current and, like a current-carrying wire, experiences a force in a magnetic field. The direction of the force is perpendicular both to the direction of motion of the particle and to the magnetic field, so that the particle is deflected from its original path. This principle can be used to focus a stream of electrons into a narrow beam and to deflect the beam by creating suitable magnetic fields, either from permanent magnets or from electromagnets. Every television receiver contains just such focusing and deflection systems to scan the face of the television tube with an electron beam.

In scientific applications the same principle is used in the electron microscope, in which the beam of electrons is passed through a series of magnetic "lenses," just as light is passed through glass lenses in a conventional microscope.

As noted above, the cyclotron makes use of a magnetic field to cause charged particles to execute a circular path. On each traverse of the circle they are accelerated and finally acquire enormous kinetic energy (energy of motion). The cyclotron has been an important tool in nuclear research and in the production of radioactive isotopes.

The same principle may be used to analyze materials in the mass spectrometer. The actual deflection of a moving charged particle in a magnetic field is determined by its charge, mass, and velocity. In a mass spectrometer the material under investigation is in the form of a gas of ionized particles that are accelerated by a fixed electric field. In passing through the magnetic field the particles are deflected by an amount determined by their mass, providing they all carry the same charge. By recording their arrival position at a fixed target, the mass of the particles can be deduced.

The electrical industry is founded on the generation and exploitation of magnetic fields. The electric motor is based on the force generated on a current-carrying conductor; the generator is based on the inverse effect that a conductor moving in a magnetic field has on a current induced in it. In general, high-flux densities are required in the magnetic circuits of motors and generators, and this requirement has led to the use of soft iron or silicon–iron electromagnets as the source of magnetic fields in them. With the advent of modern permanent-magnet materials, however, small direct-current motors, in which the field is provided by permanent magnets, are finding wide applications, particularly in the toy industry.

The principle of magnetic recording is to induce a permanent magnetization in a material by means of the signal to be recorded. The induced magnetization must be proportional to the amplitude of the signal and must remain in the material when the signal is removed. Thus, a magnetic material is required that has a high permeability, so that it will magnetize readily in a small field; a high remanent magnetization, so that the stored information can be easily "read"; and not too high (but not too low) a coercive force, so that the stored information can be erased without great difficulty.

CONCLUSION

This book examined electricity and magnetism, first as separate phenomena then as a unified whole as electromagnetism. Magnetic forces have been observed since ancient times, but it was not until William Gilbert in the Elizabethan age that the science of electricity and magnetism truly began. The study of electricity took off in 1800 with the invention of the battery. In 1820 Hans Christian Ørsted discovered that electricity and magnetism were linked, and toward the end of the 19th century, James Clerk Maxwell presented his famous equations that joined electricity and magnetism together.

Electricity is defined as being associated with a basic property of elementary particles called electric charge. If charged particles are stationary, then they can be described as affecting each other with an "inverse square" law in much the same way as particles with mass affect each other through gravitation. However, charge, unlike mass, comes in positive and negative varieties and thus can give rise to repulsive (between like charges) and attractive (between opposite charges) forces. When charged particles move, then the study of electricity becomes a study of currents.

Matter displays a wide variety of interesting electrical effects. In piezoelectricity some crystals become electrically polarized when squeezed. In electroluminescence, moving electrons can cause atoms in the material to radiate.

When electric charges move, magnetism arises. Magnetism can be seen arising from something as humble as a current flowing in a wire or from something as massive as the movement of Earth's core. As with electricity, the force between like magnetic poles is repulsive, and that between opposite magnetic poles is attractive.

Matter can be divided into paramagnetic and diamagnetic materials; that is, paramagnetic materials conduct magnetic forces well, whereas diamagnetics do not. In some cases the magnetization of a material depends on the temperature.

Many different kinds of materials can be used as magnets. Some magnets come in powdered form. Others are metallic alloys. Still others are sheets of iron with a small amount of silicon added.

In the study of electromagnetism, the separate phenomena of electricity and magnetism are understood as two sides of the same coin. Devices called electromagnets use both electricity and magnetism and are vital parts of many devices from telephones to particle accelerators.

CHAPTER 6
BIOGRAPHIES

I n this section biographies of some of the notable people who studied electricity and magnetism are presented. Hundreds of years of scientific progress are represented, from Peter Peregrinus of Maricourt, the 13th-century soldier who wrote the first book about magnets, to Louis-Eugène-Félix Néel, the 20th-century physicist who studied the different varieties of magnetism.

ANDRÉ-MARIE AMPÈRE

(b. Jan. 22, 1775, Lyon, France—d. June 10, 1836, Marseille)

French physicist André-Marie Ampère founded and named the science of electrodynamics, now known as electromagnetism. His name endures in everyday life in the ampere, the unit for measuring electric current.

Born into a prosperous bourgeois family during the height of the French Enlightenment, Ampère personified the scientific culture of his day. His father, Jean-Jacques Ampère, was a successful merchant, and also an admirer of the philosophy of Jean-Jacques Rousseau, whose theories of education, as outlined in his treatise *Émile*, were the basis of Ampère's education. Rousseau argued that young boys should avoid formal schooling and pursue instead an "education direct from nature." Ampère's father actualized this ideal by allowing his son to educate himself within the walls of his well-stocked library. French Enlightenment masterpieces such as Georges-Louis Leclerc, comte de Buffon's *Histoire naturelle, générale et particulière* (begun in 1749) and Denis Diderot and Jean Le Rond d'Alembert's

Encyclopédie (volumes added between 1751 and 1772) thus became Ampère's schoolmasters. In addition, he used his access to the latest mathematical books to begin teaching himself advanced mathematics at age 12.

His mother was a devout woman, so Ampère was also initiated into the Catholic faith along with Enlightenment science. The French Revolution (1787–99) that erupted during his youth was also formative. Ampère's father was called

André-Marie Ampère, detail of an oil painting by an unknown artist. The Mansell Collection

into public service by the new revolutionary government, becoming a justice of the peace in a small town near Lyon. Yet when the Jacobin faction seized control of the Revolutionary government in 1792, Jean-Jacques Ampère resisted the new political tides, and he was guillotined on Nov. 24, 1793, as part of the Jacobin purges of the period.

While the French Revolution brought these personal traumas, it also created new institutions of science that ultimately became central to André-Marie Ampère's professional success. He took his first regular job in 1799 as a modestly paid mathematics teacher, which gave him the financial security to marry and father his first child, Jean-Jacques, the next year. (Jean-Jacques Ampère eventually achieved his own fame as a scholar of languages.) Ampère's maturation corresponded with the transition to the Napoleonic regime in France, and the young father and teacher found new opportunities for success within the technocratic structures favoured by the new French emperor.

In 1802 Ampère was appointed a professor of physics and chemistry at the École Centrale in Bourg-en-Bresse. He used his time in Bourg to research mathematics, producing *Considérations sur la théorie mathématique de jeu* (1802; "Considerations on the Mathematical Theory of Games"), a treatise on mathematical probability that he sent to the Paris Academy of Sciences in 1803. After the death of his wife in July 1803, Ampère moved to Paris, where he assumed a tutoring post at the new École Polytechnique in 1804. Despite his lack of formal qualifications, Ampère was appointed a professor of mathematics at the school in 1809. In addition to holding positions at this school until 1828, in 1819 and 1820 Ampère offered courses in philosophy and astronomy, respectively, at the University of Paris, and in 1824 he was elected to the prestigious chair in experimental physics at the Collège de France. In 1814 Ampère was invited to join the class of mathematicians in the new Institut Impériale, the umbrella under which the reformed state Academy of Sciences would sit.

Ampère engaged in a diverse array of scientific inquiries during these years leading up to his election to the academy—writing papers and engaging in topics ranging from mathematics and philosophy to chemistry and astronomy. Such breadth was customary among the leading scientific intellectuals of the day.

Had Ampère died before 1820, his name and work would likely have been forgotten. In that year, however, Ampère's friend and eventual eulogist François Arago demonstrated before the members of the French Academy of Sciences the surprising discovery of Danish physicist Hans Christiaan Ørsted that a magnetic needle is deflected by an adjacent electric current.

Ampère was well prepared to throw himself fully into this new line of research. He immediately set to work developing a mathematical and physical theory to understand the relationship between electricity and magnetism. Extending Ørsted's experimental work, Ampère showed that two parallel wires carrying electric currents repel or attract each other, depending on whether the currents flow in the same or opposite directions, respectively. He also applied mathematics in generalizing physical laws from these experimental results. Most important was the principle that came to be called Ampère's law, which states that the mutual action of two lengths of current-carrying wire is proportional to their lengths and to the intensities of their currents. Ampère also applied this same principle to magnetism, showing the harmony between his law and French physicist Charles Augustin de Coulomb's law of magnetic action. Ampère's devotion to, and skill with, experimental techniques anchored his science within the emerging fields of experimental physics.

Ampère also offered a physical understanding of the electromagnetic relationship, theorizing the existence of an "electrodynamic molecule" (the forerunner of the idea of the electron) that served as the constituent element of electricity and magnetism. Using this physical understanding of electromagnetic motion, Ampère developed a physical account of electromagnetic phenomena that was both empirically demonstrable and mathematically predictive. In 1827 Ampère published his magnum opus, *Mémoire sur la théorie mathématique des phénomènes électrodynamiques uniquement déduite de l'experience* (*Memoir on the Mathematical Theory of Electrodynamic Phenomena, Uniquely Deduced from Experience*), the work that coined the name of his new science, electrodynamics, and became known ever after as its founding treatise. In recognition of his contribution to the making of modern electrical science, an international convention signed in 1881 established the ampere as a standard unit of electrical measurement, along with the coulomb, volt, ohm, and watt, which are named, respectively, after Ampère's contemporaries Coulomb, Alessandro Volta of Italy, Georg Ohm of Germany, and James Watt of Scotland.

The 1827 publication of Ampère's synoptic *Mémoire* brought to a close his feverish work over the previous seven years on the new science of electrodynamics. The text also marked the end of his original scientific work. His health began to fail, and he died while performing a university inspection, decades before his new science was canonized as the foundation stone for the modern science of electromagnetism.

FRANÇOIS ARAGO

(b. Feb. 26, 1786, Estagel, Roussillon, France—d. Oct. 2, 1853, Paris)

French physicist Dominique-François-Jean Arago discovered the principle of the production of magnetism by rotation of a nonmagnetic conductor. He also devised an experiment that proved the wave theory of light and engaged with others in research that led to the discovery of the laws of light polarization.

Arago was educated in Perpignan and at the École Polytechnique, Paris, where, at the age of 23, he succeeded Gaspard Monge in the chair of analytic geometry. Subsequently he was director of the Paris Observatory and permanent secretary of the Academy of Sciences. He was also active as a republican in French politics. As minister of war and marine in the provisional government formed after the Revolution of 1848, he introduced many reforms.

In 1820, elaborating on the work of H.C. Ørsted of Denmark, Arago showed that the passage of an electric current through a cylindrical spiral of copper wire caused it to attract iron filings as if it were a magnet and that the filings

François Arago, portrait on a commemorative medal. Photos.com/Jupiterimages

fell off when the current ceased. In 1824 he demonstrated that a rotating copper disk produced rotation in a magnetic needle suspended above it. Michael Faraday later proved these to be induction phenomena.

Arago supported Augustin-Jean Fresnel's wave theory of light against the emission theory favoured by Pierre-Simon Laplace, Jean-Baptiste Biot, and Siméon-Denis Poisson. According to the wave theory, light should be retarded as it passes from a rarer to a denser medium; according to the emission theory, it should be accelerated. Arago's test for comparing the velocity of light in air and in water or glass was described in 1838, but the experiment required such elaborate preparation that Arago was not ready to perform it until 1850, when his sight failed. Before his death, however, the retardation of light in denser media was demonstrated by Armand-Hippolyte-Louis Fizeau and Léon Foucault, who used his method with improvements in detail.

In astronomy, Arago is best known for his part in the dispute between Urbain-Jean-Joseph Le Verrier, who was his protégé, and the English astronomer John C. Adams over priority in discovering the planet Neptune and over the naming of the planet. Arago had suggested in 1845 that Le Verrier investigate anomalies in the motion of Uranus. When the investigation resulted in Le Verrier's discovery of Neptune, Arago proposed that the newly found planet be named for Le Verrier.

JEAN-BAPTISTE BIOT

(b. April 21, 1774, Paris, France—d. Feb. 3, 1862, Paris)

Jean-Baptiste Biot was a French physicist who helped formulate the Biot-Savart law, which concerns magnetic fields, and laid the basis for saccharimetry, a useful technique of analyzing sugar solutions.

Educated at the École Polytechnique, Biot was appointed professor of mathematics at the University of Beauvais in 1797, became professor of mathematical physics at the Collège de France in 1800, and was elected a member of the French Academy of Sciences in 1803. He accompanied Joseph-Louis Gay-Lussac in 1804 on the first balloon flight undertaken for scientific purposes. The men showed that Earth's magnetic field does not vary noticeably with altitude, and they tested upper atmospheric composition. Biot also collaborated with the noted physicist Dominique-François-Jean Arago in investigating the refractive properties of gases.

In 1820 he and the physicist Félix Savart discovered that the intensity of the magnetic field set up by a current flowing through a wire is inversely proportional to the distance from the wire. This relationship is now known as the Biot-Savart law and is a fundamental part of modern electromagnetic theory. In 1835, while studying polarized light (light having all its waves in the

Jean-Baptiste Biot. H. Roger-Viollet

same plane), Biot found that sugar solutions, among others, rotate the plane of polarization when a polarized light beam passes through. Further research revealed that the angle of rotation is a direct measure of the concentration of the solution. This fact became important in chemical analysis because it provided a simple, nondestructive way of determining sugar concentration. For this work Biot was awarded the Rumford Medal of the Royal Society in 1840.

Among his voluminous writings, the most important work was *Traité élémentaire d'astronomie physique* (1805; "Elementary Treatise on Physical Astronomy"). He was made a member of the French Academy in 1856.

CHARLES-AUGUSTIN DE COULOMB

(b. June 14, 1736, Angoulême, France—d. Aug. 23, 1806, Paris)

French physicist Charles-Augustin de Coulomb is best known for the formulation of Coulomb's law, which states that the force between two electrical charges is proportional to the product of the charges and inversely proportional to the square of the distance between them. Coulombic force is one of the principal forces involved in atomic reactions.

Coulomb spent nine years in the West Indies as a military engineer and returned to France with impaired health. Upon the outbreak of the French Revolution, he retired to a small estate at Blois and devoted himself to scientific research. In 1802 he was appointed an inspector of public instruction.

Coulomb developed his law as an outgrowth of his attempt to investigate the law of electrical repulsions as stated by Joseph Priestley of England. To this end he invented sensitive apparatus to measure the electrical forces involved in Priestley's law and published his findings in 1785–89. He also established the inverse square law of attraction and repulsion of unlike and like magnetic poles, which became the basis for the mathematical theory of magnetic forces developed by Siméon-Denis Poisson. He also did research on friction of machinery, on windmills, and on the elasticity of metal and silk fibres. The coulomb, a unit of electric charge, was named in his honour.

Charles-Augustin de Coulomb, detail of a bronze bust. H. Roger-Viollet

MICHAEL FARADAY

(b. Sept. 22, 1791, Newington, Surrey, Eng. — d. Aug. 25, 1867, Hampton Court)

English physicist Michael Faraday's many experiments contributed greatly to the understanding of electromagnetism.

Faraday received only the rudiments of an education. At the age of 14 he was apprenticed to a bookbinder. Faraday read some of the books brought in for rebinding. The article on electricity in the third edition of the *Encyclopædia Britannica* particularly fascinated him. He made a crude electrostatic generator and did simple experiments.

Faraday's great opportunity came when he was offered a ticket to attend chemical lectures by Sir Humphry Davy. He sent his notes to Davy along with a letter asking for employment, but there was no opening. Davy did not forget, however, and, when one of his laboratory assistants was dismissed for brawling, he offered Faraday a job.

Faraday's apprenticeship, under Davy, came to an end in 1820, and he achieved his early renown as a chemist. In 1820

Michael Faraday, oil on canvas by Thomas Phillips, 1841–42; in the National Portrait Gallery, London. Courtesy of The National Portrait Gallery, London

he produced the first known compounds of carbon and chlorine. In 1825, Faraday isolated and described benzene.

In 1820 Hans Christian Ørsted discovered that electric current flowing through a wire produced a magnetic field around the wire. André-Marie Ampère showed that the magnetic force was circular, producing in effect a cylinder of magnetism around the wire. No such circular force had been observed before, and Faraday was the first to understand what it implied. If a magnetic pole could be isolated, it ought to move constantly in a circle around a current-carrying wire. Faraday constructed an apparatus that confirmed this conclusion. This device, which transformed electrical energy into mechanical energy, was the first electric motor.

This discovery led Faraday to contemplate the nature of electricity. Unlike his contemporaries, he was not convinced that electricity was a material fluid that flowed through wires like water through a pipe. Instead, he thought of it as a vibration or force that was somehow transmitted as the result of tensions created in the conductor.

On Aug. 29, 1831, Faraday wound a thick iron ring on one side with insulated wire that was connected to a battery. He then wound the opposite side with wire connected to a galvanometer. He expected that a "wave" would be produced when the battery circuit was closed and that the wave would show up as a deflection of the galvanometer in the second circuit. He closed the primary circuit and saw the galvanometer needle jump. A current had been induced in the secondary coil by one in the primary. When he opened the circuit, however, he was astonished to see the galvanometer jump in the opposite direction. Somehow, turning off the current also created an induced current in the secondary circuit, equal and opposite to the original current. This phenomenon led Faraday to propose what he called the "electrotonic" state of particles in the wire, which he considered a state of tension. A current thus was the setting up of such a state of tension or the collapse of such a state. Although he could not find experimental evidence for the electrotonic state, he never entirely abandoned the concept, and it shaped most of his later work.

In the fall of 1831 Faraday attempted to determine how an induced current was produced. He now tried to create a current by using a permanent magnet. He discovered that when a permanent magnet was moved in and out of a coil of wire a current was induced in the coil. Magnets, he knew, were surrounded by forces that could be made visible by the simple expedient of sprinkling iron filings on a card held over them. Faraday saw the "lines of force" thus revealed as lines of tension in the medium, namely air, surrounding the magnet, and he soon discovered the law determining the production of electric currents by magnets: the magnitude of the current was dependent upon the number of lines of force cut by the conductor in unit time. He immediately realized that a continuous current could be produced by rotating a copper disk between the poles of a powerful magnet and taking leads off the disk's rim and centre. The outside of the disk would cut more lines than would the inside, and there would thus be a continuous current produced in the circuit linking the rim to the centre. This was the first dynamo, and it was also the direct ancestor of electric motors.

By 1839 Faraday proposed a new theory of electrical action. Electricity caused tensions to be created in matter. When these tensions were rapidly relieved, then a rapid repetition of a cyclical buildup, breakdown, and buildup of tension was passed along the substance. Such substances were called conductors. Insulators were simply materials whose particles could take an extraordinary amount of strain before they snapped. Thus, all electrical action was the result of forced strains in bodies.

In 1845 Faraday again tackled the problem of his hypothetical electrotonic state. It was at this time that a young Scot, William Thomson (later Lord Kelvin), wrote Faraday that he had studied Faraday's papers on electricity and magnetism and that he, too, was convinced that some kind of strain must exist. He suggested that Faraday experiment with magnetic lines of force, since these could be produced at much greater strengths than could electrostatic ones.

Faraday took the suggestion, passed a beam of plane-polarized light through the optical glass of high refractive index that he had developed in the 1820s, and then turned on an electromagnet so that its lines of force ran parallel to the light ray. This time he was rewarded with success. The plane of polarization was rotated, indicating a strain in the molecules of the glass. But Faraday again noted an unexpected result. When he changed the direction of the ray of light, the rotation remained in the same direction, a fact that Faraday correctly interpreted as meaning that the strain was not in the molecules of the glass but in the magnetic lines of force. The direction of rotation of the plane of polarization depended solely upon the polarity of the lines of force; the glass served merely to detect the effect.

This discovery confirmed Faraday's faith in the unity of forces, and he was certain that all matter must exhibit some response to a magnetic field. He found that this was in fact so, but in a peculiar way. Some substances, such as iron and oxygen, lined up in a magnetic field so that the long axes of their crystalline or molecular structures were parallel to the lines of force; others lined up perpendicular to the lines of force. Faraday named the first group paramagnetics and the second diamagnetics. He concluded that paramagnetics conducted magnetic lines of force better than did the surrounding medium, whereas diamagnetics conducted them less well.

From about 1855, Faraday's mind began to fail. He died in 1867, leaving as his monument a new conception of physical reality.

LUIGI GALVANI

(b. Sept. 9, 1737, Bologna, Papal States [Italy] — d. Dec. 4, 1798, Bologna, Cisalpine Republic)

Luigi Galvani was an Italian physician and physicist who investigated the nature and effects of what he conceived to be electricity in animal tissue. His discoveries led to the invention of the voltaic pile, a kind of battery that makes possible a constant source of current electricity.

Galvani followed his father's preference for medicine by attending the University of Bologna, graduating in 1759. On obtaining the doctor of medicine degree, with a thesis (1762) *De ossibus* on the formation and development of bones, he was appointed lecturer in anatomy at the University of Bologna and professor of obstetrics at the separate Institute of Arts and Sciences. In 1762, also, he married Lucia, the only daughter of Professor Galeazzi of the Bologna Academy of Science, of which Galvani became president in 1772.

Beginning with his doctoral thesis, his early research was in comparative anatomy—such as the structure of renal tubules, nasal mucosa, and the middle ear—with a tendency toward physiology, a direction appropriate to the later work for which he is noted. Galvani's developing interest was indicated by his lectures on the anatomy of the frog in 1773 and in electrophysiology in the late 1770s, when, following the acquisition of an electrostatic machine (a large device for making sparks) and a Leyden jar (a device used to store static electricity), he began to experiment with muscular stimulation by electrical means. His notebooks indicate that, from the early 1780s, animal electricity remained his major field of investigation.

Numerous ingenious observations and experiments have been credited to him. For example, in 1786, he obtained muscular contraction in a frog by touching its nerves with a pair of scissors during an electrical storm. Again, a visitor to his laboratory caused the legs of a skinned frog to kick when a scalpel touched a lumbar nerve of the animal while an electrical machine was activated. Galvani assured himself by further experiments that the twitching was, in fact, related to the electrical action. He also elicited twitching without the aid of the electrostatic machine by pressing a copper hook into a frog's spinal cord and hanging the hook on an iron railing. Although twitching could occur during a lightning storm or with the aid of an electrostatic machine, it also occurred with only a metallic contact between leg muscles and nerves leading to them. A metallic arc connecting the two tissues could therefore be a substitute for the electrostatic machine.

Galvani delayed the announcement of his findings until 1791, when he published his essay *De Viribus Electricitatis in Motu Musculari Commentarius* (*Commentary on the Effect of Electricity on Muscular Motion*). He concluded that animal tissue contained a heretofore neglected innate, vital force, which he termed "animal electricity," which activated nerve and muscle when spanned by metal probes. He believed that this new force was a form of electricity in addition to the "natural" form that is produced by lightning or by the electric eel and torpedo ray and to the "artificial" form that is produced by friction (i.e., static electricity). He considered the brain to be the most important organ for the secretion of this "electric fluid" and the nerves to be conductors of the fluid to

Galvani, detail of an engraving by A. Marchi after a drawing by F. Spagnoli. Courtesy of the Muséum National d'Histoire Naturelle, Paris

the nerve and muscle, the tissues of which act as did the outer and inner surfaces of the Leyden jar. The flow of this electric fluid provided a stimulus for the irritable muscle fibres, according to his explanation.

Galvani's scientific colleagues generally accepted his views, but Alessandro Volta, the outstanding professor of physics at the University of Pavia, was not convinced by the analogy between the muscle and the Leyden jar. Deciding that the frog's legs served only as an indicating electroscope, he held that the contact of dissimilar metals was the true source of stimulation; he referred to the electricity so generated as "metallic electricity" and decided that the muscle, by contracting when touched by metal, resembled the action of an electroscope. Furthermore, Volta said that, if two dissimilar metals in contact both touched a muscle, agitation would also occur and increase with the dissimilarity of the metals.

Thus Volta rejected the idea of an "animal electric fluid," replying that the frog's legs responded to differences in metal temper, composition, and bulk. Galvani refuted this by obtaining muscular action with two pieces of the same material. But the ensuing controversy was without personal animosity; Galvani's gentle nature and Volta's high principles precluded any harshness between them. Volta, who coined the term galvanism, said of Galvani's work that "it contains one of the most beautiful and most surprising discoveries." Nevertheless, partisan groups rallied to both sides.

In retrospect, Galvani and Volta are both seen to have been partly right and partly wrong. Galvani was correct in attributing muscular contractions to an electrical stimulus but wrong in identifying it as an "animal electricity." Volta correctly denied the existence of an "animal electricity" but was wrong in implying that every electrophysiological effect requires two different metals as sources of current. Galvani, shrinking from the controversy over his discovery, continued his work as teacher, obstetrician, and surgeon, treating both wealthy and needy without regard to fee. In 1794 he offered a defense of his position in an anonymous book, *Dell'uso e dell'atti vità dell'arco conduttore nella contrazione dei muscoli* ("On the Use and Activity of the Conductive Arch in the Contraction of Muscles"), the supplement of which described muscular contraction without the need of any metal. He caused a muscle to contract by touching the exposed muscle of one frog with a nerve of another and thus established for the first time that bioelectric forces exist within living tissue.

On June 30, 1790, Galvani's devoted wife and companion died, childless, at the age of 47. In the last years of his life, Galvani refused to swear allegiance to the new Cisalpine Republic established by Napoleon. Thereupon he was dropped from the faculty rolls, and his salary was terminated. Rejecting help and much saddened, he moved into the old Galvani home in which his brother was living. Soon, however, the politicians recanted, and the professorship was again offered to Galvani without the requirement of an oath. But the affront had cut short his days: Galvani died in the house of his birth at age 61, at a time when the world was on the threshold of the great electrical revolution.

Galvani provided the major stimulus for Volta to discover a source of constant current electricity; this was the voltaic pile, or a battery, with its principles of operation combined from chemistry and physics. This discovery led to the subsequent age of electric power. Moreover, Galvani opened the way to new research in the physiology of muscle and nerve and to the entire subject of electrophysiology.

WILLIAM GILBERT

(b. May 24, 1544, Colchester, Essex, Eng. — d. Dec. 10 [Nov. 30, Old Style], 1603, London or Colchester)

William Gilbert was a pioneer researcher into magnetism who became the most distinguished man of science in England during the reign of Queen Elizabeth I.

Educated as a physician, Gilbert settled in London and began to practice in 1573. His principal work, *De Magnete, Magneticisque Corporibus, et de Magno Magnete Tellure* (1600; *On the Magnet, Magnetic Bodies, and the Great Magnet of the Earth*), gives a full account of his research on magnetic bodies and electrical attractions. After years of experiments he concluded that a compass needle points north–south and dips downward because Earth acts as a bar magnet. The first to use the terms electric attraction, electric force, and magnetic pole, he is often considered the father of electrical studies.

In 1601 Gilbert was appointed physician to Queen Elizabeth I, and upon her death in 1603 was appointed physician to King James I. He left an unpublished work that was edited by his brother from two manuscripts and published posthumously in 1651 as *De Mundo Nostro Sublunari Philosophia Nova* ("A New Philosophy of Our Sublunar World"). He held modern views on the structure of the universe, agreeing with Copernicus that Earth rotates on its axis. He concluded that fixed stars are not all the same distance from Earth and believed that the planets were held in their orbits by a form of magnetism.

JOSEPH HENRY

(b. Dec. 17, 1797, Albany, N.Y., U.S.—d. May 13, 1878, Washington, D.C.)

Joseph Henry was one of the first great American scientists after Benjamin Franklin. He aided Samuel F.B. Morse in the development of the telegraph and discovered several important principles of electricity, including self-induction, a phenomenon of primary importance in electronic circuitry.

While working with electromagnets at the Albany Academy (New York) in 1829, he made important design improvements. By insulating the wire instead of the iron core, he was able to wrap a large number of turns of wire around the core and thus greatly increase the power of the magnet. He made an electromagnet for Yale College that could support 2,086 pounds, a world record at the time. During these studies he first noticed the principle of self-induction (1832), three years after he devised and constructed the first electric motor.

Although Michael Faraday is given credit for discovering electromagnetic induction—the process of converting magnetism into electricity—because he was the first to publish (1831) his results, Henry had observed the phenomenon a year earlier.

In 1831 Henry built and successfully operated, over a distance of one mile, a telegraph of his own design. He became professor of natural philosophy at the College of New Jersey (later Princeton University) in 1832. Continuing his researches, he discovered the laws upon which the transformer is based. He also found that currents could be induced at a distance and in one case magnetized a needle by utilizing a lightning flash eight miles away. This experiment was apparently the first use of radio waves across a distance. By using a thermogalvanometer, a heat-detection device, he showed that sunspots radiate less heat than the general solar surface.

In 1846 Henry became the first secretary of the Smithsonian Institution, Washington, D.C., where he organized and supported a corps of volunteer weather observers. The success of the Smithsonian meteorological work led to the creation of the U.S. Weather Bureau (later Service). One of Lincoln's chief technical advisers during the U.S. Civil War, he was a primary organizer of the National Academy of Science and its second president. In 1893 his name was given to the standard electrical unit of inductive resistance, the henry.

FLEEMING JENKIN

(b. March 25, 1833, near Dungeness, Kent, Eng.—d. June 12, 1885, Edinburgh, Scot.)

British engineer Henry Charles Fleeming Jenkin was noted for his work in establishing units of electrical measurement.

Jenkin earned the M.A. from the University of Genoa in 1851 and worked for the next 10 years with engineering firms engaged in the design and manufacture of submarine telegraph cables and equipment for laying them. In 1861 his friend William Thomson (later Lord Kelvin) procured Jenkin's appointment as reporter for the Committee of Electrical Standards of the British Association for the Advancement of Science. He helped compile and publish reports that established the ohm as the absolute unit of electrical resistance and described methods for precise resistance measurements. Jenkin was also professor of engineering at University College, London, and the University of Edinburgh.

GUSTAV ROBERT KIRCHHOFF

(b. March 12, 1824, Königsberg, Prussia [now Kaliningrad, Russia]—d. Oct. 17, 1887, Berlin, Ger.)

German physicist Gustav Robert Kirchhoff, with the chemist Robert Bunsen, firmly established the theory of spectrum analysis (a technique for chemical analysis by analyzing the light emitted by a heated material), which Kirchhoff applied to determine the composition of the Sun.

In 1845 Kirchhoff first announced Kirchhoff's laws, which allow calculation of the currents, voltages, and resistances of electrical networks. Extending the theory of the German physicist Georg Simon Ohm, he generalized the equations describing current flow to the case of electrical conductors in three dimensions. In further studies he

Gustav Robert Kirchhoff. Historia-Photo

demonstrated that current flows through a conductor at the speed of light.

In 1847 Kirchhoff became *Privatdozent* (unsalaried lecturer) at the University of Berlin and three years later accepted the post of extraordinary professor of physics at the University of Breslau. In 1854 he was appointed professor of physics at the University of Heidelberg, where he joined forces with Bunsen and founded spectrum analysis. They demonstrated that every element gives off a characteristic coloured light when heated to incandescence. This light, when separated by a prism, has a pattern of individual wavelengths specific for each element. Applying this new research tool, they discovered two new elements, cesium (1860) and rubidium (1861).

Kirchhoff went further to apply spectrum analysis to study the composition of the Sun. He found that when light passes through a gas, the gas absorbs those wavelengths that it would emit if heated. He used this principle to explain the numerous dark lines (Fraunhofer lines) in the Sun's spectrum. That discovery marked the beginning of a new era in astronomy.

In 1875 Kirchhoff was appointed to the chair of mathematical physics at the University of Berlin. Most notable of his published works are *Vorlesungen über mathematische Physik* (4 vol., 1876–94; "Lectures on Mathematical Physics") and *Gesammelte Abhandlungen* (1882; supplement, 1891; "Collected Essays").

JAMES CLERK MAXWELL

(b. June 13, 1831, Edinburgh, Scot.—d. Nov. 5, 1879, Cambridge, Cambridgeshire, Eng.)

James Clerk Maxwell was a Scottish physicist best known for his formulation of electromagnetic theory. He is regarded by most modern physicists as the scientist of the 19th century who had the greatest influence on 20th-century physics, and he is ranked with Sir Isaac Newton and Albert Einstein for the fundamental nature of his contributions.

The concept of electromagnetic radiation originated with Maxwell, and his field equations, based on Michael Faraday's observations of the electric and magnetic lines of force, paved the way for Einstein's special theory of relativity, which established the equivalence of mass and energy. Maxwell's ideas also ushered in the other major innovation of 20th-century physics, the quantum theory. His description of electromagnetic radiation led to the development (according to classical theory) of the ultimately unsatisfactory law of heat radiation, which prompted Max Planck's formulation of the quantum hypothesis—i.e., the theory that radiant-heat energy is emitted only in finite amounts, or quanta. The interaction between electromagnetic radiation and matter, integral to Planck's hypothesis, in turn has played a central role in the development of the theory of the structure of atoms and molecules.

Maxwell came from a comfortable middle-class background. A dull and uninspired tutor was engaged who claimed that James was slow at learning, though in fact he displayed a lively curiosity at an early age and had a phenomenal memory. Fortunately he was rescued by his aunt Jane Cay and from 1841 was sent to school at the Edinburgh Academy.

Maxwell's interests ranged far beyond the school syllabus, and he did not pay particular attention to examination performance. His first scientific paper, published when he was only 14 years old, described a generalized series of oval curves that could be traced with pins and thread by analogy with an ellipse. This fascination with geometry and with mechanical models continued throughout his career and was of great help in his subsequent research.

At age 16 he entered the University of Edinburgh, where he read voraciously on all subjects and published two more scientific papers. In 1850 he went to the University of Cambridge, where his exceptional powers began to be recognized. His mathematics teacher, William Hopkins, was a well-known "wrangler maker" (a wrangler is one who takes first-class honours in the mathematics examinations at Cambridge). Of Maxwell, Hopkins is reported to have said that he was the most extraordinary man he had ever met and that it seemed impossible for him to think wrongly on any physical subject.

In 1854 Maxwell was second wrangler. He was elected to a fellowship at Trinity, but, because his father's health was deteriorating, he wished to return to Scotland. In 1856 he was appointed to the professorship of natural philosophy at Marischal College, Aberdeen, but before the appointment was announced his father died. This was a great personal loss, for Maxwell had had a close relationship with his father.

In 1860 the University of Aberdeen was formed by a merger between King's College and Marischal College, and Maxwell was declared redundant. He then was appointed to the professorship of natural philosophy at King's College, London.

The next five years were undoubtedly the most fruitful of his career. During this period his two classic papers on the electromagnetic field were published, and his demonstration of colour photography took place. He was elected to the Royal Society in 1861. His theoretical and experimental work on the viscosity of gases also was undertaken during these years and culminated in a lecture to the Royal Society in 1866. He supervised the experimental determination of electrical units for the British Association for the Advancement of Science, and this work in measurement and standardization led to the establishment of the

National Physical Laboratory. He also measured the ratio of electromagnetic and electrostatic units of electricity and confirmed that it was in satisfactory agreement with the velocity of light as predicted by his theory.

It was Maxwell's research on electromagnetism that established him among the great scientists of history. In the preface to his *Treatise on Electricity and Magnetism* (1873), the best exposition of his theory, Maxwell stated that his major task was to convert Faraday's physical ideas into mathematical form. In attempting to illustrate Faraday's law of induction (that a changing magnetic field gives rise to an induced electromagnetic field), Maxwell constructed a mechanical model. He found that the model gave rise to a corresponding "displacement current" in the dielectric medium, which could then be the seat of transverse waves. On calculating the velocity of these waves, he found that they were very close to the velocity of light. Maxwell concluded that he could "scarcely avoid the inference that light consists in the transverse undulations of the same medium which is the cause of electric and magnetic phenomena."

Maxwell's theory suggested that electromagnetic waves could be generated in a laboratory, a possibility first demonstrated by Heinrich Hertz in 1887, eight years after Maxwell's death. The resulting radio industry with its many applications thus has its origin in Maxwell's publications.

In addition to his electromagnetic theory, Maxwell made major contributions to other areas of physics. While still in his 20s, he demonstrated his mastery of classical physics by writing a prizewinning essay on Saturn's rings, in which he concluded that the rings must consist of masses of matter not mutually coherent—a conclusion that was corroborated more than 100 years later by the first Voyager space probe to reach Saturn.

In addition to these well-known contributions, a number of ideas that Maxwell put forward quite casually have since led to developments of great significance. The hypothetical intelligent being known as Maxwell's demon was a factor in the development of information theory. Maxwell's analytic treatment of speed governors is generally regarded as the founding paper on cybernetics, and his "equal areas" construction provided an essential constituent of the theory of fluids developed by Johannes Diederik van der Waals. His work in geometrical optics led to the discovery of the fish-eye lens. From the start of his career to its finish, his papers are filled with novelty and interest. He also was a contributor to the ninth edition of *Encyclopædia Britannica*.

In 1871 Maxwell was elected to the new Cavendish professorship at Cambridge. During the Easter term of 1879 Maxwell took ill on several occasions; he returned to Glenlair in June, but his condition did not improve. He died on November 5, after a short illness. Maxwell received no public honours and was buried quietly in a small churchyard in the village of Parton, in Scotland.

LOUIS-EUGÈNE-FÉLIX NÉEL

(b. Nov. 22, 1904, Lyon, France—d. Nov. 17, 2000, Brive-Corrèze)

French physicist Louis-Eugène-Félix Néel was corecipient, with the Swedish astrophysicist Hannes Alfvén, of the Nobel Prize for Physics in 1970 for his pioneering studies of the magnetic properties of solids. His contributions to solid-state physics have found numerous useful applications, particularly in the development of improved computer memory units.

Néel attended the École Normale Supérieure in Paris and the University of Strasbourg (Ph.D., 1932), where he studied under Pierre-Ernest Weiss and first began researching magnetism. He was a professor at the universities of Strasbourg (1937–45) and Grenoble (1945–76), and in 1956 he founded the Center for Nuclear Studies in Grenoble, serving as its director until 1971. Néel also was director (1971–76) of the Polytechnic Institute in Grenoble.

During the early 1930s Néel studied, on the molecular level, forms of magnetism that differ from ferromagnetism. In ferromagnetism, the most common variety of magnetism, the electrons line up (or spin) in the same direction at low temperatures. He discovered that, in some substances, alternating groups of atoms align their electrons in opposite directions (much as when two identical magnets are placed together with opposite poles aligned), thus neutralizing the net magnetic effect. This magnetic property is called antiferromagnetism. Néel's studies of fine-grain ferromagnetics provided an explanation for the unusual magnetic memory of certain mineral deposits that has provided information on changes in the direction and strength of Earth's magnetic field.

Néel wrote more than 200 works on various aspects of magnetism. Mainly because of his contributions, ferromagnetic materials can be manufactured to almost any specifications for technical applications, and a flood of new synthetic ferrite materials has revolutionized microwave electronics.

GEORG SIMON OHM

(b. March 16, 1789, Erlangen, Bavaria [Germany]—d. July 6, 1854, Munich)

German physicist Georg Simon Ohm discovered the law, named after him, which states that the current flow through a conductor is directly proportional to the potential difference (voltage) and inversely proportional to the resistance.

Ohm became professor of mathematics at the Jesuits' College at Cologne in 1817. The most important aspect of Ohm's law is summarized in his pamphlet *Die galvanische*

Kette, mathematisch bearbeitet (1827; *The Galvanic Circuit Investigated Mathematically*). While his work greatly influenced the theory and applications of current electricity, it was so coldly received that Ohm resigned his post at Cologne. He accepted a position at the Polytechnic School of Nürnberg in 1833. Finally his work began to be recognized; in 1841 he was awarded the Copley Medal of the Royal Society of London and was made a foreign member a year later. The physical unit measuring electrical resistance was given his name.

HANS CHRISTIAN ØRSTED

(b. Aug. 14, 1777, Rudkøbing, Den.—d. March 9, 1851, Copenhagen)

Hans Christian Ørsted was a Danish physicist and chemist who discovered that electric current in a wire can deflect a magnetized compass needle, a phenomenon the importance of which was rapidly recognized and which inspired the development of electromagnetic theory.

In 1806 Ørsted became a professor at the University of Copenhagen, where his first physical researches dealt with electric currents and acoustics. During an evening lecture in April 1820, Ørsted discovered that a magnetic needle aligns itself perpendicularly to a current-carrying wire, definite experimental evidence of the relationship between electricity and magnetism.

Ørsted's discovery (1820) of piperine, one of the pungent components of pepper, was an important contribution to chemistry, as was his preparation of metallic aluminum in 1825. In 1824 he founded a society devoted to the spread of scientific knowledge among the general public. Since 1908 this society has awarded an Ørsted Medal for outstanding contributions by Danish physical scientists. In 1932 the name oersted was adopted for the physical unit of magnetic field strength.

JEAN-CHARLES-ATHANASE PELTIER

(b. Feb. 22, 1785, Ham, France—d. Oct. 27, 1845, Paris)

French physicist Jean-Charles-Athanase Peltier discovered (1834) that at the junction of two dissimilar metals an electric current will produce heat or cold, depending on the direction of current flow. The effect, known by his name, is used in devices for measuring temperature and, with the discovery of new conducting materials, in refrigeration units.

A clockmaker, Peltier retired when he was 30 years old to devote his time to scientific investigations. In 1840 he introduced the concept of

Jean-Charles-Athanase Peltier, detail of a lithograph by Maurin. Giraudon/ Art Resource, New York

electrostatic induction, a method of charging a conductor by closely juxtaposing another charged object to attract all charges of one sign and then grounding the conductor to bleed off the other group of charges, leaving a net charge behind. He wrote numerous papers on atmospheric electricity, waterspouts, and the boiling point at high elevations.

PETER PEREGRINUS OF MARICOURT

(fl. 13th century)

The French crusader and scholar Peter Peregrinus of Maricourt wrote the first extant treatise describing the properties of magnets.

Almost nothing is known about Peregrinus's life, except that he wrote his famous treatise while serving as an engineer in the army of Charles I of Anjou that was besieging Lucera (in Italy) in August 1269 in a "crusade" sanctioned by the pope. Peregrinus's abilities as an experimenter and technician were highly praised by his contemporary Roger Bacon.

Peregrinus's letter on the magnet, *Epistola Petri Peregrini de Maricourt ad Sygerum de Foucaucourt, militem, de magnete* ("Letter on the Magnet of Peter Peregrinus of Maricourt to Sygerus of Foucaucourt, Soldier"), commonly known by its short title, *Epistola de magnete,* consists of two parts: the first treats the properties of the lodestone (magnetite, a magnetic iron oxide mineral), and the second describes several instruments that utilize the properties of magnets. In the first part, Peregrinus provides the first extant written account of the polarity of magnets (he was the first to use the word "pole" in this regard), and he provides methods for determining the north and south poles of a magnet. He describes the effects magnets have upon one another, showing that like poles repel each other and unlike poles attract each other. In the second part of his treatise he treats the practical applications of magnets, describing the floating compass as an instrument in common use and proposing a new pivoted compass in some detail.

In the *Epistola* Peregrinus added his own fundamental observations to the existing contemporary knowledge of magnets and organized the whole into a body of scholarship that formed the basis of the science of magnetism. It is widely regarded as one of the great works of medieval experimental research and a precursor of modern scientific methodology.

JOHN HENRY POYNTING

(b. Sept. 9, 1852, Monton, Lancashire, Eng. — d. March 30, 1914, Birmingham, Warwickshire)

John Henry Poynting was a British physicist who introduced a theorem that assigns a value to the rate of flow of electromagnetic energy known as the Poynting vector.

He was a professor of physics at Mason Science College (later the University of Birmingham) from 1880 until his death. In papers published in 1884–85, he showed that the flow of energy at a point can be expressed by a simple formula in terms of the electric and magnetic forces at that point. This is Poynting's theorem. He also wrote papers on radiation and the pressure of light. After 12 years of experiments he determined in 1891 the mean density of Earth and in 1893 the gravitational constant, a measure of the effect of gravity. He published his results in *The Mean Density of the Earth* (1894) and *The Earth; Its Shape, Size, Weight and Spin* (1913).

WILLIAM STURGEON

(b. May 22, 1783, Whittington, Lancashire, Eng.—d. Dec. 4, 1850, Prestwich, Lancashire)

English electrical engineer William Sturgeon devised the first electromagnet capable of supporting more than its own weight. This device led to the invention of the telegraph, the electric motor, and numerous other devices basic to modern technology.

Sturgeon, self-educated in electrical phenomena and natural science, spent much time lecturing and conducting electrical experiments. In 1824 he became lecturer in science at the Royal Military College, Addiscombe, Surrey, and the following year he exhibited his first electromagnet. The 7-ounce (200-gram) magnet was able to support 9 pounds (4 kilograms) of iron using the current from a single cell.

Sturgeon built an electric motor in 1832 and invented the commutator, an integral part of most modern electric motors. In 1836, the year he founded the monthly journal *Annals of Electricity,* he invented the first suspended coil galvanometer, a device for measuring current. He also improved the voltaic battery and worked on the theory of thermoelectricity. From more than 500 kite observations he established that in serene weather the atmosphere is invariably charged positively with respect to Earth, becoming more positive with increasing altitude.

ALESSANDRO VOLTA

(b. Feb. 18, 1745, Como, Lombardy [Italy] — d. March 5, 1827, Como)

Alessandro Giuseppe Antonio Anastasio Volta was an Italian physicist whose invention of the electric battery provided the first source of continuous current.

In 1775 Volta's interest in electricity led him to invent the electrophorus, a device used to generate static electricity. He became professor of physics at the Royal School of Como in 1774 and discovered and isolated methane gas in 1778. One year later he was appointed to the chair of physics at the University of Pavia.

In 1780 Volta's friend Luigi Galvani discovered that contact of two different metals with the muscle of a frog resulted in the generation of an electric current. Volta began experimenting in 1794 with metals alone and found that animal tissue was not needed to produce a current. This finding provoked much controversy between the animal-electricity adherents and the metallic-electricity advocates, but, with his demonstration of the first electric battery in 1800, victory was assured for Volta. In 1801 in Paris, he gave a demonstration of his battery's generation of electric current before Napoleon, who made Volta a count and senator of the kingdom of Lombardy. The emperor of Austria made him director of the philosophical faculty at the University of Padua in 1815. The volt, a unit of the electromotive force that drives current, was named in his honour in 1881.

WILHELM EDUARD WEBER

(b. Oct. 24, 1804, Wittenberg, Ger.—d. June 23, 1891, Göttingen)

Wilhelm Eduard Weber was a German physicist who, with his friend Carl Friedrich Gauss, investigated terrestrial magnetism and in 1833 devised an electromagnetic telegraph. The magnetic unit, termed a weber, formerly the coulomb, is named after him.

Weber was educated at Halle and later at Göttingen, where he was appointed professor of physics in 1831. He was professor at the University of Leipzig from 1843 to 1849, and he then returned to Göttingen and became director of the astronomical observatory there. He played an important role in the development of electrical science, particularly by his work to establish a system of absolute electrical units. Gauss had introduced a logical arrangement of units for magnetism involving the basic units of mass, length, and time. Weber repeated this for electricity in 1846. Occasionally he collaborated with his brothers, the physiologists Ernst Heinrich Weber (1795–1878) and Eduard Friedrich Weber (1806–71). During his final years at Göttingen, Weber studied electrodynamics and the electrical structure of matter.

He received many honours from England, France, and Germany, among which were the title of *Geheimrat* (privy councillor) and the Copley Medal of the Royal Society. Many of his extensive articles are in the six volumes of *Resultate aus den Beobachtungen des magnetischen Vereins* (1837–43), edited by himself and Gauss.

SIR CHARLES WHEATSTONE

(b. Feb. 6, 1802, Gloucester, Gloucestershire, Eng.—d. Oct. 19, 1875, Paris, France)

English physicist Sir Charles Wheatstone popularized the Wheatstone bridge, a device that accurately measured electrical resistance and became widely used in laboratories.

Wheatstone was appointed professor of experimental philosophy at King's College, London, in 1834, the same year that he used a revolving mirror in an experiment to measure the speed of electricity in a conductor. The same revolving mirror, by his suggestion, was later used in measurements of the speed of light. Three years later, with Sir William Fothergill Cooke of England, he patented an early telegraph. In 1843, he brought to notice the Wheatstone bridge, a device invented by British mathematician Samuel Christie.

Sir Charles Wheatstone, detail of a chalk drawing by Samuel Laurence; in the National Portrait Gallery, London
Courtesy of the National Portrait Gallery, London

His own inventions include the concertina, a type of small accordion, and the stereoscope, a device for observing pictures in three dimensions still used in viewing X-rays and aerial photographs. He initiated the use of electromagnets in electric generators and invented the Playfair cipher, which is based on substituting different pairs of letters for paired letters in the message. He was knighted in 1868.

APPENDIX:
OTHER CONCEPTS

E lectricity and magnetism are associated with a variety of fascinating concepts and instruments. For example, there is the analog to the elementary charge, the magnetic monopole. Electrons themselves can be used like light in the field of electron optics.

AMMETER

An ammeter is an instrument for measuring either direct or alternating electric current, in amperes. An ammeter can measure a wide range of current values because at high values only a small portion of the current is directed through the meter mechanism; a shunt in parallel with the meter carries the major portion.

Ammeters vary in their operating principles and accuracies. The D'Arsonval-movement ammeter measures direct current with accuracies of from 0.1 to 2.0 percent. The electrodynamic ammeter uses a moving coil rotating in the field produced by a fixed coil. It measures direct and alternating current with accuracies of from 0.1 to 0.25 percent. In the thermal ammeter, used primarily to measure alternating current with accuracies of from 0.5 to 3 percent, the measured current heats a thermoconverter (thermocouple); the small voltage thus generated is used to power a millivoltmeter. Digital ammeters, with no moving parts, use a circuit such as the dual slope integrator to convert a measured analogue (continuous) current to its digital equivalent. Many digital ammeters have accuracies better than 0.1 percent.

BARKHAUSEN EFFECT

The Barkhausen effect is a series of sudden changes in the size and orientation of ferromagnetic domains, or microscopic clusters of aligned atomic magnets, that occurs during a continuous process of magnetization or demagnetization. The Barkhausen effect offered direct evidence for the existence of ferromagnetic domains, which previously had been postulated theoretically.

Heinrich Barkhausen, a German physicist, discovered in 1919 that a slow, smooth increase of a magnetic field applied to a piece of ferromagnetic material, such as iron, causes it to become magnetized, not continuously but in minute steps. The sudden, discontinuous jumps in magnetization may be detected by a coil of wire wound on the ferromagnetic material; the sudden transitions in the magnetic field of the material produce pulses of current in the coil that, when amplified, produce a series of clicks in a loudspeaker. These jumps are interpreted as discrete changes in the size or rotation of ferromagnetic domains. Some microscopic clusters of similarly oriented magnetic atoms aligned with the external magnetizing field increase in size by a sudden aggregation of neighbouring atomic magnets; and, especially as the magnetizing field becomes relatively strong, other whole domains suddenly turn into the direction of the external field.

DISPLACEMENT CURRENT

In electromagnetism a displacement current is a phenomenon, analogous to an ordinary electric current, posited to explain magnetic fields that are produced by changing electric fields. Ordinary electric currents, called conduction currents, whether steady or varying, produce an accompanying magnetic field in the vicinity of the current. The

British physicist James Clerk Maxwell in the 19th century predicted that a magnetic field also must be associated with a changing electric field even in the absence of a conduction current, a theory that was subsequently verified experimentally. As magnetic fields had long been associated with currents, the predicted magnetic field also was thought of as stemming from another kind of current. Maxwell gave it the name displacement current, which was proportional to the rate of change of the electric field that kept cropping up naturally in his theoretical formulations. As electric charges do not flow through the insulation from one plate of a capacitor to the other, there is no conduction current; instead, a displacement current is said to be present to account for the continuity of the magnetic effects. In fact, the calculated size of the displacement current between the plates of a capacitor being charged and discharged in an alternating-current circuit is equal to the size of the conduction current in the wires leading to and from the capacitor. Displacement currents play a central role in the propagation of electromagnetic radiation, such as light and radio waves, through empty space. A traveling, varying magnetic field is everywhere associated with a periodically changing electric field that may be conceived in terms of a displacement current. Maxwell's insight on displacement current, therefore, made it possible to understand electromagnetic waves as being propagated through space completely detached from electric currents in conductors.

ELECTRIC DISPLACEMENT

The electric displacement is an auxiliary electric field or electric vector that represents that aspect of an electric field associated solely with the presence of separated free electric charges, purposely excluding the contribution of any electric charges bound together in neutral atoms or molecules. If electric charge is transferred between two originally uncharged parallel metal plates, one becomes positively charged and the other negatively charged by the same amount, and an electric field exists between the plates. If a slab of insulating material is inserted between the charged plates, the bound electric charges comprising the internal structure of the insulation are displaced slightly, or polarized; bound negative charges (atomic electrons) shift a fraction of an atomic diameter toward the positive plate, and bound positive charges shift very slightly toward the negative. This shift of charge, or polarization, reduces the value of the electric field that was present before the insertion of the insulation. The actual average value of the electric field E, therefore, has a component P that depends on the bound polarization charges and a component D, electric displacement, that depends on the free separated charges on the plates. The relationship among the three vectors D, E, P in the metre–kilogram–second (mks) or SI system is: $D = \varepsilon_o E + P (\varepsilon_o$ is a constant, the permittivity of a vacuum). In the centimetre–gram–second (cgs) system the relationship is: $D = E + 4\pi P$.

The value of the electric displacement D may be thought of as equal to the amount of free charge on one plate divided by the area of the plate. From this point of view D is frequently called the electric flux density, or free charge surface density, because of the close relationship between electric flux and electric charge. The dimensions of electric displacement, or electric flux density, in the metre–kilogram–second system are charge per unit area, and the units are coulombs per square metre. In the centimetre–gram–second system the dimensions of D are the same as those of the primary electric field

E, the units of which are dynes per electrostatic unit, or statvolts per centimetre.

ELECTRON OPTICS

Electron optics is the branch of physics that is concerned with beams of electrons, their deflection and focusing by electric and magnetic fields, their interference when crossing each other, and their diffraction or bending when passing very near matter or through the spacings in its submicroscopic structure. Electron optics is based on the wave properties of electrons, which, according to quantum theory, can be treated either as particles or as waves. The wave behaviour was predicted and then experimentally established in the 1920s. Beams of electrons exhibit behaviour similar to those of light and X-rays, and all these are subject to the same mathematical descriptions. One of the applications of electron optics is the electron microscope.

FERRITE

Ferrite is a ceramic-like material with magnetic properties that are useful in many types of electronic devices. Ferrites are hard, brittle, iron-containing, and generally gray or black, and are polycrystalline—i.e., made up of a large number of small crystals. They are composed of iron oxide and one or more other metals in chemical combination.

A ferrite is formed by the reaction of ferric oxide (iron oxide or rust) with any of a number of other metals, including magnesium, aluminum, barium, manganese, copper, nickel, cobalt, or even iron itself.

A ferrite is usually described by the formula $M(Fe_xO_y)$, where M represents any metal that forms divalent bonds, such as any of the elements mentioned earlier. Nickel ferrite, for instance, is $NiFe_2O_4$, and manganese ferrite is $MnFe_2O_4$; both are spinel minerals. The garnet mineral known as YIG, containing the rare-earth element yttrium, has the formula $Y_3Fe_5O_{12}$; it is used in microwave circuitry. The most familiar ferrite, known since biblical times, is magnetite (lodestone, or ferrous ferrite), $Fe(Fe_2O_4)$. Ferrites exhibit a form of magnetism called ferrimagnetism, which is distinguished from the ferromagnetism of such materials as iron, cobalt, and nickel. In ferrites the magnetic moments of constituent atoms align themselves in two or three different directions. A partial cancellation of the magnetic field results, and the ferrite is left with an overall magnetic field that is less strong than that of a ferromagnetic material. This asymmetry on the part of the atomic orientations may be due to the presence of two or more different types of magnetic ions, to a peculiar crystalline structure, or to both. The term ferrimagnetism was coined by the French physicist Louis-Eugène-Félix Néel, who first studied ferrites systematically on the atomic level. There are several types of ferrimagnetism. In collinear ferrimagnetism the fields are aligned in opposite directions; in triangular ferrimagnetism the field orientations may be at various angles to each other. Ferrites can have several different types of crystalline structures, including spinel, garnet, perovskite, and hexagonal.

The most important properties of ferrites include high magnetic permeability and high electrical resistance. High permeability to magnetic fields is particularly desirable in devices such as antennas. High resistance to electricity is desirable in the cores of transformers to reduce eddy currents. Ferrites of a type known as square-loop ferrites can be magnetized in either of two directions by an electric current. This property makes them useful in the memory cores of digital computers, since it enables a tiny ferrite ring to store binary bits of information. Another type of computer memory can be made of certain single-crystal ferrites in which tiny magnetic domains called bubbles can be individually manipulated. A number of ferrites absorb microwave energy in only one direction or orientation; for this reason, they are used in microwave wave guides.

FERROELECTRICITY

Ferroelectricity is a property of certain nonconducting crystals, or dielectrics, that exhibit spontaneous electric polarization (separation of the centre of positive and negative electric charge, making one side of the crystal positive and the opposite side negative) that can be reversed in direction by the application of an appropriate electric field. Ferroelectricity is named by analogy with ferromagnetism, which occurs in such materials as iron. Iron atoms, being tiny magnets, spontaneously align themselves in clusters called ferromagnetic domains, which in turn can be oriented predominantly in a given direction by the application of an external magnetic field.

Ferroelectric materials—for example, barium titanate $(BaTiO_3)$ and Rochelle salt—are composed of crystals in which the structural units are tiny electric dipoles; that is, in each unit the centres of positive charge and of negative charge are slightly separated. In some crystals these electric dipoles spontaneously line up in clusters called domains, and in ferroelectric crystals the domains can be oriented predominantly in one direction by a strong external electric field. Reversing the external field reverses the predominant orientation of the ferroelectric domains, though the switching to a new direction lags somewhat behind the change in the external electric field. This lag of electric polarization behind the applied electric field is ferroelectric hysteresis, named by analogy with ferromagnetic hysteresis.

Ferroelectricity ceases in a given material above a characteristic temperature, called its Curie temperature, because the heat agitates the dipoles sufficiently to overcome the forces that spontaneously align them.

GALVANOMETER

The galvanometer is an instrument for measuring a small electrical current or a function of the current by deflection of a moving coil. The deflection is a mechanical rotation derived from forces resulting from the current.

The most common type is the D'Arsonval galvanometer, in which the indicating system consists of a light coil of wire suspended from a metallic ribbon between the poles of a permanent magnet. The magnetic field produced by a current passing through the coil reacts with the magnetic field of the permanent magnet, producing a torque, or twisting force. The coil, to which an indicating needle or mirror is attached, rotates under the action of the torque; the angle through which it rotates to balance the torsion of the suspension provides a measure of the current flowing in the coil. The angle is measured by the movement of the needle or by the deflection of a beam of light reflected from the mirror.

The ballistic galvanometer is designed to deflect its indicating needle (or mirror) in a way that is proportional to the total charge passing through its moving coil or to a voltage pulse of short duration. Any conventional galvanometer may also be employed as a ballistic type, but the latter has smaller torque and higher inertia in the coil.

GAUSS'S LAW

Gauss's law is either of two statements describing electric and magnetic fluxes. Gauss's law for electricity states that the electric flux across any closed surface is proportional to the net electric charge enclosed by the surface. The law implies that isolated electric charges exist and that like charges repel one another while unlike charges attract. Gauss's law for magnetism states that the magnetic flux across any closed surface is zero; this law is consistent with the observation that isolated magnetic poles (monopoles) do not exist.

Mathematical formulations for these two laws— together with Ampère's law (concerning the magnetic effect of a changing electric field or current) and Faraday's law of induction (concerning the electric effect of a changing magnetic field)—are collected in a set that is known as Maxwell's equations, which provide the foundation of unified electromagnetic theory.

GUNN EFFECT

The high-frequency oscillation of electrical current flowing through certain semiconducting solids is called the Gunn effect. The effect is used in a solid-state device, the Gunn diode, to produce short radio waves called microwaves. The effect was discovered by J.B. Gunn in the early 1960s. It has been detected only in a few materials.

In materials displaying the Gunn effect, such as gallium arsenide or cadmium sulfide, electrons can exist in two states of mobility, or ease of movement. Electrons in the state of higher mobility move through the solid more easily than electrons in the lower mobility state. When no electrical voltage is applied to the material, most of its electrons are in the high mobility state. When an electrical voltage is applied, all its electrons begin to move just as in ordinary conductors. This motion constitutes an electrical current, and in most solids greater voltages cause increased movement of all the electrons and hence greater current flow. In Gunn-effect materials, however, a sufficiently strong electrical voltage may force some of the electrons into the state of lower mobility, causing them to move more slowly and decreasing the electrical conductivity of the material. In electronic circuits incorporating the Gunn diode, this unusual relationship between voltage and current (motion) results in the generation of high-frequency alternating current from a direct-current source.

MAGNETIC MIRROR

A magnetic mirror is a static magnetic field that, within a localized region, has a shape such that approaching charged particles are repelled back along their path of approach.

A magnetic field is usually described as a distribution of nearly parallel nonintersecting field lines. The direction of these lines determines the direction of the magnetic field, and the density (closeness) of the lines determines its strength. Charged particles such as electrons tend to move through a magnetic field by following a helical path about a magnetic field line. If the field lines along the path of the particle are converging, the particle is entering a region of stronger magnetic field. The particle continues to circle about the field line, but its forward motion is retarded until it is stopped and finally forced back along its original path. The exact location at which this mirroring occurs depends only upon the initial pitch angle describing its helical path. Two such magnetic mirrors can be arranged to form a magnetic bottle that can trap charged particles in the middle.

MAGNETIC MONOPOLE

The magnetic monopole is a hypothetical particle with a magnetic charge, a property analogous to an electric charge. As implied by its name, the magnetic monopole consists of a single pole, as opposed to the dipole, which is comprised of two magnetic poles. As yet there is no evidence for the existence of magnetic monopoles, but they are interesting theoretically. In 1931 the English physicist P.A.M. Dirac proposed that the existence of even a single magnetic monopole in the universe would explain why electric charge comes only in multiples of the electron charge. Since the quantization of electric charge remains a great theoretical mystery, physicists have repeatedly renewed their search for monopoles whenever particle accelerators attain a new energy level or when a new source of matter is discovered. Lunar rock samples brought back by U.S. astronauts in 1969, for example, were extensively studied because it was thought that monopoles might be trapped in the surface material of the Moon. Research showed, however, that such was not the case.

MAGNETIC POLE

The region at each end of a magnet where the external magnetic field is strongest is called a magnetic pole. A bar magnet suspended in Earth's magnetic field orients itself in a north–south direction. The north-seeking pole of such a magnet, or any similar pole, is called a north magnetic pole. The south-seeking pole, or any pole similar to it, is called a south magnetic pole. Unlike poles of different magnets attract each other; like poles repel each other.

The magnetic force between a pole of one long bar magnet and that of another is described by an inverse square law. If, for example, the separation between the two poles is doubled, the magnetic force diminishes to one-fourth its former value.

Breaking a magnet in two does not isolate its north pole from its south pole. Each half is found to have its own north and south poles. Magnetic forces, in fact, cannot be traced to unit magnetic poles of submicroscopic size in direct contrast to electric forces that are caused by actual discrete electric charges, such as electrons and protons. Indeed, magnetic forces themselves also fundamentally arise between electric charges when they are in motion.

MAGNON

The magnon is a small quantity of energy corresponding to a specific decrease in magnetic strength that travels as a unit through a magnetic substance.

In a magnetic substance, such as iron, each atom acts as a small individual magnet. These atomic magnets tend to point in the same direction, so that their magnetic fields reinforce each other. When the direction of one atomic magnet is reversed, the total magnetic strength of the group is decreased. A definite amount of energy is required to reverse such a magnet. This energy, involving the decrease in magnetic strength of the group of atoms, constitutes a magnon.

According to the laws of quantum mechanics, the reversal of a single atomic magnet is equivalent to a partial reversal of all the atomic magnets in a group. This partial reversal spreads through the solid as a wave of discrete energy transferal. This wave is called a spin wave, because the magnetism of each atom is produced by the spin of unpaired electrons in its structure. Thus, a magnon is a quantized spin wave.

As the temperature of a magnetic substance is increased, its magnetic strength decreases, corresponding to the presence of a large number of magnons.

PINCH EFFECT

The pinch effect is the self-constriction of a cylinder of an electrically conducting plasma. When an electric current is passed through a gaseous plasma, a magnetic field is set up that tends to force the current-carrying particles together. This force can compress the plasma so that it is heated as well as confined, but such a self-pinched plasma cylinder is unstable and will quickly develop kinks or break up into a series of lumps resembling a string of sausages. The pinch effect, therefore, must be augmented with other magnetic-field configurations to produce a stable magnetic bottle.

POLARON

A polaron is an electron moving through the constituent atoms of a solid material, causing the neighbouring positive charges to shift toward it and the neighbouring negative charges to shift away. This distortion of the regular position of electrical charges constitutes a region of polarization that travels along with the moving electron. After the electron passes, the region returns to normal. An electron accompanied by this kind of electrical displacement of neighbouring charges constitutes a polaron.

A polaron behaves as a negatively charged particle with a mass greater than that of an isolated electron because of its interaction with the surrounding atoms of the solid. The effect is most pronounced in ionic solids, composed of positively and negatively charged atoms called ions, because the forces between the electron and ions are strong. The strength of these forces is reflected in the mass of the polaron. In common table salt, or sodium chloride, the mass of a polaron is more than twice the mass of a free electron.

SEEBECK EFFECT

The Seebeck effect is the production of an electromotive force (emf) and consequently an electric current in a loop of material consisting of at least two dissimilar conductors when two junctions are maintained at different temperatures. The conductors are commonly metals, though they need not even be solids. The German physicist Thomas Johann Seebeck discovered (1821) the effect. The Seebeck effect is used to measure temperature with great sensitivity and accuracy and to generate electric power for special applications.

SKIN EFFECT

In electricity the tendency of alternating high-frequency currents to crowd toward the surface of a conducting material is called the skin effect. This phenomenon restricts the current to a small part of the total cross-sectional area and so has the effect of increasing the resistance of the conductor. Because of the skin effect, induction heating can be localized at the surface and the heated area controlled by a suitable choice of the inductor coil. The skin effect becomes more pronounced as the frequency is increased.

SPACE CHARGE

Electrical charge distributed through a three-dimensional region is called space charge. In an electron tube, for example, a negative charge results because electrons that are emitted from the cathode do not travel instantaneously to the plate (anode) but require a finite time for the trip. These electrons form a cloud around the cathode, the cloud being continually depleted by electrons going to the plate and replenished by electrons emitted from the cathode. It is this cloud of electrons that produces the negative space charge.

Another example of space charge occurs when two different semiconductor materials are brought together. Electrons very near the interface in one of the materials (the donor) typically migrate into the other material (the acceptor) in order to establish thermodynamic equilibrium. Atoms that lose electrons are positively charged and form a fixed space charge layer within the donor.

THOMSON EFFECT

The Thomson effect is the evolution or absorption of heat when electric current passes through a circuit composed of a single material that has a temperature difference along its length. This transfer of heat is superimposed on the common production of heat associated with the electrical resistance to currents in conductors. If a copper wire carrying a steady electric current is subjected to external heating at a short section while the rest remains cooler, heat is absorbed from the copper as the conventional current approaches the hot point, and heat is transferred to the copper just beyond the hot point. This effect was discovered (1854) by the British physicist William Thomson (Lord Kelvin).

ampere A unit of electrical current, named for the French physicist and founder of electromagnetics, André-Marie Ampère.

capacitor A device for storing electrical energy, consisting of two conductors in close proximity and insulated from each other.

coulomb Unit of electric charge, equal to as much electricity transported in a single second by a current of one ampere.

dielectric A material that insulates against the transport of electrical current.

electric dipole A pair of electrical charges that are of equal strength and opposed polarities.

electrodynamics The study of moving charged-particle interaction within the electromagnetic field.

electromagnetism The science of charge, as well as the forces and fields associated with charge.

faraday A unit of electrical charge used to study electrochemical reactions; named for electromagnetic physicist Michael Faraday.

gauss A unit of magnetic induction, equal to the magnetic flux density necessary to induce an electromotive force of one abvolt per centimetre.

joule A unit of energy equal to the work done by a force of one newton acting through one metre.

Lorentz force The force exerted on a charged particle moving through an electric and magnetic field.

magnetostatics The study of steady-state magnetic fields.

newton The force necessary to provide a mass of 1 kg with an acceleration of 1 m per second per second.

oersted Unit of magnetic-field strength, named for physicist Hans Christian Ørsted, a forefunner in electromagnetic theory.

ohm A unit of electrical resistance, named for physicist Georg Simon Ohm.

piezoelectricity The appearance of an electric field in certain nonconducting crystals as a result of the application of mechanical pressure.

polarization Property of certain types of electromagnetic radiation in which the direction and magnitude of the vibrating electric field are related in a specified way.

reactance Measure of the opposition that an electrical circuit or a part of a circuit presents to electric current, insofar as the current is varying or alternating.

remanence The magnetic induction remaining in a magnetized substance no longer under external magnetic influence.

sinusoidal Shaped like a sine wave or curve.

solenoid A cylinder of tightly wound coil whose total length is greater than its diameter.

superconductivity Almost total lack of electrical resistance in certain materials when they are cooled to a temperature near absolute zero.

tesla Unit of magnetic induction or magnetic flux density equaling one weber per square metre, corresponding to 10,000 gauss.

thermocouple Temperature-measuring instrument consisting of two wires of different metals joined at each end.

valence band The electronic energy band in a semiconductor that is filled with the highest number of electrons.

vitreous Having a glass-like quality, in colour, texture, or translucence.

ELECTRICITY

P.C.W. Davies, *The Forces of Nature*, 2nd ed. (1986), is an interesting, readable account. Edward M. Purcell, *Electricity and Magnetism*, 2nd ed. (1985), is superbly illustrated and treats key principles and phenomena with remarkable insight. Many examples and problems on electricity, as well as elementary discussions of vectors and other aspects of physics, are found in David Halliday, Robert Resnick, and Jearl Walker, *Fundamentals of Physics*, 7th ed., extended (2005). Useful physics textbooks with illustrations, examples, and problems include Richard Wolfson and Jay M. Pasachoff, *Physics*, 3rd ed., 2 vol. (1999); and Hugh D. Young, *University Physics*, 8th ed. (1992).

Overviews of uses of electricity may be found in the following texts: Gordon R. Slemon, *Electric Machines and Drives* (1992); Syed A. Nasar (ed.), *Handbook of Electric Machines* (1987); Syed A. Nasar and L.E. Unnewehr, *Electromechanics and Electric Machines*, 2nd ed. (1983); Vincent Del Toro, *Electric Machines and Power Systems* (1985); and George McPherson and Robert D. Laramore, *An Introduction to Electrical Machines and Transformers*, 2nd ed. (1990).

MAGNETISM

Gerrit Verschuur, *Hidden Attraction: The Mystery and History of Magnetism* (1993) and J.D. Livingston, *Driving Force: The Natural Magic of Magnets* (1997) are delightful, popular accounts of the history and contemporary uses of magnetism. Edward Purcell, *Electricity and Magnetism*, 2nd ed. (1985), is a superbly written and illustrated college-level introduction to the basic physics and mathematics of magnetism.

ELECTROMAGNETISM

Richard P. Feynman, Robert B. Leighton, and Matthew Sands, *The Feynman Lectures on Physics*, vol. 2, *The Electromagnetic Field* (1964, reprinted 1977), is highly recommended for its lucid discussion of fundamentals. The same is true for Edward M. Purcell, *Electricity and Magnetism*, 2nd ed. (1985). John R. Reitz, Frederick J. Milford, and Robert W. Christy, *Foundations of Electromagnetic Theory*, 3rd ed. (1979), is a fine, compact, college-level text using vector calculus. Richard Fitzpatrick, *Maxwell's Equations and the Principles of Electromagnetism* (2008), and J.D. Jackson, *Classical Electrodynamics*, 3rd ed. (1998), are more expansive treatments of the subject.

J.L. Heilbron, *Electricity in the 17th and 18th Centuries: A Study of Early Modern Physics* (1979), provides a readable survey of significant developments, as do Edmund Whittaker, *A History of the Theories of Aether and Electricity*, rev. and enlarged ed., 2 vol. (1951–53, reprinted 1973) and Patricia Fara, *An Entertainment for Angels: Electricity in the Enlightenment* (2003). Charles Singer and T.I. Williams (eds.), *A History of Technology*, 8 vol. (1954–84), begins in the prehistoric period and concludes around 1950.

INDEX

A

Adams, John C., 220
Albany Academy, 232
Alfvén, Hannes, 239
Alnico alloys, 169
alternating current (AC), 25, 26,
    55, 74–85, 87, 184, 185, 193,
    195, 196, 197, 205, 206, 250,
    257, 261
Ampère, André-Marie, 14, 19, 20,
    85, 198, 215–219, 224
Ampère, Jean-Jacques, 215, 216
Ampère's law, 19, 198–199, 200,
    201, 218, 256
Annals of Electricity, 244
antiferromagnetism, explained,
    160–161
Arago, François, 14, 217,
    219–220, 221
Audion, 27
Avogadro's number, 31

B

Bacon, Roger, 243
Bardeen, John, 104
barium ferrites, 170, 172
Barkhausen, Heinrich, 249
Barkhausen effect, 249
battery, development of the,
    10–13

BCS theory, 104, 106, 110, 120
Bednorz, Johannes Georg,
    118, 120
Bell, Alexander Graham, 26
Bevis, John, 183
bioelectric effects, 89,
    100–102, 230
Biot, Jean-Baptiste, 126, 220,
    221–222
Biot-Savart law, 126–127, 199, 221
Bologna Academy of Science,
    11, 227
Boltzmann's constant, 96, 110
Brillouin function, 153
British Association for the
    Advancement of Science,
    234, 237
British Broadcasting
    Corporation, 27
Bunsen, Robert, 234, 235

C

capacitance, 6, 29, 47–55, 75,
    78, 79, 80, 83, 84, 87, 100,
    182–185, 189, 198, 199, 250
Carlisle, Anthony, 12
Cavendish, Henry, 9, 13
Cay, Jane, 236
Center for Nuclear Studies, 240
charge conservation, principle
    of, 7–8, 9, 178–179

Charles I, 242

Christie, Samuel, 247

*Commentary on the Effect of
Electricity on Muscular
Motion*, 228

Committee of Electrical
Standards, 234

Cooke, Sir William
Fothergill, 247

Cooper, Leon N., 104

Cooper pairings, 106, 110, 114,
115, 117, 120

Copernicus, 232

Copley Medal, 241, 246

Coulomb, Charles-Augustin de,
8–9, 12, 86, 137, 176, 177, 218,
219, 222–223

Coulomb's law, 9, 32, 33, 38, 45,
137–138, 176–178, 200, 222

Crookes, Sir William, 21

Curie, Pierre, 20, 148

Curie's law, 148, 150, 154, 156

Curie temperature, 156, 157,
158, 255

Curie-Weiss law, 148, 156, 158

D

d'Alembert, Jean Le Rond,
215–216

Davy, Sir Humphrey, 12, 223

De Forest, Lee, 27

demagnetization, explained,
166–167

diamagnetism, 119, 131, 140,
147, 149, 151–153, 154, 162,
214, 227

Diderot, Denis, 215

Dirac, P.A.M., 258

direct current (DC), 25, 26,
55–74, 80, 83, 87, 117, 184,
206, 212, 238, 257

displacement currents, 185, 199,
200, 201, 238, 249–252

DuFay, Charles François de
Cisternay, 5–6, 7, 8

E

*Earth: Its Shape, Size, Weight and
Spin, The*, 244

École Polytechnique, 217,
219, 221

Edison, Thomas A., 25

Einstein, Albert, 1, 2, 23, 174,
198, 236

Einstein relation, 97–98

electric displacement, explained,
250–252

electric field, calculating the
value of an, 34–36

electricity and magnetism,
biographies, 215–247
effects in matter, 140–145
electrostatics, 29–55
fields and forces, 126–135,
179–185, 202
fundamentals, 122–126, 174–214
introduction to, 1–28
properties of matter, 89–121,
146–162
units, 85–88, 172–173

electric potential, 37–47

electrochemistry and electrodynamics, foundations of,
10–24

electroluminescence, 21,
98–100, 213

electrolysis, 12–13
electromagnetic technology, development of, 24–28
electromagnets, explained, 202–213
electromotive force, explained, 64–68
electron, discovery of the, 20–22
electron optics, 252
electro-optic phenomena, 92
electrostatics and magneto-statics, formulation of the quantitative laws of, 8–10
electroweak force, 3
"Elementary Treatise on Physical Astronomy," 222
Elizabeth I, 4, 231, 232
Émile, 215
energy gaps, 104, 110–111, 114, 119

F

Faraday, Michael, 9–10, 14, 15–18, 24, 25, 26, 49, 86, 175, 190, 191, 197, 220, 223–227, 232–233, 236, 238
Faraday's law, 19, 77, 80, 188, 191–193, 195, 197, 201, 238, 256
Fermi levels, 93, 95
ferrimagnetism, explained, 161–162
ferrites, 161–162, 170, 252–254
ferroelectricity, 254–255
ferromagnetism, explained, 154–160
Fizeau, Armand-Hippolyte-Louis, 220

Foucault, Léon, 220
Franklin, Benjamin, 7–8, 232
French Academy of Sciences, 217, 219, 221, 222
Fresnel, Augustin-Jean, 15, 220

G

Galeazzi, Lucia, 227
Galvani, Luigi, 11, 12, 227–231, 245
Galvanic Circuit Investigated Mathematically, The, 241
Gauss, Carl Friedrich, 9, 173, 246
Gauss's law, 46–47, 200, 255–256
Gay-Lussac, Joseph-Louis, 221
Geissler, Heinrich, 21
Gilbert, William, 4–5, 213, 231–232
Ginzburg, Vitaly Lazarevich, 105
Ginzburg-Landau coherence length, 119
Gramme, Zénobe Théophile, 24–25
Gray, Stephen, 5
Guericke, Otto von, 5
Gunn, J.B., 256
Gunn effect, 256–257

H

Hall, Edwin Herbert, 133
Hall effect, 133, 134
Helmholtz, Hermann von, 18
Helmholtz coil, 145
Henry, Joseph, 15, 16–17, 18, 86, 195, 232–233
Hertz, Heinrich, 19, 26, 200, 238
History and Present State of Electricity, 8

Hopkins, William, 237
Humboldt, Alexander von, 12

I

inductance, self- and mutual,
    194–197

J

James I, 4, 232
Jeans, Sir James Hopwood, 21
Jenkin, Fleeming, 233–234
Josephson, Brian D., 105
Josephson currents, 111,
    115–117, 119
Joule, James Prescott, 18, 63
Joule's law, 63

K

Kammerlingh-Onnes, Heike,
    20, 103, 104, 117
Kelvin, Lord, 18, 163, 226,
    234, 262
Kerr, John, 92
Kerr effect, 92
Kirchhoff, Gustav Robert, 18,
    72, 234–235
Kirchhoff's laws, 72–74, 77, 78,
    79, 234–235
Kleist, Ewald Georg von, 6, 183
Kohlrausch, Rudolf, 18

L

Landau, Lev Davidovich,
    104–105
Laplace, Pierre-Simon, 220

Laplace's equation, 42
Leclerc, Georges-Louis, 215
"Lectures on Mathematical
    Physics," 235
Lenz, Heinrich F.E., 18, 192
Lenz's law, 152, 192
"Letter on the Magnet,"
    3–4, 243
Le Verrier, Urbain J.J., 220
Leyden jar, 6–8, 12, 183, 228, 229
Lincoln, Abraham, 233
Lorentz, Hendrik A., 22, 23, 132
Lorentz force, 132–135
Louis XV, 7
Lucretius, 3

M

magnetic anisotropy, explained,
    166, 167–168
magnetic dipoles,
    induced and permanent
        atomic, 149–151
    repulsion or attraction
        between two, 136–140
magnetic field of steady cur-
    rents, 126–131
magnetic-flux quantization,
    114–115, 119
magnetic monopoles, 123,
    257–258
magnetic poles, 4, 9, 258–259
magnetic resonance imaging
    (MRI), 138–139
magnetization, process of, 165
magnetohydrodynamics (MHD),
    145–146
magnetomotive force (mmf),
    203–204

magnetostriction, 145

magnets, explained, 162–172

Marconi, Guglielmo, 27

Mason Science College, 244

Maxwell, James Clerk, 2, 14, 18–20, 22, 23, 174, 175, 189, 190, 197, 198, 199, 200, 201, 213, 235–239, 250

Maxwell's equations, 2, 19, 20, 23, 256

Maxwell's theory of electro-magnetism, 200–201

Mean Density of the Earth, The, 244

Meissner effect, 104, 111, 112–114, 119

Memoir on the Mathematical Theory of Electrodynamic Phenomena, 218, 219

Michelson, Albert Abraham, 23

Millikan oil-drop experiment, 30

Monge, Gaspard, 219

Morley, Edward W., 23

Morse, Samuel F.B., 232

Müller, Karl Alex, 118, 120

Musschenbroek, Pieter van, 6, 183

N

Napoleon, 216, 230, 245

National Academy of Science, 233

National Physical Laboratory, 238

Neckam, Alexander, 3

Néel, Louis-Eugène-Félix, 160, 162, 215, 239–240, 253

Néel temperature, 160, 161

Neumann, Franz Ernst, 18

"New Philosophy of Our Sublunar World, A," 232

Newton, Sir Isaac, 8, 23, 176, 236

Nicholson, William, 12

Nobel Prize, 103, 104, 118, 239

Nollet, Jean-Antoine, 7

O

Ohm, Georg Simon, 13, 59, 63, 75, 87, 219, 234, 240–241

Ohm's law, 13, 57, 58, 59, 63, 69, 74, 75, 79, 80, 81, 87, 88, 203, 240–241

"On the Magnet, Magnetic Bodies, and the Great Magnet of the Earth," 4, 231

"On the Nature of Things," 3

"On the Use and Activity of the Conductive Arch in the Contraction of Muscles," 230

Ørsted, Hans Christian, 13–14, 15, 173, 190, 213, 217, 218, 219, 224, 241

Ørsted Medal, 241

P

paramagnetism, 131, 140, 147, 148, 149, 153–154, 157, 158, 160, 214, 227

Paris Observatory, 219

Pauli exclusion principle, 60, 154, 155

Peltier, Jean-Charles-Athanase, 94, 242

Peltier effect, 94, 242

Peltier refrigerators, 95

Peregrinus of Maricourt, Peter, 3–4, 215, 242–243
Permalloy, 171–172
permeable materials, 131, 141–142, 163, 170–172, 204–205, 212
photoelectric conductivity, 97–98
piezoelectricity, 89–91, 213
pinch effect, 260
Planck, Max, 22, 23, 236
Planck's constant, 22, 114, 115, 139
Playfair cipher, 247
Pliny the Elder, 3
Plücker, Julius, 21
Pockels, F.R., 92
Pockels effect, 92
Poincaré, Henri, 23
Poisson, Siméon-Denis, 9, 220, 223
Poisson's equation, 9, 42
powder magnets, 168, 214
Poynting, John Henry, 243–244
Poynting vector, 243
Priestly, Joseph, 8, 9, 222
pyroelectricity, 102

Q

quantum electrodynamics, 10, 20, 23–24, 201

R

rare-earth elements, 169, 253
Rayleigh, Lord, 21, 22
resistors in series and parallel, 70–72
Reynolds number, 146
Richardson, Owen W., 96
Richardson's law, 96

Robinson, John, 9
Rousseau, Jean-Jacques, 215
Royal Society, 222, 237, 241, 246
Rumford Medal, 222
Rutherford, Sir Ernest, 26–27

S

Savart, Félix, 126, 221
Schrieffer, John Robert, 104
secondary electron emission, 96–97
Seebeck, Thomas Johann, 93, 261
Seebeck effect, 93, 94, 261
Siemens, Sir William, 87
Siemens, Werner von, 87
skin effect, 261
Smithsonian Institution, 233
solenoids, explained, 205–207
space charge, 261–262
special theory of relativity, 1, 2, 22–24, 174, 198, 236
static electricity, 31–47, 91, 101–102, 245
St. Louis Exposition, 23
Stokes, Sir George Gabriel, 18
Strutt, John William, 21
Sturgeon, William, 15, 244–245
superconductivity, 20, 63–64, 103–121, 152–153, 196
superposition principle, 36–37, 76
Swan, Sir Joseph Wilson, 25

T

Tacoma Narrows Bridge, collapse of, 83
Tesla, Nikola, 26, 173

Thales of Miletus, 3
Theory of Electrons and Its Applications to the Phenomena of Light and Radiant Heat, The, 22
thermionic emission, 95–96
thermoelectricity, 93–95, 245
Thomson, Sir J.J., 21, 22
Thomson, William, 18, 163, 226, 234, 262
Thomson effect, 262
Treatise on Electricity and Magnetism, 238

U

ultrasound, 91
U.S. Weather Bureau, 233

V

Van de Graaff, Robert J., 65
Van de Graaff generator, 65–66
van der Waals, Johannes Diedrik, 239

Volta, Alessandro, 11–12, 88, 219, 229–230, 231, 245
Voyager space probe, 238

W

Watson, William, 6–7
Watt, James, 88, 219
Weber, Eduard Friedrich, 246
Weber, Ernst Heinrich, 246
Weber, Wilhelm Eduard, 18, 20, 88, 246
Weiss, Pierre-Ernest, 148, 159, 239
Wenström, Jonas, 25
Westinghouse Electric Company, 26
Wheatstone, Sir Charles, 246–247
Wien, Wilhelm, 21, 22

Y

Young, Thomas, 90
Young's modulus, 90